The Battle of RICHMOND, KENTUCKY

The Battle of RICHMOND, KENTUCKY

1862 Weather and Civil War Digest

PAUL ROMINGER

Acclaim Press
MORLEY, MISSOURI

Acclaim Press
— Your Next Great Book —
P.O. Box 238
Morley, MO 63767
(573) 472-9800
www.acclaimpress.com

Editor: Randy Baumgardner
Book & Cover Design: Rodney Atchley

Library of Congress Control Number: 2020950517
ISBN: 978-1-948901-77-2 / 1-948901-77-3

First Printing 2021
Printed in the United States of America
10 9 8 7 6 5 4 3 2 1

Contents

The Battle of Richmond Association was formed in 2001 by the Madison County Historical Society, the Richmond Chamber of Commerce and Madison County Civil War Round Table to act as the lead organization to preserve the Battle of Richmond battlefield. Preservation progress resulted in removal of this battlefield from the Civil War Trust's list of ten most endangered sites. The Battle of Richmond Association continues to support the preservation of Civil War land, Battlefield Park Visitors Center, park and museum through events that seek to education the public about those who participated in or were affected by the 1862 battle. We are particularly proud of our Living History for Students in May with approximately 1,100 students in attendance, and our Living History Civil War Battle Reenactment for the public in August. This event has had 8,000 visitors in each of the recent years from forty counties in Kentucky and a dozen other states. Approximately 20,000 visitors come to Battlefield Park each year. They have visited from almost all of the states and two dozen foreign countries.

The association provided an initial $25,000 to keep open an option to buy Pleasant View house and farm. It also promoted and served as a conduit of funds donated by over 200 persons to purchase the static three-inch ordnance rifle in front of Battlefield Park Visitors Center. This cannon was produced by Steen Cannon and Ordnance Works of Ashland, Kentucky. Another recent successful drive by the Battle of Richmond Association has been to purchase the commission as major general of William Nelson signed by Lincoln and Stanton. While many individuals have been instrumental is acquiring artifacts and promoting Battlefield Park, vital leadership and vision have been provided by Phillip Seyfrit and Robert Moody.

Promotion and funding of history education and Battlefield Park activities have been enhanced by the crucial partnership with Richmond Tourism and Richmond Chamber of Commerce, and with Berea Tourism and Berea Chamber of Commerce. There is also a valued relationship with the Kentucky Historical Society.

This book is intended to support the education mission of the Battle of Richmond Association, a 501c3 non-profit. Sections on American Indians supplement the education mission of Richmond Pow Wow Association, also a 501c3 non-profit. Sharon Farthing Graves serves as Battle of Richmond Association Executive Director. Phillip Seyfrit is Superintendent of Battlefield Park.

The Madison County Historical Society was formed in 1891. Its mission is to promote, protect and preserve the history and heritage of

Madison County. The historical society is noted for its excellent bi-annual publication *Heritage Highlights*. The society was at the forefront of acquisition of land and work in the Pleasant View house with decisive leadership provided by Charles Hay. The national organization Civil War Trust has also provided significant funds for purchase of land. In the writing of this book, the archive of photographs held by the Madison County Historical Society as well as two books the society published by Warren Lambert and by Lavinia Harvey Kubiak have been very valuable.

Dr. D. Warren Lambert — without his research, the Battle of Richmond would have remained merely a footnote on the 1862 Confederate campaign into Kentucky.

The Madison County Civil War Round Table was founded in 1977. It meets in Berea on odd numbered months alternating with the Central Kentucky World War Two Round Table. The Civil War round table through its members purchased the Union Brig. Gen. Jefferson C. Davis pistol on display at Battlefield Park Visitors Center. The round table continues to sponsor Civil War interpretive signs and programs of Battlefield Park. Phillip Seyfrit is the contact for both round tables.

Nicholas Bauer provided technical support with initial research, photography, illustrations and changing the original interpretive museum brochures to book format. He has a B.A. in Education Studies with a focus on History from Berea College. He served as an intern at Battlefield Park Visitors Center Civil War Park and Museum, and as an intern in the Education Department of the Kentucky Historical Society. He is an Eagle Scout from Corbin, Kentucky.

Sherman Rominger provided additional technical support and several photographs. He has a B.A. from Clemson University in Criminal Justice, Sociology and Business. His skill in organization, logistical focus and business analysis proved a benefit in the organization of this book. He is an Eagle Scout from Saint Simons Island, Georgia, and is enrolled in the Cherokee of Georgia Tribal Council.

Paul Rominger holds doctorates in history. He has a Kentucky Rank 1 Teaching Certificate with Continuing Life Endorsements for Grades 7-12: History and English, and for School Superintendent. He is Executive Director Emeritus of the Battle of Richmond Association, board chair of the Richmond Pow Wow Association, former President of the Madison County Historical Society, Cherokee of Georgia Tribal Council, enrolled, former council member; two-term member of the Georgia Council on American Indian Concerns, member of Phi Delta Kappa Professional Education Fraternity and Kappa Delta Pi Honor Society in Education. He was certified by the Kentucky Personnel Cabinet in 2007 as Education Academic Program Consultant and as Historic Preservation Coordinator.

This book is dedicated with love to the alumni of Fruitjar,
a.k.a. Berea High School.

—Paul Rominger, Class of 1963

The Battle of RICHMOND, KENTUCKY

1862 Weather and Civil War Digest

Chapter One

Weather and the Battle of Richmond

Kentucky Weather, 1862

Many hardships, deprivations and the disruptive nature of the war itself were endured by people in Kentucky during the years of 1861-65. These were made severely worse by the extremely wet and dry spells in Kentucky during those years. These weather conditions are known because the Smithsonian Institution began collecting climate data in 1847. Seven years later, there were observers in Kentucky and in thirty other states. Ten stations in Kentucky reported throughout the war period and seven other stations reported for shorter periods of time.

Kentucky was one of the many areas enduring the last years of the Little Ice Age, a period between about 1300 and 1870 during which Europe and North America were experiencing much colder winters than those of the 20th century. The period can be divided in two phases, the first beginning around 1300 and continuing until late the 1400s. There was a slight warmer period in the 1500s, after which the climate deteriorated substantially. The years between 1600 and 1800 mark the height of the Little Ice Age. These years were characterized by the expansion of European trade and formation of European empires, directly linked to advances in the ability of technology to harness more of nature's power and the increase in fossil fuel power.

The cause of the Little Ice Age is unknown, but research has indicated that there was low sunspot activity during those years. This "Maunder Minimum" coincided with the coldest years, particularly 1645 to 1715. This was named for E.W. Maunder, who discovered the absence of sunspots during that period. Solar observers such as Giovanni Domenico Cassini and John Flamsteed calculated a minimum in sunspots, which indicates a much less active and possibly a colder sun with less energy output to warm the earth. Recent published data suggests that the sun expanded during the Maunder Minimum and its rotation slowed.

Of concern is the north Atlantic region, which is one of the most climatically unstable regions in the world. This is caused by the complex interaction of atmosphere and ocean. There is a seesaw of atmospheric pressure between a normal persistent high pressure cell over the Azores, and an equally persistent low pressure cell over Iceland. Sometimes the pressure cells trade places, which has severe consequences for the weather. Also for consideration are volcanic eruptions. The year after the Tamora eruption in Indonesia, 1815, was known as the year without a summer. However, the effect of such eruptions is limited to only a few years.

The *National Geographic Magazine* published an article by Habibulla Abdussamatov in 2007, who said that observations of Mars indicate a shrinking of the Martian Ice Caps of the Martian South Polar region. He said that a long-term increase in solar radiance is heating both earth and Mars. He predicted that Earth would enter a little ice age as early as 2014 and could last as long as two centuries. He contended that "Long-term variations in the amount of solar energy reaching the earth are the main and principal reasons driving and defining the climate change." Abdussamatov is an astrophysicist and head of space research at Pulkovo Astronomical Observatory in St Petersburg, Russia.

U.S. solar scientists have announced that the sun appears to be headed into a lengthy spell of low activity. Geophysicist Victor Manuel Velasco Herrera at the University of Mexico stated that in about five years the "Earth will enter a 'Little Ice Age' that will last from sixty to eighty years and may be caused by the decrease in solar activity." It would appear that after a warming period of over hundred and forty years, resembling the trend of the 1500s, we may be entering the third installment of the Little Ice Age. Future students may understand better how weather affects battles, logistics and troop movements.

In the final years of the second cold phase, Kentucky in 1862 began with unusually wet winter months. January had twenty-two days of warmer temperatures and rain or snow. Many roads were in terrible condition. February saw additional heavy rains that caused extensive flooding, sweeping away wooden fences and worsening already muddy roads. March followed with nineteen more days of rain and April was about the same.

At the Battle of Middle Creek, January 10, 1862, Union troops at Louisa, Kentucky, attempted to advance on Confederate troops recruited at Paintsville by Brig Gen. Marshall. Federal movement south of Prestonsburg was slowed by streams swollen by runoff from heavy rains. Confederates retired southward, hampered by bad road conditions, with rain on the 11th and 12th, an inch of snow on the 13th, sleet on the 14th and a mix of rain, sleet and snow on the 15th.

The Battle of Mill Springs was fought January 19, 1862. Confederate troops under Brig. Gen. Zollicoffer had been guarding Cumberland Gap. A portion of these moved to Mill Springs near Somerset and set up fortifications. They attacked Union Brig. Gen. Thomas' troops at Logan's Crossroads about dawn. Troop movements were difficult and miserably disagreeable. Federal troops left Lebanon, Kentucky, and marched about forty miles, slogging through roads of deep mud for two and a half weeks. They stopped at Logan's Crossroads on January 17. The Confederates moved toward them during the night of the 18th through a thunderstorm that dropped one and half inches of rain. The Confederates attacked during unrelenting weather. The temperature climbed to 68 degrees F. Many flintlocks, still in use during the Civil War, were unable to fire because of the wet weather.

By August, the drought of 1862 was in full effect. Crops were suffering and grass in the pastures was dry enough to burn. The last rain of significance was a half-inch from a violent thunderstorm on August 14. There were sprinkles on the 21st and the 23rd, but hardly enough to settle the dust. An evening shower on August 27th produced a quarter of an inch, which was promptly absorbed by the dry soil, and dusty conditions quickly followed. During the Battle of Richmond, August 29th and 30th, evening temperatures cooled to the middle seventies, with relative humidity at sixty to seventy per cent. It was an uncomfortable night for troops of both armies.

Chris Kolakowski writes that in the middle of oppressive heat and drought on August 25, the Confederate Army of Kentucky again took to the road. On August 30, by midday, the temperature stood at about one hundred degrees and both sides suffered heavily from lack of water. Warren Lambert wrote that Lieutenant Cox, adjutant of the 16th Indiana, thought the day was "gorgeous." Kirby Smith wrote that "The day dawned bright, clean and beautiful." Twelve-year-old Anderson Chenault Quisenberry, picking peaches with his little brother, later agreed that Saturday, August 30, 1862, was "one of the most beautiful days that has ever dawned in all the sensuous summer time. It was a perfect summer day." Mattie Wheeler wrote in her diary, "Before the morning was far advanced the deep peace of that lovely day was broken by a sullen, muffled boom, boom, boom in the direction of Richmond."

B. Kevin Bennett writes of the oppressive heat and humidity, which with the strain of battle left troops exhausted. The morning of Saturday, August 30th, dawned bright and clear with the promise of sweltering heat. Meal preparations and filling of canteens proved difficult inasmuch as Kentucky was in the grips of a severe drought that was already several weeks old and would last until October. The summer drought had not relented, and water supplies were falling. Spring branches stopped flowing and ponds had dried up. A couple of weeks later, the actions at Munfordville occurred from September 14-17. Gen. Bragg's Confederates attacked a much smaller Federal force under Colonel Wilder at dawn on Sunday, the 14th. A truce was called for tending the wounded, who were moved to hospitals, and the dead were buried. The truce continued, and Col. Wilder surrendered the Union troops on the 17th.

October saw the drought deepen and the shortage of water became critical. Many people in Kentucky faced the prospect of winter with a severe shortage of food. The bloody Battle of Perryville was fought on October 7th and 8th between U.S. Maj. Gen. Buell's army and the army of Confederate Gen. Bragg. Doctor's Creek, Bull Run and Wilson's Creek are tributaries of the Chaplin River, which flows through Perryville. The drought prevented these streams from flowing and remaining pools in them were usually covered with scum. These were the sources of water for both soldiers and horses. In the two-day battle, over 1,300 men were killed and over 5,400 were wounded. October 8th was the 21st consecutive dry day. The temperature rose to 90 degrees by 2 p.m. October 9th was another hot and dry day, with the temperature reaching 88 degrees. Fall arrived the next day after the battle, when a half inch of rain fell and the temperature rose only to 66 degrees in the afternoon. The following day saw only 52 degrees. Soldiers who had been suffering from the heat now endured shivering from the cold.

Stuart Sanders writes that Ormond Hupp of the 5th Indiana Light Artillery was wounded on the 8th, his wounds were dressed, and he was placed under a tree. He noted, "I laid under this tree two nights with but the one quilt, the weather was quite cold and chilling and in consequence many suffered." A member of the 33rd Alabama wrote that "we carried wheat straw for the wounded to lie upon...we were up with the wounded boys and assisting the doctors nearly all night. Since it was frigid some complained of being cold, their clothing being wet with blood."

R. S. Matthews of the 6th Tennessee wrote, "One night I was left in the ambulance, and the driver fed and watered his mules in the back part of it. My blanket got wet and froze, and my feet became frostbitten." James I. Hall of the 9th Tennessee Infantry was wounded in the torso. He lay on the battlefield all evening and was taken to the Goodnight farm near midnight. Hall remained outside for several days. His clothes had been ripped away so doctors could examine his wound. He was eventually placed under a lean-to made from old planks, where he lay when a heavy snow fell. He remained at that farm for approximately two weeks.

In 1968, a small black book the size of a pocket testament was found in Bristol, Tennessee. It contained a badly deteriorated diary written by a Confederate soldier, possibly an officer. Leaving Salyersville, Kentucky, October 26, the author wrote, "A heavy snow has fallen today, continued falling all day, very wet, never knew so much timber broken to pieces by snow. Late in the afternoon it is one continual crashing – Roads very bad – no one team able to draw its load across the mountains – slow progress – great deal trouble."

For much of the mid-1800s, the Smithsonian Institution in Washington, D.C. was the center of weather observation for the United States. Major tornado disasters during the spring and summer of 1860 resurfaced previous concerns about tornadoes, and by 1862 the Smithsonian distributed circulars alerting people to their dangers. Ian Livingston in *Tornado History*, March 12, 2012.

In 1862 there were forty-four tornadoes. Nine affected war efforts and eight affected troops. In Kentucky, there were up to three tornadoes on April 2, resulting in twenty-one deaths. One tore the roofs off thirty houses in Paducah, Kentucky, sank the steamer *Philadelphia* and moved toward Fort Holt, Kentucky. The Confederate defenses on Island No. 10 were badly weakened, resulting in the eventual surrender of 6,000 Confederate troops, three generals and the opening of the Mississippi River to just above Memphis by April 17, 1862. The ship eventually rechristened the USS *Red Rover*, the first hospital ship, was originally a Confederate vessel acquired in the capture of Island No. 10.

Information on tropical storms is more difficult to ascertain. There are some written reports at the time, but the existence of others has been determined by recent analysis of data. There were eight tropical systems in 1861. Six attained Category 1 or higher, and three affected the United States. One of these struck in November along the Atlantic Seaboard; 220 people were killed in a ship wrecked off the New England coast. There were three tropical storms and three hurricanes in 1862, with one making landfall. Five tropical systems made landfall in the U.S. in 1863. One came ashore in the Florida panhandle in May and has since been called Amanda because it ran ashore the bark (a sailing ship of three or more masts) USS *Amanda*, which was used as a stationary gunboat off Confederate ports in the Gulf of Mexico. There were other vessels damaged, and there were 110 fatalities. There were five tropical systems in 1864, but there was no hurricane landfall.

The Battle of Richmond, Kentucky

Braxton Bragg arrived in Chattanooga on July 30, 1862, to confer with Edmund Kirby Smith on a joint campaign. Kirby Smith had been wounded at Manassas and returned to duty as commander of a newly formed Department of East Tennessee. (Henry) He was to proceed from Knoxville to the Union position at Cumberland Gap. Bragg was to make a feint toward Nashville, but then move into Kentucky to draw Buell out of Tennessee. Bragg expected Buell to chase after him. In Kentucky, Bragg and Kirby Smith were to combine their armies to confront Buell. This action would enable Price and Van Dorn to secure West Tennessee for the Confederacy. Then with Buell defeated, Kirby Smith would move on Cincinnati and Bragg would go to Louisville. From there, the war would be carried north. (Bobrick)

At Chattanooga, Braxton Bragg did not assert his rank over Edmund Kirby Smith. Evidently they agreed to continue their independent commands until they would join forces in Kentucky, at which time Bragg would assume over-all command. This strongly suggested that the campaign would be poorly coordinated. Kirby Smith did not like to serve under anyone, and this assured him that he could continue to be independent as long as possible. (Harrison)

> General Kirby Smith wrote his wife, "I am with my advance in the bluegrass region…We have marched 110 miles through a mountain region over almost impassable roads, through a country destitute of supplies of all kinds—ragged bare footed almost starved marching day and night, exhausted from want of water. I have never seen such suffering…. Such fortitude, patriotism and self control has never been surpassed by any army that ever existed." (Parks)

Two recent opinions conclude: "Richmond was potentially more decisive that Bull Run—it opened Kentucky to Confederate invasion giving the rebels a possible route to the aorta of the Union war effort, the Ohio River. (Leigh) And, "Attempting to draw Kentucky into the Confederacy, the rebels risked it all at the 1862 Battle of Richmond."(Garcia)

In that same article, Col. Walter Taylor on General Lee's staff is quoted as saying, "Just now it does appear as if God was truly with us. All along our lines the movement is onward. Ohio, Maryland they expect to see invaded. We are here & I trust Kirby Smith will ere long shell Cincinnati." (Garcia)

However, Dr. Clement Eaton, in a biography of Jefferson Davis, concluded that President Davis made a serious mistake in not forcing the two armies to operate in a unified plan. Kirby Smith was young and ambitious and operated without much regard for Bragg who was his senior officer. (Eaton) Bragg seemed reluctant to exercise too much authority in East Tennessee, Kirby Smith's official territory. With this awkward situation, it is little wonder that uncertainty and muddling developed. (Horn)

Kirby Smith's campaign started off smoothly. Reinforced by General Cleburne's two brigades from Hardee's corps, Kirby Smith on August 14 moved from Knoxville into Kentucky, bypassing the Union force holding Cumberland Gap. (Horn) He rested at Barbourville, with his men carrying their provisions in their haversacks. Kirby Smith compared his expedition to Hernan Cortes, the Spanish conquistador, who burned his ships before the invasion of the Aztec Empire. (Hess) At that point, his army consisted of the following:

Confederate Units at the Battle of Richmond

Brig. General Patrick Cleburne

Marion (Florida) Light Artillery Battery (Capt. John Martin {w})
1st Texas Artillery Battery (Capt. James Douglas)
12th Tennessee Infantry (Col. Tyree Bell {ill}
47th Tennessee Infantry (Lt. Col. W.E. Holmes)
13th Tennessee Infantry (Col. Alfred Vaughan)
154th Senior Tennessee Infantry (Col. Edward Fitzgerald {killed})
13th & 15th Arkansas Infantry (Consolidated) (Col. Lucius Polk {w})
2nd Tennessee Infantry (Lt. Col. John Butler {killed})
5th / 35th Tennessee Infantry (Col. Benjamin Hill/Lt. Col. Joseph Smith)
48th Tennessee Infantry (Col. George Nixon)

Brig. General Thomas Churchill

10th Texas Dismounted Cavalry (Col. E.C. Earp)
11th Texas Dismounted Cavalry (Col. John C. Burks)
14th Texas Dismounted Cavalry (Col. Matthew Ector)
15th (aka 32nd) Texas Dismounted Cavalry (Lt. Col. James Weaver)
31st Arkansas Sharpshooters (Col. Thomas McCray/Major James W. Clark)
Humphrey's Arkansas Artillery Battery (Capt. Thomas Humphreys)
1st Arkansas Dismounted Rifles (Col. Daniel Reynolds)
2nd Arkansas Dismounted Rifles (Col. Harris Flanigan/Col. Robert Harper)
4th Arkansas Infantry (Col. Evander McNair/Lt. Col Henry Bunn)
4th Arkansas Battalion (Major J.A. Ross)
30th Arkansas Infantry (Col. Charles Turnball)

Cavalry Units (Col. John S. Scott)

1st Louisiana Cavalry (Col. John Scott/Lt. Col. James Nixon)
1st Georgia Cavalry (Col. James J. Morrison)
Buckner Guards from Kentucky (co.) (Capt. Willaim L. Gariott)
3rd Tennessee Cavalry (detachment) (Col. James Starnes)
1st Florida Cavalry (Comps. A, E, & F) (Capt. Footman)
Section of Georgia Cavalry as Headquarters Escort (Capt. Nelson)
Holmes Mountain Howitzer Battery (Lt. William Holmes)

Additional Unit
Huwalt's Tennessee Artillery Battery (arrived late)

Brig. General Henry Heth
(These units not engaged in the fight)
1st Florida Dismounted Cavalry
6th Florida Infantry
7th Florida Infantry
43rd Alabama Infantry
55th Georgia Infantry
(Seyfrit)

As he assumed command of the Army of East Tennessee, Kirby Smith had about 8000 troops. Major General John McCown's division was moved to Knoxville and assigned to Brig. General Thomas Churchill. Two brigades under Brig. General Patrick Cleburne and Colonel Preston Smith were loaned to Kirby Smith by General Bragg. As the Army of East Tennessee moved north, Kirby Smith carried arms for an additional 24,000 soldiers in expectation of augmenting his army. In a telegram to him on July 24, 1862, John Hunt Morgan said that his cavalry was "sufficient to hold all the country outside Lexington and Frankfort. These places are garrisoned chiefly with Home Guards…25,000 to 30,000 will join you at once." (Morgan)

Kirby Smith's army moved toward Kentucky but avoided Cumberland Gap. Union Brig. General George Morgan's 10,000 soldiers were judged to be too strong in number and too well fortified to attack (Henry), and with a view of taking central Kentucky and heading toward Cincinnati, Cumberland Gap was not a necessary target. As Kirby Smith left Tennessee and entered the Commonwealth of Kentucky, his army was renamed the Army of Kentucky.

He was opposed by the forces of General William Nelson, known as Bull because of his size and temper. Nelson had headquarters in Lexington. He had a command of 16,000 to defend the Bluegrass region of central Kentucky. Of this number, 7000 were assigned to Brig. General Mahlon Manson located near Richmond, Kentucky. (Dorris) General Horatio Wright in Cincinnati had been determined to not fight at Richmond unless the Federals could be certain of a victory. (Dorris) General Cassius M. Clay of Richmond had advocated a strategy of retreating to the Fayette County (Lexington) side of the Kentucky River and defending from the palisades of the river. This is what General Wright endorsed.

Gen. Nelson discarded the advantage of this plan by removing Gen. Clay from command and sending his two regiments and artillery to Richmond. This deployed Union troops exactly where the Confederate command wanted them. Of other units available to him, Gen. Nelson kept some in Lexington and others in the areas near Lancaster and Danville. On August 29, Nelson informed Gen. Wright that "Kirby Smith's game plan is now clear. He will assail Buell in left and rear." Expecting Kirby Smith to shift toward Lancaster, Nelson planned to have 16,000 Union troops there. If this plan seemed sensible, it was absolutely incorrect. (Brown)

General Manson was evidently not aware of this plan. Not knowing Nelson's location, Manson sent a message to him in Lexington and in Lancaster informing him of the army opposing him and asking for directions. An answer did not arrive from Nelson until Saturday afternoon when the battle had been engaged for several hours.

According to a fellow officer, Gen. Nelson was "ardent, loud-mouthed and violent." He was awakened in his bedroom in Lexington at 2:30 on the morning of August 30, and told that Confederate troops had crossed Big Hill the previous day but were prevented from taking Richmond because his brigadiers were alert and had intercepted Kirby Smith's army. He dressed quickly and rode to Richmond, taking back roads to avoid capture. His concern was that he had two small divisions of raw recruits under two ex-civilian brigadier generals. It would be difficult for his troops to hold against the battle seasoned Confederates. He arrived in Richmond in the early afternoon. (Foote)

Manson's brigade consisted of new recruits who had enlisted approximately two weeks earlier, 3,415 troops. In his command were 3,085 troops in Brig. General Charles Cruft's 2nd Brigade, who did not arrive until four days before the Battle of Richmond. (Ellis, Everman and Sears) Union cavalry under Colonel Metcalfe were also recruited about two weeks before the battle. The Union army at Richmond was as follows:

Brig. General Mahlon Manson

16th Indiana Infantry (Col. Thomas Lucas {w})
55th Indiana Infantry (Lt. Col. John R Mahan)

69th Indiana Infantry (Lt. Col. Hermann J. Korff {w})
71st Indiana Infantry (Lt. Col. Melville Topping {k})
Portions of Batteries F & G 1st Michigan Artillery (Lt. Edwin Lamphere/Lt. Luther Hale)

Brig. General Charles Cruft
12th Indiana Infantry (Col. William H. Link {mw})
66th Indiana Infantry (Major Thomas Morrison)
95th Ohio Infantry (Col. William McMillen {w})
18th Kentucky Infantry (Col. William Warner {w})
3rd Tennessee Infantry (detachment) (Lt. Col. William Chiles)
7th (aka 3rd) Kentucky Infantry (detachment) (Captain Elisha Treadway)

Col. Leondias Metcalfe, Cavalry Commander
7th Kentucky Cavalry (Col Leonidas Metcalfe)
6th Kentucky Cavalry (portion) (Lt. Col. Reuben Munday)
9th Kentucky Cavalry (portion) (Col. Richard Jacob)
9th Pennsylvania (portion) (Col. Edward Williams)
(Seyfrit)

Robert Collins Suhr wrote, "Scott's cavalry brigade had preceded the infantry into Kentucky. On August 23, near Big Hill, he had attacked a Union supply train heading for the Cumberland Gap, capturing fifty wagons and driving the guards back toward Richmond. On the 28th, Scott's mounted pickets warned of the approach of a large Federal force. (Kirby) Smith was at the Rockcastle River with Churchill and Cleburne when he found out about the Union advance. He ordered both infantry divisions to march to Scott's support, and at 3 a.m. the next day, he started toward Big Hill himself.

"A Union cavalry detachment under Lt. Col. Reuben Munday reported at 11 a.m. on the 29th that the Confederate force was advancing. Manson ordered Munday to continue watching the Confederates and to inform him if they left the road. Meanwhile he sent messages to Nelson, warning him of the Confederate advance. Since Manson was unsure of Nelson's location, he sent one message to him at Lexington and one to Lancaster. For some reason, it took sixteen hours for Manson's message to reach Nelson at Lexington. A response from Gen. Nelson did not reach Gen. Manson until Saturday afternoon.

"At 2 p.m. on the 29th, Manson learned that his pickets were retreating, with 5,000 Confederates close behind. 'The only question for me now to determine was whether I should allow the enemy to attack me in my camp or whether I should advance and meet him,' he said later. Because there were hills one and a half miles to the south that dominated the Union camp, Manson ordered his troops forward to higher ground a little further south to make a stand there."

"Three-quarters of a mile from their camp, Union pickets spotted a large Confederate cavalry force a half mile east of the road. When the Union cannons opened fire, the Confederates retreated into the woods. Manson deployed part of his brigade across the road on the high ground…Scott's horse artillery returned fire, shells crashing all around the Union guns and the 55th Indiana."

Late in the afternoon, Union Col. Metcalfe's cavalry chased Confederate cavalry to Joe Lick Knob just south of Mount Zion Church. At about 5 o'clock in the afternoon, Confederate cavalry encountered Federal cavalry and were driven back. Gen. Cleburne alerted his officers to form a line of battle, but this was not completed until after dark. A battery was placed to the left of the road supported by two companies of sharpshooters. Scott's cavalry dashed down the road, followed by Metcalfe's cavalry. When the Union cavalry was within twenty-five paces, the Confederates unleashed a tremendous follow of fire that stopped the Federals, who lost thirty prisoners, 100 stands of rifles and several horses. (Stewart) Metcalfe did not mention this engagement to General Manson.

In a dispatch to the *Cincinnati Commercial*, Murat Halstead wrote that the result of fighting on Friday was insignificant. That night, there were many and varied rumors that the Confederates had been defeated and disappeared. The sun rose on Saturday in a clear and cloudless day. The early morning was delightful, but there was a drought and as in previous days, the temperature hovered at about a hundred degrees. (Halstead) Kirby Smith said it began as one of the most beautiful mornings he had ever seen.

Kirby Smith learned that Union troops at Richmond were expected, and he decided to attack before they arrived. (Harrison) "(Kirby) Smith, who was afraid that Manson would do what Wright had suggested, [and] entrench on the high bluffs of the Kentucky River, wanted to press forward and begin the battle before the Union troops withdrew. He ordered Cleburne to begin the attack rather than withdraw. Manson prepared to fight south of Richmond. At 4 a.m. he ordered the men to stand to arms. He brought Cruft's brigade forward and placed it on his left flank."(Suhr)

Nathaniel Shaler wrote in 1884, that the Union force, "was under the command of the able but erratic General William Nelson. General Nelson was an excellent division commander, as was well proved at Shiloh, where he won distinguished credit. He was, however, unfitted by his furious nature for independent command. Nelson expected the attack, but was surprised by the amazing swiftness of the Confederate advance, for in three days they had marched nearly ninety miles. Nelson himself was in Lexington, when he should have been with his army." (Shaler)

Ellis, Everman and Sears wrote in 1985, "That night, the Union soldiers slept on their arms, those who slept at all. Some of the troops assembled for this battle had seen service less than a month, some a little over a week. "Some of the regiments never had had a battalion drill and knew not what a line of battle was. They were undisciplined, inexperience, and had never been taught in the manual of arms." … To add to the problem, the men were ill-equipped, with no "ordinary camp equipage or conveniences. They were lying exposed to the hot sun by day and heavy dews by night." In addition, the Union army had insufficient ammunition, as events of the day would demonstrate. According to Manson, reporting after the battle, some pieces of artillery had run out of ammunition during the first engagement in the morning, while all ammunition had been exhausted by the end of the last battle in the evening.

"In the Confederate camp, the troops may have been seasoned, but they had every reason to be fatigued. They had been, E. Kirby Smith reported, on "a forced march, almost day and night, for three days, over a mountainous wilderness, destitute alike of food and water." He stated that his men had undergone "without murmur the fatigues and privations of one of the most difficult marches of this war. For several days and parts of nights…over stony roads, with their almost bare feet, and with green corn and beef without salt as their only food…." Some of them slept in the "line of battle without any supper" the night before the Battle of Richmond." (Ellis, Everman and Sears)

At seven o'clock Saturday morning, the fighting began with cannon exchanges. The Union batteries were well trained. Confederate batteries at that time were some of the best in any Southern army. The number of Union cannon engaged is easy to ascertain. There were nine, and all of them were captured. The number of Confederate cannon is much more difficult to determine. There may have been fourteen. Most of the artillery on both sides consisted of field howitzers. There was one three-inch ordnance rifle and possibly one or two Napoleons. There were a few mountain howitzers most likely only on the Confederate side, but it is not probable that these were engaged in the battle. Union artillery was on the south side of Mount Zion Church. Confederates formed artillery less than a mile south on a ridge above Bethel Church, where Hays Fork Baptist Church is now located. One opening Confederate round apparently bounced on the hard, sun-baked dirt and struck the south side of Mount Zion Christian Church, causing minor damage still visible today.

General Cleburne reported to General Kirby Smith that the Union battery opened in rapid fire. In response to Kirby Smith's order not to engage in battle until General Churchill was in place, he said he sent out skirmishers and ordered his artillery to fire slowly and not waste any rounds. The exchange between cannon and skirmishers lasted two hours. (Cleburne) Early in the battle on Saturday, Brig. Gen. Cleburne reported to Lt. Gen. Kirby Smith that he had been wounded in the mouth by a minie ball, losing two teeth. The wound was painful, and he had difficulty talking. Cleburne was taken to the home of John White Parks near Mt. Zion Christian Church, where he spent several days. His reports were written from that house.

Despite his wound early in the battle, Gen. Cleburne greatly distinguished himself as a combat leader. His adept generalship enabled his men to vanquish the Federals. Kirby Smith said he was, "one of the most gallant, zealous, and intelligent" of officers. (Parks) This victory at Richmond and subsequent combat leadership earned for the Irish-born general a promotion to major general, one of only two foreign born Confederate officers to earn this commission. (Hattaway-Jones)

Halstead reported, "Gen. Manson's brigade was called out and formed the line of battle about half a mile beyond Rogersville…Manson had not yet been reinforced by any part of Cruft's brigade. The rebels were prompt in their response to Manson's artillery, and it became apparent that their four guns of Friday had increased in number and caliber during the night. Confederates formed their line of battle very differently from that of Friday, describing an arc of a circle with a flanking regiment at each end of their line so as to bring our men between a cross fire which no troops could stand for any length of time. Many of their men were concealed behind trees and fences, and did terrible execution as sharp shooters." (Halstead)

The Confederates began attacking Manson from a shallow ravine to his left. He turned his troops to face them and began pulling soldiers across the road from Mount Zion Church. General Churchill located a ravine to Manson's right through which flowed a rivulet, Mound Branch Creek or Mounce's Creek, which was reasonably flat where the brook joined Hays Fork of Silver Creek. It quickly became deep with sharply plunging sides. This is today called Churchill's Draw. As the Confederate dismounted cavalry charged out of this, they flanked Union troops at the Christian church. The first phase of the battle was effectively ended. Manson and Cruft began retreat to Senator White's Farm about three miles closer to Richmond. The roads did not intersect squarely, and the two brigades could not form an even line.

"As the Confederate infantry began to advance, Manson feared that he could not defend the ground. He ordered his infantry to turn about and march toward the rear, leaving the ground he had held the day before. Cruft's brigade was on the right of the road on high ground, while Manson's brigade was on the left behind a fence. After about an hour of fighting, Cruft's right collapsed at about the same time Manson's line on the left broke for the rear. The entire Union line began to fall back toward Richmond, unit integrity disintegrating with every step." (Suhr)

"Manson ordered the remnants of the army to make a stand at their camp near Richmond. Nelson arrived on the battlefield at about 2 p.m. He ordered Manson to fall back to a better position closer to the town. Nelson immediately realized that he could not hold Richmond, and he ordered the army's wagon trains to assemble on the road to Lexington." (Suhr) Against this last Union line, Kirby Smith concentrated the full weight of his army against the remaining Union force, lasting about an hour and a half. These two armies met with a ferocity that came near to equaling the worst Gettysburg and Chickamauga. (Lambert) The three phases of the Battle of Richmond, Mount Zion Christian Church, White's Farm and the Richmond Cemetery were all decisive Confederate victories.

"Early on Saturday Scott's Louisiana cavalry with three mountain howitzers were sent to intercept our retreat. They dismounted about two miles from the expected point of attack, tied their horses to the fences and lay in ambush, waiting our appearance. "By 4 p.m., Scott was in position; he placed most of his men on the Lexington road, with one company on the Lancaster road and the remainder between the two. Almost as soon as he arrived, Union stragglers began passing across his front. At about 6 p.m., the main Union force arrived. Manson rode to the front of the column, where he found a small group of Confederate cavalry on the road. There he organized an advanced guard of 100 men who managed to drive off the cavalrymen. Farther down the road, he found the Confederates in the woods. When he tried to drive them off, his force was cut to pieces." (Suhr)

Early in the afternoon Gen. Nelson had ordered all the wagons and supplies to be ready for removal. A portion of Col. Metcalfe's cavalry and Col. Jacob's regiment were ordered to the front as an advance guard. Col. Mundy's cavalry was detailed to cover the retreat. "Nothing occurred to disturb the monotony of a very slow march until we had passed the third mile-stone on our way to the Kentucky River. Suddenly an officer dashed along the line with the order "Cavalry to the front!" We all knew what that meant, and unfortunately the cavalry that should have formed our advance, but had lagged behind, also knew what it meant. (Halstead) Instead of forming line to oppose Scott's cavalry, many in the Union cavalry left their horses and weapons and began running to escape.

In addition to their cannon, the Union lost their entire wagon train. The number of Union soldiers killed was 206, wounded was 844 and captured was 4,303, for a total of 5,353 Union casualties. (Hattaway-Jones) General Nelson, who had arrived at the Richmond Cemetery about 2 p.m., was wounded twice. General Manson suffered a slight injury when his horse fell on him in the engagement against Scott north of Richmond. This attempted engagement and Manson's capture enabled Nelson to escape capture. He was taken by his aide Major Green Clay to Nicholasville, and then to Louisville to recover. The Confederates captured nine cannon, 10,000 stands of small arms and a large quantity of supplies. Confederates lost 78 killed, 372 wounded and one missing. (Hattaway-Jones) A few hundred Union soldiers escaped, some fording the Kentucky River to Winchester. The remainder were scattered through the woods and by-paths, finally making their way to the Ohio River all the way from the Little Sandy River to Louisville. (Shaler)

Following the victory at Richmond, Kirby Smith quickly took Lexington and sent his cavalry raiding as far as the vicinity of Louisville and Covington, across the Ohio River from Cincinnati. He occupied Frankfort, the capital of Kentucky, with 1,500 cavalry, causing officials of the state government to flee to Louisville where the state archives and treasury had already been transferred. (Horn)

Of the arms Kirby Smith brought into Kentucky for new recruits, only about 1,600 were used. President Davis wrote to General Theophilus Homes in Arkansas after the Battle of Richmond to affirm that the only justification for the invasion of Kentucky was the belief that Kentuckians would rise up en masse to support the Confederate army. In his report on the battle, Kirby Smith wrote with a degree of bitterness, "the Kentuckians are slow and backward in rallying to our standard. Their hearts are evidently with us but their blue-grass and fat cattle are against us." (Eaton) The Battle of Richmond was perhaps the most decisive Confederate victory of the Civil War, but the campaign in Kentucky failed. When Braxton Bragg left for Tennessee after withdrawing from the Battle of Perryville in early October, Edmund Kirby Smith had no choice but to follow him.

The advantage of the victory at Richmond was squandered. Braxton Bragg had realized from his position near Louisville that he was outnumbered by Buell. He sent a request to Kirby Smith after Richmond to join him at Bardstown. Bragg believed that the two combined forces could defeat Buell. This would bring Kentucky with the Ohio River as its northern boundary conclusively into the Confederacy. (Keegan) An eventual joint command was what Bragg thought was agreed to at Chattanooga. There was a vagueness and lack of decision, not uncommon in Civil War battles. The fault lay with Jefferson Davis' policy of creating independent departments within larger departments. Bragg did not order a joint campaign; such an order would have probably been ignored by Kirby Smith, who had no intention of subverting his command to Bragg. Davis would not enforce a joint venture (Lambert). A decisive Kentucky campaign came to naught.

Chapter Two

Along the Line of Battle

Boone's Trace, The Old State Road and U.S. 421

The road in front of the Battlefield Park Visitors Center and Museum, Mt. Zion Christian Church and the Pleasant View home of the Battlefield Park is U.S. 421, a spur of U.S. 21, which runs 941 miles from Michigan City, Indiana, to Fort Fisher, North Carolina. It was commissioned in 1930. This highway generally follows the route of the Old State Road from Cumberland Gap to the Falls of the Ohio, the city of Louisville. Some of this route was the Wilderness Road, a term that came to be applied to much of the early road system. The Wilderness Road ran through the Gap passed through Danville on its way to Louisville. At Hazel Patch in what later became Laurel County, a road veered northward toward the settlement of Boonesborough. This was Boone Trace or Boone's Trace. The Old State Road followed this route. It has in the past been mistakenly called the Wilderness Road, but that route followed Skaggs Trace, which veered from Boone Trace at Hazel Patch and went to Crab Orchard. The Battle of Camp Wildcat was fought near Skaggs Trace.

Boone's Trace

Boone's Trace was blazed in March and April of 1775 by thirty men with axes accompanying Daniel Boone. Starting at the Watauga settlements on the Holston River, now Kingsport, Tennessee, these explorers went through the Cumberland Gap, followed the Shawnee – Cherokee warriors' trail for fifty miles, then continued on a bison (buffalo) trail to the Rockcastle River. From there, they followed Roundstone Creek to the gap at Big Hill, and descended north to Otter Creek and a site called Boonesborough on the Kentucky River. It was a dirt path, steep and rough, traversed only on foot or horseback.

In 1792, the new Kentucky legislature provided money to upgrade Boone Trace, the Old State Road, extended through Richmond to Lexington and Frankfort as it headed to the Falls of the Ohio at Louisville and also Skaggs Trace from Hazel Patch through Danville to Louisville, the Wilderness Road. These roads were considered all-weather with a corduroy surface of logs over dirt. Boone's Trace significantly improved as it came down off the Cumberland Plateau near Berea. The improved roads allowed for wagon and carriage travel and were used by thousands of people.

Because of the threat of Native attacks, the road was so dangerous that most pioneers traveled well-armed. The Shawnee had not been part of the land sale treaty and the Chickamauga Cherokees were traditionalists who rejected the land sale treaty. Robbers and criminals could also be found on the road. Defensive log blockhouses were built alongside the road, with portholes in the walls for firing at attackers. They were often called stations.

The Old State Road served as a great path of commerce for the early settlers. Horses, cattle, sheep and hogs found a waiting market in the Carolinas, Maryland and Virginia. Hogs in groups of 500 or more were driven down the road to market. Beef in Eastern markets had become a main source of income for farmers in Kentucky.

A postal road was opened in 1792 from Bean Station, Tennessee, through Cumberland Gap to Danville, Kentucky, due to the efforts of Kentucky's first Governor Isaac Shelby. This connection of Kentucky to the East was a great advantage. Frontier settlers eagerly waited for the arrival of postal riders to get mail, newspapers and local news from other settlements. Use of the older roads declined when the National Road was opened in 1818, allowing travel to the Ohio River on level ground from the East. At about this time, steamboats first appeared on the Ohio and Mississippi Rivers.

During the Civil War, both the Union Army and the Confederate Army used the Old State Road. An early battle at Camp Wildcat stopped the first attempt of the Confederates to gain control of Kentucky. The Cumberland Gap changed hands four times throughout the war. Southern armies used the road for marches into Virginia. General U. S. Grant came down the road for the Union campaign in Tennessee in 1864. He said of the road, "With two brigades of the Army of the Cumberland, I could hold that pass against the army which Napoleon led to Moscow."

A segment of the Old State Road was among the first roads in the United States to be paved. The old road from the town of Cumberland

Gap, Tennessee, to Middlesboro, Kentucky, was paved and completed on October 3, 1908. This was a new kind of paved macadam construction funded by local communities with Federal supervision. It was later linked to the famous Dixie Highway that connected Detroit, Michigan, to Miami, Florida. The name was later changed to US Highway 25. The new road brought in new industry and tourism to rural areas.

US 421 enters Tennessee from North Carolina in Trade, Tennessee, the oldest crossroads community in Tennessee and the easternmost town in the state. After Trade, US 421 goes to Mountain City then towards Bristol. From there it goes through the Cumberland and Powell Mountains. For much of the length of 421 in Kentucky, there are many curves. The road becomes more level as it joins US 25 at the Blue Grass Army Depot south of Richmond, and roughly parallels I-75 towards Lexington. US 421 still provides the most direct route between Lexington and Frankfort, the state capital of Kentucky.

Merritt Jones Tavern
Compiled from various newspapers and Kubiak: Madison County Rediscovered

There is no record of a person named Merrick Jones from Madison County serving in the Confederate military, but there is record of Merritt Jones. Aunt Sally and Uncle John Anderson, who lived in the house and were interviewed for the older of the two articles, always referred to the previous owner as "Merrick." In these newspaper accounts and in local tradition, the old home was called the Grant House. It was thought that in February 1864, Gen. Grant stopped for the night. The log cabin was known as Jones Tavern. It was sold in 1883 by Jones to Mrs. John Anderson's grandparents. Aunt Sally, formerly an Ambrose and age 73 at the time she was interviewed, was four years old when she moved with her grandparents to the house. She could remember when Mrs. Jones sat on the front porch talking with neighbors and friends about Grant's visit.

Early in 1864, General Grant was on his way to Washington to receive a gold medal struck in his honor and to assume command of the Armies of the United States. He came through Cumberland Gap on his way to Lexington to entrain for the Capital. He was delayed and decided to spend the night at Jones Tavern. That spot had already become well known. A fierce battle had been fought in the neighborhood in August 1862. The tavern was used as a hospital after the Battle of Big Hill, August 23, 1862. There are thirteen Confederates buried behind the garden at the foot of Big Hill. Two Union soldiers found nearby were reburied in the Berea Cemetery. After the Battle of Perryville, Confederates used the home in their return to Tennessee. Federal soldiers later took possession and built a commissariat from which goods were forwarded over rough corduroy roads.

In February 1864, Grant was riding with perhaps a dozen staff officers. A member of his staff reached the "stand" a little before supper time and told the Jones family they must prepare for the general a nice supper and "be real particular to have a warm bedroom ready." Gen. Grant came to the home and was waited on by daughters of the tavern owner. Mrs. Jones was in bed ill. Gen. Grant was very courteous. They later spoke of him as being taciturn, but polite. As he prepared to leave the next morning, he paid for his lodging and asked one girl where her father was. She replied that he was in the Confederate Army. When asked about her mother, the girl told Gen. Grant that she was ill. He asked to see her. When he entered her room, she was in the company of several of John Hunt Morgan's cavalrymen. Gen. Grant thanked her for her hospitality and said he hoped her husband and sons would return safely. He then departed for Lexington. Rumors spread that the General had stayed in Madison County, but they were not confirmed until about 1915 by Dr. William F. Francis of St. Louis. As a young man, he had been a very close friend of the Jones family, and later he lived in the house. At that time, it was occupied by the Jarvis Carrier family. They rented the house from Berea College.

Jones Tavern was a log and clapboard house. The older half was built c.1800, with the latter half about 1830. It was situated at the base of Big Hill in southern Madison County along the old state road from Cumberland Gap to Louisville. It was unusual in having three entrances. Two of these went into the main part of the house, the third was to the "saddle room," an area where saddles were kept secure so that guests could not leave on their journey without paying. One door had walnut panels with wooden pegs. The home was built on a stone foundation and had four stone fireplaces, planked pine floors and dove-tailed log walls.

After the war, railroads made the old state road of little use. However, some people still remember it. Sherman Robinson told of traveling on it from Clay County in the 1880s, and that it was a corduroy road. Mrs. Carrier said that she came on it from Jackson County in 1883. The house was bypassed when the highway was straightened and repaved. Jones Tavern burned in the early 1990s. The road at Big Hill is now part of U.S. 421, with that section to the junction of 421 and U.S. 25 in front of Battlefield Park Visitors Center designated as Battlefield Memorial Highway. Berea College is studying the feasibility of keeping the area around Jones Tavern cleared, mowed and accessible to the public. This will require that the old section of road be reconstructed to Highway 421 for the safety of cars entering and exiting the property.

Joe Lick Knob

Stand on the front porch of Pleasant View, 1546 Battlefield Memorial Highway (part of Highway 421) and look south. The pleasant view is Joe Lick Knob or Joe's Lick Knob. It is located just beside the road and was used by Confederates during the Battle of Richmond. A skirmish took place there on Friday, August 29, 1862. Joe Lick Knob is one of thirty-four knobs in Madison County. It is fourth in height in the county, with an elevation of 1,483 feet.

Joe Lick Knob is a part of the Knobs Region of Kentucky. This is a narrow, horseshoe shaped region of hundreds of isolated hills. The region wraps around the Bluegrass region in the center of the state. The Knobs region begins near Louisville and stretches in an arc for more than 100 miles. It is never more than thirty miles wide. The knobs are often cone-shaped hills and in physiographic terms are monadnocks or erosional remnants. They were originally continuous with the Mississippian Plateau, but were separated from the plateau by stream erosion. Many of the knobs are still capped by erosion-resistant limestone or sandstone. The sharp slopes of the knobs are mostly composed of shale from the Mississippian-age Borden Formation. The base of the knobs commonly contains Devonian black shale.

In *Glimpses of Historic Madison County*, Jonathan and Maude Dorris wrote about the Squire Boone Rock found at Joe Lick Knob, saying that Daniel Boone and his brother Squire came to Kentucky in 1769 to hunt and explore. To replenish their supply of ammunition, salt and other necessities, Squire returned to North Carolina. Daniel remained and traveled alone as far away as the Falls of the Ohio (present day Louisville). Squire carved his name on the rock in 1770 so his brother would know he had returned. The rock was about four feet in the ground. It is eleven feet in length, four feet wide at the bottom to twenty-two inches wide at the top. The rock is sixteen to twenty inches wide and weighs 7,500 pounds. The inscription is large, bold and distinct. It reads "1770 Squire Boone." About 1900, the rock was moved into Richmond in front of the Madison County Courthouse. Because of further erosion concerns, it is now encased in the foyer of the courthouse.

Concerning Joe Lick Knob, Warren Lambert wrote in his booklet *The Decisive Battle of Richmond, Kentucky*, "The roads from Barbourville to Big Hill were through almost impassable mountains. Though a terrible march, the two lead (Confederate) divisions made it to Big Hill in three days.... Uneasy with the enemy so near, however, Pat Cleburne formed his Southern infantry (north of Big Hill) in a line of battle near the present road junction of U.S. Highway 421 and Kentucky 1016 near Bobtown (this is at the base of Joe Lick Knob). After instructing his officers to form their troops accordingly if an alarm was sounded, he dismissed his men and a left small rearguard deployed on both sides of the Richmond Road. Within a short time and in pitch blackness, Metcalfe's Union cavalry chased Scott's cavalry into Cleburne's prepared position. The Southern gunfire repulsed the Union nearly as badly as they had been routed at Big Hill, and the fighting on August 29 came to an end."

When a name includes "Lick," it refers to a salt lick. A salt lick is a mineral lick, a natural mineral deposit providing sodium, calcium, iron, phosphorus and zinc required in the springtime by animals for bone and muscle growth. Many animals visited mineral licks regularly to supplement their food intake with other micronutrients, including magnesium, sulfur, potassium, selenium, cobalt and molybdenum. Licks are often, but not always, near creeks or springs. Licks were good locations for hunting. Perhaps Joe Lick was an attempt to pronounce in English the name of the area in Shawnee, an Algonquin language. More likely, it refers to one of the fourteen early settlers at Fort Boonesborough with the first name of Joseph and two with the name of Josiah. Several of the last names of these persons indicate families that remained in the area. Natural salts are chemicals dissolved in water. Electrolytes are essential for a body to remain alive.

Prior to arriving at Joe Lick Knob and Bobtown, the area at its base, the Confederate army came to Big Hill. It is 4.9 miles from Berea and

14.2 miles from Richmond. Big Hill has an elevation of 1,550 feet. The counties of Madison, Jackson and Rockcastle come together at the top of Big Hill. Confederate Cavalry Col. John Scott arrived at Big Hill at 1 p.m. on August 23, 1862. His seasoned First Louisiana Cavalry Regiment, First Georgia Cavalry Regiment and a regiment of the Kentucky Buckner Guard assembled at Big Hill by 3 p.m. Scott also had a battery of mountain howitzers. They encountered Union Col. Leonidas Metcalfe's Seventh Kentucky Cavalry, recruited a week earlier, and the Third Tennessee Infantry Battalion. Scott charged Metcalfe's forces. The Union cavalry quickly retreated to Richmond and Paris, Kentucky. The Third Tennessee Infantry rescued Metcalf and Union Lt. Col W. M. Odin. Scott captured 148 Union wagons and teams, plus twenty-seven wagons and teams later, 600 horses and mules, and much needed military supplies headed to resupply Union forces at Cumberland Gap. Scott also captured Metcalfe's horse and uniform, with vital information about Richmond. Cavalry used the next few days to scout the entire area.

Within the Big Hill area is Pilot Knob, with an elevation of 1,411 feet. Also within sight is Indian Fort Mountain. It has five lookout points on two peaks—East Pinnacle with an elevation of 1503 feet and West Pinnacle at 1487 feet. There is a natural rock outcropping used as a cliff dwelling by Hopewell Indians from 100 B.C. to 400 or 500 A.D. Later American Indians have also used the site. The rock shelter was initially thought to have been a fortification used for defense. Recent evaluation suggests that it was a sacred place used for rituals. Indian Fort, owned by Berea College, is open year-round for visitors. With about eight miles of trails, the pinnacles are a popular hiking and picnic area for local residents and students.

Kingston

The Old State Road ran through the community of Kingston. The village of Kingston was named for Theodore King, the first merchant and tailor in the community. In 1846, a post office was built. After the Carl F. Day Law of 1904, a school for Berea College colored students was built in the community. With the establishment of Lincoln Memorial Institute by Berea College near Shelbyville, the Kingston school was abandoned and the building acquired by Kingston Masonic

Lodge. Some family names have remained in Kingston since the Civil War. Robert C. Moody still owns the family farm, and soldiers of both armies would have walked by the Moody general store in Kingston.

Masonic Fraternity

Soldiers would also have marched by Kingston Masonic Lodge Number 315. This lodge was organized in 1855 and continues to be active. Of the six generals involved in the Battle of Richmond, five were Freemasons: Edmund Kirby Smith, Thomas Churchill and Patrick Cleburne of the Confederates; Mahlon Manson and Charles Cruft of the Union. Within an army, while there might possibly have been cordiality between Freemasons, there certainly was consideration given. This consideration was also shown to members of the Masonic Fraternity in an opposing army. At the time of the Battle of Richmond, there were several lodges in Madison County: Richmond Lodge 25, 1813; Madison Lodge 183, 1848; Moss Lodge 254, 1852; Kingston Lodge and Waco Lodge 338, 1856. Berea Lodge 617 was organized in 1882.

The Freemasons were a vital component of the establishment of the American republic. Church attendance at the time of the Revolutionary War was less than twenty percent. On the frontier areas, a much lower percentage of persons had the opportunity for church. Many early leaders were Deist. This was a belief that it might be reasonable to think that a creator had been present when the earth was formed, but Deism rejected the belief that any supernatural deity continued to interact with humans. God might have made the world, but then remained aloof and did not intervene.

Some of our Founders of the republic were Freemasons. They brought a different set of beliefs. At the core of the Masonic Fraternity were the requirements of Brotherly Love, Relief and Truth. Relief means charity for others and mutual aid for fellow Masons. Truth requires a search for answers to questions of morality and salvation of the soul that only a person's faith and relationship with God can provide.

Mount Zion Church

The most iconic structure on the battlefield at Richmond is the Mt. Zion Christian Church. For many, many years the church was one of two "public" buildings on the battlefield, the other being the Madison County Courthouse. The church building was built in 1851-52. It was built in a large grove of old growth trees, with some of those trees being used to build the structure. The pews in use today are original. The deed to the lot on which the Mt. Zion Church stands was recorded in June of 1852. Bricks were made on-site in an area behind the present church building. The building is four bricks thick. There is not a foundation; the walls originally extended fifteen feet into the ground. The building was surrounded by oak, poplar and sycamore trees. One sixty-three-foot-long tree trunk from those trees was placed the full length of the ceiling and one of equal length in the floor. Each was sixteen inches square. The pews were made from four poplar boards each cut from the property. The church still has the two original front doors. In earlier days, men entered the left door to sit on the left side and women entered the right door to sit in their section on the right.

Being less than ten years old at the time of the battle, Mt. Zion Church was one of the largest church buildings in Madison County. It originally was one large room. It has since added interior walls for Sunday school rooms and offices on the main floor. A basement was dug for a fellowship hall, requiring the ground around the church to be excavated and lowered three feet. But you still can get a good feel of what the church looked like at the time of the Battle of Richmond in August 1862. With the exception of the outside entrance to the basement, the exterior of the church remains virtually unchanged.

Federal forces occupied Richmond and the Federal Medical Director, Capt. Bernard J.D. Irwin, M.D., commandeered the Madison County Courthouse and Madison Female Institute as hospitals. Irwin noted that he had "few medical officers, instruments, ambulances, tents or other camp equipage to enable them to perform their duties."

Mt. Zion became a field hospital early in the fight on August 30, and a yellow flag denoted that fact. However, the church was struck by Confederate artillery, scars of which remain to this day on the south side near the top of the electrical service.

Confederate forces took control of the church as the Union soldiers fled toward Richmond. Treatment of wounded became a cooperative effort between both sides, with many members of the surrounding church community and other settlements helping out. In addition to military personnel, several local doctors, Dr. William Chase,

Dr. Charles Wilmore and others, assisted in the treatment of scores of wounded. The dead were buried across the road from Mt. Zion, and were eventually moved to Richmond Cemetery. The Union dead were moved to Camp Nelson National Cemetery in 1867-68. The church served as a surgery during and after the battle. Confederate and Union surgeons were working together, which was common. When they ran out of surgical supplies, the surgeons collected $400 in federal money and the Union surgeon went through the Confederate line to Richmond to buy more supplies. Approximately forty soldiers died in the church. Others, whether Confederate or Union, were taken home by church members in the hope that they would recuperate.

Mt. Zion Christian Church is still an active congregation and has a strong sense of its unique history. The congregation has been a great partner in the preservation and interpretive efforts at the Battle of Richmond. Looking at the church, walk to the left or south side, toward the back and high up on the building is a repair from a solid shot cannon ball. Michigan Light Artillery was formed in line there and it is believed that a Confederate solid cannon ball fired toward them to determine the range hit the ground and bounced to the top of the church. Despite hitting the ground, it would have still been traveling very fast. A Michigan Historical Marker denoting the initial position of Federal artillery from Michigan was dedicated in the summer of 2012 about thirty yards south of Mt. Zion Church.

Chapter Three

Medical Attention

Bernard J.D. Irwin

Bernard John Dowling Irwin was born in Ireland in 1830. After immigrating to the United States, he served in the Army from 1856 to 1894. He died in Canada in 1917 and is buried in the West Point Cemetery, New York. His son, George Leroy Irwin graduated from West Point in 1888, served in World War One, and held the rank of Major General. His grandson, Stafford Leroy Irwin graduated from West Point in 1915, served in World War Two and held the rank of Lieutenant General.

Bernard Irwin graduated from New York Medical College in 1852 and was appointed house surgeon and physician at State Emigrant Hospital until 1855, when he became acting assistant surgeon, U.S. Army. In 1856 he became assistant surgeon, Regular Army, was sent to Fort Union, New Mexico, and then to Fort Defiance, Arizona. In 1861, Irwin led a detachment fourteen men of the 7th Infantry to the aid of Lieut. George Bascom, who with sixty men was surrounded by 500 Apaches under Cochise. Irwin's detachment defeated the Apaches and relieved the besieged soldiers. For this action above and beyond the call of duty, Irwin was the first person (chronologically by action) to receive the Medal of Honor, which was created in 1862. His Medal of Honor was belatedly awarded at his retirement.

Dr. Irwin was appointed medical director under Gen. William "Bull" Nelson in 1862, and at Shiloh, April 1862, improvised one of the first field hospitals used by the Army. This was the beginning of the M.A.S.H. units, mobile army surgical hospitals. Dr. Irwin was captured during the Battle of Richmond while saving the wounded Gen. Nelson. Nelson escaped across the Kentucky River to Winchester, then to Nicholasville. Irwin was released in September 1862 and became medical director of the Army of the Southwest.

Following the Civil War, he remained in the Army and was promoted to lieutenant colonel in 1885 and to colonel in 1890. He was a delegate and vice president of the Pan American Medical Congress in 1893 and a delegate to the 1894 International Medical Congress, which met in Rome. At his retirement in 1894, he was the second ranking officer in the medical corps. In 1904, by Act of Congress, Dr. Irwin was promoted to brigadier general. Despite the title of "fighting doctor" that had often been bestowed on him, Irwin was always primarily interested in his work as a physician.

There were anesthetics during the Civil War. Morphine, a pain medication, was isolated from opium about 1804. Nitrous oxide, used in dentristry, was developed in 1844. Ether was first used in surgery by Crawford Long in 1842. Chloroform was synthesized about 1831 and first used in surgery in 1847. It was preferred over ether because less was required, it acted more quickly and was non-flammable. But it had higher risk. A low dose of ether to chloroform was administered which produced a lighter sleep than in modern anesthesiology, but at least 95% of all Civil War surgeries were performed using one of these agents.

In 1860, Joseph Lister, a young surgeon at the Edinburgh Royal Infirmary, took the position of Regius Professor of Surgery at the University of Glasgow. He promoted the use of a sterile surgery with sterilized surgical instruments. In 1877, he accepted the Chair of Clinical Surgery at King's College Hospital, London. At first his ideas were widely criticized and mocked, but the principles of surgery hygiene he deveoped were adopted worldwide by 1890. Knighted in 1883, he was created Baron Lister of Lyme Regis in 1897 and was appointed one of twelve original members of the Order of Merit in 1902.

Men Who Served as Surgeons

Medical schools in Kentucky founded prior to the Civil War were the Medical Department of Transylvania University, established in 1816; Louisville Medical Institute, established in 1833; University of Louisville Medical Department, 1845, and Kentucky School of Medicine, 1849.

During the Battle of Richmond, Dr. Irwin commandeered the Madison County Courthouse and the Madison Female Institute as hospitals in Richmond. He reported that there were very few medical officers, instruments and ambulances. At Mount Zion Church, local physicians

Dr. William Chase and Dr. Charles Wilmore, with others, worked tirelessly when the church was in Union control and then in Confederate control. They were assisted by area residents who furnished food and water, and took the wounded of both sides to their homes in Berea and Richmond. The first three burials in the Berea Cemetery were from the Battle of Richmond.

Dr. James McCune Smith 1813-1865
physician (surgeon), apothecary, abolitionist, author

Smith was born in slavery in New York of parents from South Carolina. He was the first African American man to receive a medical degree from a medical college, graduating top of his class from the University of Glasgow, Scotland in 1837 and interned in Paris. Dr. Smith returned to New York City where he owned a pharmacy and served as a surgeon for twenty years.

Dr. Smith was financially successful. He was a member of the Committee of Thirteen that opposed the Fugitive Slave Law. Frederick Douglass said that James Smith was the single most important influence on his life.

The first African American male to receive a medical degree from a college in the United States was David Jones Peck, who graduated from Rush Medical College in Chicago in 1847. Alexander Thomas Augusta was the first African American to receive a medical degree in Canada, Medical College, University of Toronto, 1856. He was the highest ranking African American man in the Union Army. By the end of the Civil War, twenty-two African American men had received medical degrees, and at least twelve were serving in the Union Army.

In 1861, there were 113 surgeons in the U.S. Army. Of these, twenty-four resigned to join the Confederate Medical Service. There were sixty-one surgeons in the U.S. Navy and twenty-five resigned. Neither the Confederate and Union services nor these physicians were prepared for what would take place over the next four years. By the end of the war, there were over 12,000 surgeons in the Union Army and over 3,000 surgeons in the Confederate Army. In the Federal Navy, about 425 surgeons were serving at the end of the war. The Confederate Navy, never very large, had a total of 107 surgeons who had served during the war.

Civil War Disease, Wounds and Medicine

During the period just before the Civil War, a physician received minimal training. Nearly all the older doctors served as apprentices instead of having other formal education. Even those who attended one of the few medical schools were poorly trained, studying for two years or less. In Europe, four-year medical schools were common, lab training was widespread and there was a greater understanding of disease and infection.

When the war began, the Federal army had a total of ninety-eight medical officers and the Confederacy had twenty-four. By 1865, 13,000 Union doctors had served in the field and the hospitals; in the Confederacy, 4,000 medical officers served and an unknown number of volunteers. It is estimated that 4,000 women served as nurses for the Union, and a large number of Confederate women served.

The most common Civil War small arms ammunition was the dreadful minie ball, which tore an enormous wound on impact. A wound to the abdominal area or head was usually fatal. A shot to the arm or leg shattered any bone it hit.

Contrary to popular myth, most amputees did not experience surgery without an anesthetic. Ample doses of chloroform were given beforehand. Those who survived the surgery still had a high risk of infection. Surgeons were not aware of the relationship between cleanliness and infection. They did not know how to sterilize their equipment.

While soldiers thought that wounds were the biggest problem, disease was the major cause of death of the war. Of the Federal dead, three out of five died of disease. In the Confederate armies, two out of three died from disease.

About half of the deaths were caused by intestinal disorders, mainly typhoid fever, diarrhea and dysentery. The remainder died from pneumonia and tuberculosis. Camps were populated by young soldiers who had never before been exposed to common diseases and were plagued by measles, mumps, chickenpox and whooping cough. The Union army reported that more than 995 of every 1,000 men eventually contracted chronic diarrhea or dysentery.

Typhoid fever was even more devastating. Perhaps one-quarter of noncombat deaths in the Confederacy resulted from this disease. Epidemics of malaria spread throughout camps located next to stagnant swamps. Poor diet and exposure to the weather added to the problem.

A simple cold often developed into pneumonia, which was the third leading killer disease. Typhoid fever was called Camp Fever. It was very severe, caused a high fever, intense headache, intense rash and delirium.

Smallpox was also deadly. In normal times, it would not have required medication. During the Civil War, many men with smallpox were already suffering from fatigue, malnutrition, typhoid or dysentery. Recovery often took a long time. In addition, there were pockmarks left on the skin from this disease.

Hygiene was very poor. Civil War soldiers did not get a daily shower. Also, they used the same pots to cook food and to boil lice-infested clothing. There was filth in camp. Latrines were dug too close to streams, which contaminated the water supply. Diet was improper. Normal foods were hardtack for Union soldiers and cornbread for the Confederates. Fresh fruit and vegetables were rare. Soldiers received some meat, but it was often spoiled or too full of preservatives to eat. Impure water was another problem. If a stream looked good, it was assumed that the water was good, but this was not always true. Outdoor exposure was severe. Soldiers existed in all types of conditions, extreme hot and cold, rain, sleet, snow, dust and mud.

Sisters of Charity of Cincinnati

In 1861, Cincinnati Mayor George Hatch and Archbishop John Purcell sent a request to the Sisters of Charity Motherhouse at Mount St. Vincent to attend sick troops at Camp Dennison, Ohio. There were only sixty-nine sisters in that congregation. This was at a time when women were not considered suitable to serve as nurses. However, the sisters were highly regarded because they had skills that few of the other nurses had, according to Sister Judith Metz, present archivist of the Sisters of Charity. Eventually forty-two sisters left Cincinnati to serve as nurses in the Civil War. Their leader was Sister Anthony O'Connell, who had served as director of nursing at St. John's Hospital, which was run by the order, later to become Good Samaritan Hospital. All the sisters were trained in medicine by the physicians there. While they served as U.S. Army nurses, they also treated Confederates.

Sister Anthony was born Mary O'Connell in Ireland in 1814. She migrated with her family to Massachusetts and at the age of twenty-one joined the Sisters of Charity founded by St. Elizabeth Seton in Maryland. Two years later she was sent to Cincinnati to open an orphanage, and she became head of nursing at St. John's. She was a natural born leader. In the spring of 1862, Sister Anthony and others from that congregation boarded a hospital ship in Cincinnati to Pittsburg Landing in Tennessee and the Battle of Shiloh. Most of the wounded they treated were Protestants, if they had any church affiliation. The sisters were not fully accepted at first. Sister Judith Metz says soldiers were equally uncomfortable with women serving as nurses and with Catholics. However, the care which the wounded received was so good and was given with such kindness, that attitudes changed. Sister Anthony became known as the Angel of the Battlefield. At Shiloh, one soldier wrote in his diary, "Amid this sea of blood, she performed the most revolting duties for those poor soldiers. She seemed like a ministering angel and many a young soldier owes his life to her care and charity."

After Shiloh, the sisters served in Cumberland, Maryland; Corinth, Mississippi; Nashville, Tennessee; and Richmond, Kentucky. After the Union defeat at Richmond in August 1862, Sister Anthony and six sisters along with forty horse-drawn ambulances tended the wounded at the Madison Female Institute. This was a large brick structure built in 1858 with ten acres for lawns, gardens and tennis courts. Teachers and students at the school assisted the sisters. The wounded were treated in the field and at the institute, and hundreds were taken back to Cincinnati to receive further care. The Sisters of Charity were not the only ones to serve. From various religious orders, over 600 nuns served as volunteer nurses in the Civil War.

Today the motherhouse in Cincinnati has the battered medical kit she carried throughout the war, along with her eyeglasses, her rosary, a small pair of scissors and a pocket knife. Sister Anthony's belongings are treasured by the sisters. Quoting Sister Judith Metz, "The fact that these things survived and are preserved tells you something. It is a testimony to how highly she was thought of and always will be." In the cemetery next to the motherhouse, sisters of the congregation are buried high on a hill overlooking the Ohio River. The graves of those who served as nurses are easy to locate. There is a headstone cross and a second marker that reads U.S. Army Nurse. Sister Anthony died in 1897.

Surgeons Who Were Women

Women were not accepted as surgeons at the start of the Civil War. There were few female physicians. Dr. Elizabeth Blackwell from England was the first woman to receive a medical degree in the United States. She ran an infirmary for women and children in New York City slums. She and her sister, Dr. Emily Blackwell, organized 4,000 women into the New York Women's Central Association of Relief. Dr. Chloe Annette Buckel worked with the Blackwell sisters at the New York Infirmary. She trained nurses for the Union Army and helped establish hospitals in Memphis, Tennessee. Dr. Buckel co-founded a hospital for women and children in San Francisco. Dr. Sarah Ann Chadwick Clapp served as assistant surgeon of the Seventh Illinois Volunteer Cavalry. Dr. Mary Frame Thomas was appointed by Gov. Oliver Morton of Indiana to work alongside her surgeon husband in an Army Hospital in Nashville, Tennessee.

Dr. Rebecca Lee Crumpler attended the prestigious West-Newton English and Classical School in Massachusetts. She received her medical degree in 1864 from New England Female Medical College, which merged with Boston University School of Medicine. She was the first American female Black physician. Dr. Crumpler worked in the Freedmen's Bureau in Richmond, Virginia, after the war. She wrote *Book of Medical Discourses,* published in 1883. Dr. Esther Hill Hawks joined her surgeon husband and assisted him as much as the Union Army would allow. She also worked with the National Freedmens' Relief Association. During the war, she lived and worked in Beautfort and Charleston, South Carolina and Jacksonville, Florida. She helped establish Hospital Number 10 for black soldiers and cared for the wounded of the 54th Massachusetts Colored Infantry. Her diary, *A Woman Doctor's Civil War*, in three volumes, was found in 1975.

Dr. Orianna Moon Andrews of Virginia graduated from Female Medical College of Pennsylvania in 1857. She married another southerner, John Summerfield Andrews, in 1861. She assisted him in turning several buildings of the University of Virginia into hospital units and was recognized with a surgeon's commission in the Confederate Army.

Dr. Mary Edwards Walker, 1832-1919, was from a New York abolitionist family. She studied at Syracuse Medical College and graduated with honors in 1855. She married a fellow classmate, Dr. Albert Miller. At the start of the Civil War, the War Department rejected her for service as a surgeon because she was a woman. She refused a job as a nurse, but may have served as a nurse at the First Battle of Bull Run.

She was an unpaid field surgeon at the Battle of Fredericksburg and the Battle of Chickamauga. She organized the Women's Relief Organization to aid wives and mothers of wounded soldiers. In 1863, she was employed as acting assistant surgeon assigned to the 52nd Ohio Volunteers. Dr. Walker was captured by Confederates and held for four months. Following her exchange, the War Department assigned her first as surgeon at a hospital for women prisoners in Louisville, Kentucky, then at a Tennessee orphans' asylum. Dr. Walker was commended for meritorious service by Gen. William T. Sherman and Gen. George H. Thomas and awarded the Medal of Honor on November 11, 1865.

Studies at the Women's Medical College of Pennsylvania included chemistry, anatomy, physiology, histology, pharmaceutical science, obstetrics and general medicine with clinical work in Philadelphia.

By 1870, there were 525 trained American physicians who were women. Opposition to women in medical schools and as professionals was strong. The American Medical Association did not admit its first female member until 1915.

Of additional interest will be DeAnne Blanton and Lauren M. Clark: *They Fought Like Demons: Women Soldiers in the American Civil War*, 2002. Concerning the Battle of Richmond, they state, page 11, Confederate soldier Mary Ann Clark was "wounded in the thigh a considerable piece above the knee at the Battle of Richmond, Kentucky, August 30, 1862. One of 451 Confederate casualties, Clark fell into Union hands and became a prisoner of war. She survived her wound, survived her incarceration, and was ultimately paroled."

Women Who Served as Nurses

Prior to the Civil War, most nurses were males. Army leadership quickly realized that more help was needed. Women were accepted into service and thousands served as nurses. They played a significant role during the Civil War. Men serving as nurses became increasingly rare. One male nurse of interest to people in Berea and Mt. Vernon was *Sylvester Freeman Storrs*. He was born in 1816 in Essex County,

New York, where he earned a life-time teaching certificate. He and his wife *Catharine Pickering Storrs* moved to Rockcastle County, Kentucky area prior to the Civil War. During the war, he became a nurse at Armory Square Hospital, Washington, D.C. According to the memoirs of his granddaughter Flora Shockley Robinson, he and Walt Whitman served as nurses to Secretary of State William Seward, who was wounded on the night of Abraham Lincoln's assassination. After the war, he started schools in Rockcastle and Madison Counties. They no longer exist. The stone spring house trough at Berea Tourism came from the Storrs farm off Walnut Meadow Road. It was used to hide and water their horses when Union troops and Confederate troops came to the farm looking for food and fresh horses and mules.

Chapter Four

Richmond

Virginia created Kentucky County in 1776, which was abolished in 1780 when the county was divided into Jefferson, Fayette and Lincoln Counties. Madison County was formed in 1785 with land taken from Lincoln County. Madison County was the first county named for James Madison. The original borders of the county extended from Dix River to the Big Sandy River, and south of the Kentucky River. Fort Boonesborough and Paint Lick were in contention for the location of the Madison County seat of government. To settle the dispute, Gov. Patrick Henry selected a spot half-way between the two — Milford, overlooking Taylor's Fork of Silver Creek. Kentucky was admitted into the Union as the fifteenth state on June 1, 1792. John M. Miller was one of the first members of the new state legislature.

After repeated flooding in Milford, Madison County records were moved secretly in 1798 to a barn belonging to John Miller. The move was adamantly opposed by the 300 citizens of Milford, but the Kentucky legislature approved. In March 1798, the county also approved the move and purchased two acres of land from John Miller. On July 4, 1798, the area was named Richmond in honor of Col. Miller's birthplace. The city was incorporated in 1809. The first two constitutions of Kentucky specified the appointment of justices of the peace, but indicated neither their duties nor the governance of counties. The first mayor of Richmond, T.T. Covington, served in 1896-97.

The first courthouse of Madison County was built in 1799 and was used for fifty years. It was built on the spot where John Miller's barn had been located and where Mt. Nebo Church previously stood, the walls of which are still within the foundation of the present courthouse. This second courthouse was built in 1849 and was a holding site for Union prisoners after the Battle of Richmond within a large fence made of best quality Swedish steel surrounding the courthouse. Portions of the fence are located today at the Richmond Cemetery. The courthouse is an impressive building and is still in service with courtrooms and main administrative offices.

The Madison County Historical Society states on its website:

> May 1775. The Baptists represented the first religious denomination in the county, with the Tates Creek Baptist Church being organized between 1783 and 1785. The first Methodist congregation, Proctor's Chapel, now Red House Methodist Church, was organized in 1790 near Boonesborough. A Presbyterian congregation, called the Silver Creek Church, was also formed in 1790 at Round Top near Milford.
>
> Congregations of the Disciples of Christ were established in the 1830s in several rural areas and in Richmond in 1844. The First Baptist Church congregation of Irvine Street in Richmond, the earliest church organized by blacks, was also founded in 1844. Before that time blacks and whites had worshiped together. Roman Catholics organized in 1858 and the Episcopalians in 1871 in Richmond.
>
> Madison Countians enjoyed a variety of cultural and social activities. Mills served as social gathering places as well as marketplaces. Another source of both social and economic exchange was Richmond's public marketplace that opened officially in 1810 on the east side of the courthouse square. A 26'x40' roofed markethouse was constructed on Main Street in 1812 and removed in 1852 after the construction of the new courthouse. In spite of the loss of a markethouse, Court Day in Richmond offered social exchange and entertainment as much as the opportunity to trade farm goods and livestock.
>
> The county fair, begun in 1833, advertised and sold local produce in a carnival atmosphere which included livestock shows and horse racing.... More formal entertainment was offered at Green's Opera House in Richmond which operated from 1872 until it was destroyed by fire in 1887. Throughout the nineteenth century citizens were entertained and enriched by their participation in philosophical societies; men's and women's organizations, such as the Cecilian Club and the Masons; and county events ranging from militia musters and political debates to circuses, traveling shows, foxhunting, and chicken fights.

Colonel John Miller was a Revolutionary War soldier from Richmond, Virginia. He was a member of the Virginia Militia, fought in the siege and battle at Yorktown and was present when Gen. Charles Cornwallis surrendered at Yorktown in 1781. Col. Miller was attracted to the area that became Richmond. Kentucky, by the good spring water and friendly American Indians. Col. Miller and his wife Jane Dulaney Miller and their seven children settled in 1784 on the headwaters of Otter Creek, where Richmond is now located. He built the first house in the area where he lived until his death in 1808. He built and operated the first hotel. He was appointed Justice of the Peace of Kentucky County by Gov. Henry of Virginia in 1787.

At the time of Battle of Richmond, the population of the city was less than 600 persons, with 457 of these being free. There were approximately seventy-three homes for the citizens and a small number of separate houses for slaves. The city had a thriving commercial district. During the Battle of Richmond, the county had a population of 17,213. Of these, 6,040 residents were slaves. Approximately 3,000 residents of Madison County were under the age of ten years, and 2,720 were from ten to twenty years of age. There were about 2,726 households in the county.

James Bennett McCreary

Richmond has been home to five governors, two of Kentucky, two of Missouri, one of a territory, and one federal Supreme Court justice. James B. McCreary had served in the 11th Kentucky Cavalry, CSA, under John Hunt Morgan. He served in the Kentucky House of Representatives and was Speaker. He served his first term as Governor of Kentucky from 1875-79, was elected to six consecutive terms as member of the U.S. House of Representatives, then one term in the U.S. Senate, then in 1911-15 to his second term as Governor.

Keen Johnson

Keen Johnson served as Governor of Kentucky from 1939-1943. He published the *Richmond Daily Register* and was the only journalist to serve as governor. He was later U.S. Secretary of Labor in the Truman Administration. David R. Francis was 27th Governor of Missouri, served as U.S. Secretary of the Interior and as U.S. Ambassador to Russia. William J. Stone was the 28th Governor of Missouri, 1893-97.

Green Clay Smith

Green Clay Smith was a nephew of Cassius M. Clay. He graduated from Transylvania University at the age of eighteen, and three years later took a law degree from Lexington Law School. He was commissioned a Second Lieutenant of Infantry during the Mexican War. He enlisted in the 4th Kentucky Volunteer Cavalry, USA, during the Civil War and was made Brigadier General of Volunteers in 1862 and Major General before resigning his commission in the fall of that year and election to Congress. He resigned from Congress in 1866 to accept the position of Governor of the Montana Territory. He was ordained as a minister in 1869 and became pastor of First Baptist Church in Frankfort, Kentucky.

Samuel Freeman Miller

Samuel Freeman Miller lived from 1816 to 1890. He practiced as a physician for twelve years and became a lawyer in 1847. He was appointed Associate Justice of the U.S. Supreme Court by Abraham Lincoln, serving 1862-1890. He played a major role in restricting the reach of the fourteenth amendment into areas of law reserved to states. His concern was that a broad interpretation of that amendment would give too much power to the federal government and would distort the balance of power between the states and the central government Justice Miller wrote the opinion on the Slaughter-House cases in 1873. In the 1880s, some Republican leaders promoted him as a presidential candidate.

Madison Campbell

A Baptist Church was first organized in Richmond in 1843 by a group of consecrated individuals including a man named Madison Campbell. The church was named the United Baptist Church, Colored, of Richmond. Their first church was a log structure. Rev. Campbell was called as pastor of the church in 1858. Madison Campbell, a former slave, was born in 1823 in an area between Joe Lick Knob, Pilot Knob, and Silver Creek. He received a degree of Doctor of Divinity from a Louisville seminary in 1892. United Baptist Church is now First Baptist Church, and the congregation continues to worship on Irvine Street in Richmond.

African American churches were often of an invisible nature. Through signals, passwords, and messages not known to the white population, they called believers to "hush harbors" where they freely mixed African music and beliefs with evangelical Christianity. There is little remaining written record of these religious gatherings. It was in these, however, that the spirituals developed. They had double meanings of salvation and freedom from slavery. Black preachers, believing that God had called them to speak His word, polished their sermons with rhythmic, intoned extemporaneous preaching. These meetings within the Black communities provided a way for enslaved African Americans to express their hopes for a better future.

Cassius Marcellus Clay

General Cassius Marcellus Clay, son of General Green Clay, was born in Madison County, October 19, 1810. His father, a first cousin of Henry Clay, served as an officer in the Revolutionary War and the War of 1812. Cassius graduated with distinction from Yale University in 1832, having the singular honor of delivering the Washington Centennial address in New Haven, on February 22, 1832, then and there delivering his "first anti-slavery speech." In an 1840 political campaign, he asked workers to look after their own best interests rather than following the dictates of slave owners. He declared, "I believe slavery to be an evil, an evil morally, economically, physically, intellectually, socially, religiously, politically — an unmixed evil." He used statistics to show how Kentucky's economic development lagged far behind such free-state neighbors as Ohio.

Clay owned slaves until 1844, when he began freeing all of those who did not belong to the Clay Estate, whom he was not legally entitled to sell. In June 1845, he founded at Lexington, Kentucky, an anti-slavery paper called *The True American*, which he published for more than a year at the peril of his life. Though opposed to slavery and to the annexation of Texas, he served as captain in the Mexican War, and so endeared himself to his company of Kentuckians that, on his return, Lexington gave him a public reception, and Madison County presented him with a beautiful sword.... In 1848, Harpers and Brother published *The Writings of Cassius Marcellus Clay, including Writings and Addresses*. Horace Greeley, the distinguished editor of the *New York Tribune*, wrote a Preface and a Memoir for the volume. The book contains Clay's Washington Centennial Address and much of the contents of *The True American*.

Mr. Clay served several terms in the Kentucky legislature; he gave land and money to the movement that produced Berea College, and he was a candidate for the Vice Presidency before the Republican convention in 1860. He was one of the earliest emancipators, and no man of prominence in the United States manifested greater courage in fearlessly asserting his constitutional rights in assailing the institution of slavery. In 1862 he was commissioned Major General of Volunteers by President Lincoln. He was minister to Russia during Lincoln's and Johnson's administrations, and he always claimed the credit for the purchase of Alaska in 1867. In 1886 he published the first volume of *The Life, Memoirs, Writings and Speeches of Cassius M. Clay*. The second volume was never finished. Mr. Clay escaped death by violence many times and survived his bitterest and greatest enemies. He died July 22, 1903. The grave of Madison County's most picturesque and prominent son is in the Richmond Cemetery.

Mention might well be made of the influence Mr. Clay probably had at Chicago on the nomination of Lincoln in 1869. "Madison G. Proctor of St. Joseph, Michigan, who was one of the five surviving members of the split rail convention" stated in 1911 in an address before the Hamilton Club of Chicago that during the confusion over the choice of a candidate of the Republican Party for President, Clay spoke as follows: "We are on the eve of a great civil war," began Mr. Clay, but we of Kansas were used to strong words and smiled. The Kentuckian looked at us sternly and continued: "We know what your platform plans are and I am here to say that if a candidate is nominated on that platform the South will make an attempt to dissolve the Union. Your southern border extends from Maryland to Missouri and on this side stands a determined body of men, resolute that the Union shall not be destroyed except after a most desperate struggle."

"It makes a great difference to you whom you nominate," thundered the tall Kentuckian, "and it makes a much more vital difference to us. Our homes and all we possess are in peril. We demand of you a candidate who will inspire our courage and confidence. We call upon you to nominate Abraham Lincoln, who knows us and understands our aspirations. Give us Lincoln and we will push back your battle line from the Ohio River to the Tennessee where it belongs. Give us Lincoln and we will unite the strength of our Union sentiment with the Union army and bring success to your legions. Do this for us," pleaded the speaker, "and we will go home and prepare for the conflict."

We saw things from a new angle, according to Madison Proctor. It was no longer a question of fighting slavery, but of saving the Union.

Lincoln was nominated. (This was taken from E. Polk Johnson's *A History of Kentucky and Kentuckians*, vol. II, page 822.)

Soon after Mr. Clay's death, *The Literary Digest* for August 8, 1903, quoted Henry Waterson, the able editor of the Louisville *Courier-Journal* as stating: "He [Clay] was a man such as the world sees but once, and a character known to all. He, more than any other one man stood for the world's idea of a Kentuckian — bold, fearless, generous, kind, quick to avenge an insult and equally quick to forgive a wrong, an orator and a hand-to-hand fighter. By some he was loved, by others he was hated, but by all he was feared and by most he was respected. He made his mark in whatever department of life he was thrown. Possessed of a will that brooked no obstacle when once he set his hand to the plow, there was no turning back until the end of the furrow. He rode roughshod and cared not a whit whose toes were injured in the riding. He was an editor, politician, duelist, author and statesman, and acted each part with an originality and spice which lent him new interest."

The New York *Mail and Express* ... said: "Henry Waterson describes Clay as a giant and a lion. He was a giant who never directed his own strength, a lion who lashed his power into the shreds of aimless rage. Yet throughout his fretted years there runs a strain of great-heartedness and of lovable quality that made men condone his eccentricities.

Undoubtedly, the entire life of Clay was changed when he was a college lad at New Haven. There, thirty years before the Civil War, he listened to the eloquence of William Lloyd Garrison. The emotional youth became at once an abolitionist, although his parents were slaveholders. Returning to Kentucky, he plunged into politics; but his campaigns were those of 'fiery epithet' and 'fierce denunciation,' breathing alike defiance to his foes and independence of his allies. His stump speeches were delivered with a bowie knife in his boot-let and a brace of revolvers at his hand. When he edited *The True American*, an anti-slavery paper, his desk was fortified with iron doors, behind which were cannon loaded to the muzzle...."

Note: Some remarks about C.M. Clay are not complimentary. The reader might wish to look at *Mr. Lincoln's White House, Notable Visitors: Cassius M. Clay (1810-1893)*. This is a website of the Gilder-Lehrman Institute of American History, a non-profit organization devoted to the improvement of history education. The institute works in all fifty states with an array of programs for teachers, schools and students. There are over 65,000 unique documents in the Gilder-Lehrman Collection, some online. There are Gilder-Lehrman Teacher Institutes held in the U.S. and abroad each year.

Laura Clay and Mary Barr Clay

Laura Clay, 1849-1941, and Mary Barr Clay, 1839-1924, were daughters of Cassius Marcellus Clay. They were born at White Hall in Madison County. Both sisters worked for women's voting rights and women's property rights. Mary Clay became president of the American Women's Suffrage Association in 1883. Laura Clay was educated at Sayre School, Mrs. Sarah Hoffmen's Finishing School in New York City, at the University of Michigan and the University of Kentucky. She leased a three hundred acre farm from her father in 1883 and became its owner at his death in 1903. She described herself as a practical farmer and was a skillful farm manager. Laura Clay was an officer in the Women's Christian Temperance Union and the Kentucky Federation of Women's Clubs. She and Josephine K. Henry founded the Kentucky Equal Rights Association in which Laura served as president until 1912. She was succeeded by her cousin Madeline McDowell Breckinridge. Laura Clay was a powerful speaker and became the best known suffragist in the National American Woman Suffrage Association. She became the first woman to have her name placed in nomination for the office of President of the United States in a major party at the Democratic National Convention in 1920.

The Clay – Fee Disagreement

Rev. Fee in his autobiography wrote, "The Fourth of July was near at hand. We had previously, on this national holiday, celebrated liberty prospectively — Mr. Clay leading and I following. The place of the celebration had, by previous arrangements, been fixed. Mr. Clay and I were on hand, and when the hour for addresses came, Mr. Clay said that I must speak first. I declined. He insisted. I thought I saw his policy — have me utter my radical sentiments, and he then review me.

"I decided, in my own mind, to meet the issue squarely; and rising with a copy of the Declaration of Independence in my hand, I repeated the words: 'All men are created free and equal' and 'endowed by their Creator with certain inalienable rights.' I said, if inalienable, then such are man's relations to God, to himself and his family, that he cannot alienate; society cannot; governments cannot alienate. 'Endowed by their Creator,' if so, then it is impious in us to attempt to take away.... That which thus outrages natural right and divine teaching is mere usurpation, and, correctly speaking, is incapable of legalization...that when the American colonies became States of this Union, they did not attempt to legalize slavery — it exists only by usurpation.... A law confessed contrary to the law of God ought not by human courts to be enforced; and referred to the Fugitive Slave Law, and said I would refuse to obey, then suffer the penalty.

"Mr. Clay followed, and after expressions of high personal regard for me, ...'As long as a law is on the statute book, it is to be respected and obeyed until repealed by the republican majority.... When he came to the Fugitive Slave Law, he said, 'So far as this is concerned, I would not obey it myself; it is contrary to natural right....'"

In his *Memoirs*, Gen. Clay wrote, "To deny the potency of the Constitution and the laws, is to set up an independent government in opposition to the existing government and laws; the two necessary policies and jurisdictions of which must inevitably at last come into physical conflict. And whilst I am opposed to slavery on all possible grounds, my love and respect for my constitution and my country override all other political considerations. My theory is that slavery is a creature of law and the subject of support, modification, increase or destruction, as any other policy, and to be reached in the same way only, by moral suation [suasion], by speeches, by the press, by the law and by the constitution."

"The political differences of opinion between us is fully set forth in these volumes—so that all the world may judge us. He has always been free to criticise [criticize] my course, but my friendship for him has never abated. Any other man saying what he has at times said of me would have brought on him my greatest indignation. But as I know his sincerity of purpose, and his idiosyncracies [idiosyncrasies] of thought, I have not believed it necessary to defend myself.... I hold and have held from the beginning, that there is an inborn sentiment of justice and humanity which is the basis of all human laws, and to which they should be conformed; that the existence of slavery, though sanctioned by constitutions and laws, was in opposition to that higher law, and that it should be abolished — not by indirection, or slave-escaping, or by armed assault upon the master, but by free discussion and the ballot — to peaceably conform them to the higher law."

Chapter Five

Berea

The area known today as Berea was a settlement prior to 1853 known as The Glade. John G. Fee first preached there in a church, The Old Glade Meeting House, located about where the present Glades Christian Church facility was later built.

The large area of land in southern Madison County and bordering counties was owned by Cassius M. Clay, who began in the 1840s to bring into the vicinity white and free black families who were opposed to slavery. There eventually were possibly as many as 200 free black families living on farms they owned interspersed with white families on their own farms. It is probable that many of these farmers had formerly been slaves who were freed by Clay and relocated from White Hall to the Glade. This farming community may have stretched five to six miles from what is now the center of Berea. George White, who was freed in 1828, began buying property at White Hall, The Glade, and Big Hill in 1832.

This community supported the preaching of Rev. Fee. He moved to the Glade in 1854 and named the community Berea after the Greek city mentioned in Acts 17 where Paul and Silas went from Thessalonica to Berea, preached at the synagogue and were well accepted by the citizens. Rev. Fee founded a school in 1855. He had been given ten acres of land with the early support of Cassius M. Clay. Fee selected land on the ridge above the Glade. A small town began to grow along the ridge. Berea was incorporated in 1890. John L. Gay became the first mayor and served from 1910 to 1958.

Berea College

The school founded by Rev. Fee was named Berea College. It was coeducational and enrolled equal numbers of black students and white students. The college has thrived.

Berea College emphasizes Learning, Labor, and Service. Berea is one of seven members of the National Work Colleges Consortium. There is no tuition. Each student receives the equivalent of a full-tuition scholarship worth at present $24,100. Students work ten to fifteen hours a week in any one of over a hundred campus offices, departments and programs off-campus. Berea College was listed in *Princeton Review*'s "The Best 371 Colleges" in 2009 and was listed as the top liberal arts college in 2011 by *Washington Monthly*. Current enrollment is about 1,600, with a twenty-two percent minority enrollment. Students at this time represent forty-four states, the District of Columbia, US territories, and fifty-eight countries other than the United States.

John G. and Matilda H. Fee

John Gregg Fee (September 9, 1816 - January 11, 1901) was an abolitionist, minister, and educator. He was the founder of Berea College in 1855, the first school in the state with interracial and coeducational admissions. Fee was born in Bracken County, Kentucky, to Vincent Hamilton and Elizabeth Gregg, a slave-holding family. He was education at Augusta College, Miami University, and Lane Seminary, where he became an abolitionist. He and a few followers in 1845 styled themselves a non-denomination Church of Christ. He had written to C.M. Clay the previous year introducing himself and sent several articles for *The True American*. In 1851, Fee wrote a pamphlet using biblical scholarship to refute assertions that the Bible sanctioned slavery, in which he stated that, "freedom is the natural state of all men, as soon as they attain the age of manhood." This belief allowed him to appeal to higher law when confronted with the argument that slavery was legal in the United States. Fee also attacked slavery on economic terms, but this was subordinate to his moral argument.

He married Matilda Hamilton, also from Bracken County, on September 26, 1844. She was also an abolitionist, egalitarian, and a reformer. They eventually had six children. She was public spirited and was a member of the Women's Christian Temperance Union. She rode horseback throughout the area with Rev. Fee, or by herself or with one of their children, visiting and helping families. In 1895, Berea College President Frost said in her eulogy that Mrs. Fee was a person who was willing to be happy, that she believed in her friends and always saw the good in other people. She was a restraining influence. While she was not afraid to speak in support of what she believed, extreme positions and severe judgments of others were modified by her kindly presence.

In 1853, Clay invited Fee to visit him in Madison County and preach in the southern part of the county where Clay owned land and was building a following of people with thoughts similar to his on slavery. C.M. Clay had begun selling farm land to people of his emancipationist mindset. There was not a black section and a white section of the area. All families lived as neighbors. Other people of similar thinking began to move there. With his wife, Matilda, John A.R. Rogers, a gifted mathematician and linguist, Fee's cousin John Hanson and a few others, a school was opened in 1855 to whites and blacks, co-educational named Berea College. Fee preached in neighboring counties, often running into violent opposition to his anti-slavery views. His autobiography is filled with his accounts on the volatility of the decade before the war, when he was often challenged and threatened because of his stand on abolition and equal treatment of blacks.

There was great interest in the college, as small as it was. Governor Salmon P. Chase of Ohio attended its commencement ceremonies as one of the speakers. Fee, J.A.R. Rogers, who acted as principal, and other supporters drew up a constitution for the school and pledged their own support with more than 100 acres of land for the college's campus.

With social tensions increasing in the years leading up to the American Civil War, and especially after John Brown's Raid, in December 1859 a band of armed pro-slavery men came to Berea while Fee was still away in the East. They delivered notice to J.A.R. Rogers and others to leave the state within ten days because of the group's opposition to Fee, their church, and college. In 1864, Fee returned to the college. Although the people of Berea appealed to the governor of the state for protection, he said he was unable to do so. Townspeople abandoned the village and school for a time. Abolitionists were expelled from Lewis and Bracken counties as well. After Fee's return to Bracken County, where he and his family were staying with his in-laws, a committee of sixty-two men of "high standing" told Fee he and his supporters had to leave Bracken County.

In a series of pamphlets from the mid-1840s, Fee offered a full arsenal of biblical antislavery armament. In fact, he provided so many arguments, and of so many kinds, that his sharp analysis of the racial situation seems to have been lost in the tussle. As an example, in 1851 he published a substantial pamphlet that included the bold declaration that American Slavery "by whomsoever caused, is always sinful," and he did not hesitate to claim that "the plain principles of the Bible (justice, mercy, impartial love) are opposed to slavery. Fee argued that if the slavery of African Americans was defended because as a race they were less intelligent or had darker skin, the logic led to an absurd conclusion: "The fact that one man, or race of men, may have more intellectual capacity than other man, or race of men, gives no ground for enslaving the inferior; otherwise the most intellectual man that exists may have a right to enslave every other man white and black.... Otherwise he who has a fairer skin... than you or I, may have a right to enslave us; and the fairest man in the world may enslave other men."

"Love thy neighbor as thyself" rang in my ears. I also considered the condition of the slave-owner. I knew he was willingly deceived by the false teachings of the popular ministry. I knew also that the great part of the non-slave-owners, who were by their votes and action the actual slaveholders, did not see their crime; that they despised the slave because of his condition, and that these non-slave-owners were violently opposed to any doctrine or practice that might treat the slave as a "neighbor," a brother, and make him equal before the law. I knew also that the great body of the people were practically without the fundamental principle of the Gospel, love to God and love to man; that, as in the days of Martin Luther, though the doctrine of justification by faith was plainly written in the Bible, yet the great body of people did not then see it; so now the great doctrine of loving God supremely and our neighbor as ourselves, "on which hang all the law and the prophets," though clearly written in the Bible, was not seen in its practical application by the great mass of the people. Such was my relation to this people, and theirs to God and the world that I felt I *must* return and preach to them the gospel of impartial love."

In his autobiography, Fee wrote, "We came up to Bracken County, and my wife, taking her horse and carriage, took the two eldest children and started across the country for Berea. I took the younger son and started around by Cincinnati, that I might there arrange for the publication of another anti-slavery tract, and also ship our household goods back to Berea. I found that our goods could not then be shipped. The government had the entire use of the railroad in shipping munitions of war. My son and I got as far as Richmond, Ky. There I engaged a single horse on condition that I would not take the horse into rebel lines. We mounted the horse, Howard behind me, and came seven miles toward our home.

"We there met the Union forces retreating before the advance of Kirby Smith's invading army. Some Union troops were gathered at and near to Richmond. These resisted the approach of the rebel army, but were over-powered and fell back to Richmond, thence to Lexington, and afterwards dispersed in various directions. I fell back with the Union forces to Lexington, and from thence to Bracken County. There I left my son Howard, then eleven years old, with his grandfather. I went on to Augusta, a town on the Ohio River, intending, if possible, to get around to my wife and the other children, then at Berea.

"Whilst out hunting up some simple cooking utensils which two years previously she had distributed among neighbors, rebel soldiers came into her house, took her borrowed blanket, her coarse and fine comb, her better shoes and Burritt's hat, and the carriage harness. The horse and carriage were hid in the woods. My daughter Laura had a very nice Union flag which her mother had made, and with this a set of silver spoons her grandfather had given to her; these she had hid up in the eaves-trough. These the rebels did not find; so the present loss of the little family was not great, and they could say with Col. Slack's slave, 'Blessed be nothing; I has nothing to lose, and nothing to be sorry for.'

"Thousands of Kirby Smith's men were then encamped nearby. With some other women my wife went to the encampment to see the complexion of the rebel soldiers. Whilst sitting with other women a rebel officer rode up, and addressing himself politely, inquired of my wife for her home, and then for the "politics" of the region. My wife said, 'My home is nearby; and, as for politics, we are for the Union, and believe slavery is wrong, and that the rebels are fighting for a lost cause.' The officer inquired, 'Madam, ain't you from the North?' She replied, 'No, this is my home and my native State.' Again he inquired in a tone derisive, 'Madam, are you an Abolitionist?' She replied, 'I am.' 'Well,' said he, 'I have seen some men who were Abolitionists, but I never before this saw a woman who was. ' My wife then asked, 'Why are you here with the uniform of our men on you?' He had a Union belt on him with U.S. inverted. He replied, 'Madam, don't you see that is S.U. - Southern Union?' and rode off. Not long after this she heard the Cannon's roar at Perrysville. Soon this was followed by the retreating rebel army with trains of wagons laden with plunder, and herds of lowing cattle famishing for the want of water. Three rebel officers came up to her house and asked for food. My wife had some potatoes, meal, coarse flour and milk. She gave to them bread and milk, with baked potatoes. They received this kindly, and were very respectful. Soon after they were gone my wife learned that some rebel soldiers were in her potato patch, grabbing her potatoes. "A friend who had occupied the house for a time, left for her a small plat of ground planted with potatoes. Taking her son Burritt with her, she went for her potatoes. Something to live on then was an item of concern. She came to the fence and said, 'Men, I have fed your officers, and now you are taking the last potato I have; this is no credit to you.' One young fellow looked up pertly and. said, 'Madam, credit has gone up long ago.' They filled their haversacks and went on. Scenes of privation, anxiety and toil went on from day to day."

"Moved by a sense of duty I went, during the latter part of our late war into Camp Nelson, Ky, for the purpose of giving religious instruction & encouragement to soldiers — white and colored. I instituted a school for the instruction of non-commissioned soldiers. This was especially needed among the colored that they might write their names and muster rolls. The instruction was heartily endorsed by Gen. Fry. I also there organized an undenominational church & Sunday school. For the purpose of calling together these two classes for instruction I needed a good bell that should be heard far & wide. I so wrote to two personal friends, Edward Harwood & Levi Coffin, old wol-died abolitionists, then living in Cincinnati Ohio. Speedily they sent to me this bell which we properly call the 'Freedman's Bell'. The bell was in no sense government property. When the war closed I removed the bell to Berea Ky where it again rang for freedom. The College at Berea had the use of the bell with this proviso, that when the College should secure another bell or for any reason ceased to use the old historic bell, then it should revert to me. I now gladly transfer it to the 'Church of Christ at' Berea here known as the Second Church. May the old bell ring loud & long & alike for all men."

—John G. Fee; March 23, 1896; Berea Ky

John Greg Hanson

John Hanson was a first cousin once removed of Rev. Fee. His parents were Greenbury Griffith and Rebecca Gregg Hanson. He was one of four brothers and two sisters. He was born in Bracken County in

1832. At one point, he taught at Oberlin College. The entire Hanson family was converted to abolitionism. John Hanson and his wife Ellen moved to Berea in 1858, where they served as the third and fourth teachers at the school. He and his brother Samuel Griffith Hanson were lumbermen. John bought a lumbermill and in 1859, he converted it to steam power. It began to bring in money to the Berea community.

John Hanson was forced to leave Berea during the war, taking refuge in Rockcastle and Jackson Counties before heading back to northern Kentucky. Ellen died in 1865. John returned in August 1865. He married Elizabeth Preston, also a teacher at the school. John Hanson was one of the original trustees and served as secretary of the board of trustees until his death in 1885. His financial acumen helped make the college successful. With his steam powered sawmill back in operation, John Hanson supplied all the wood for college buildings. He eventually owned sawmills in Madison, Rockcastle and Jackson Counties. His steam circular sawmill was probably bought from Lee and Leavitt Saw Mill Works in Cincinnati. That may have been the only Ohio firm producing steam sawmill engines prior to the Civil War. Its Cincinnati location suggests that Hanson would have known about it.

James Shelton Hathaway

James Shelton Hathaway was born in Mt. Sterling, March 29, 1859, the son of Lewis and Ann Hathaway, who were slaves. He graduated from Berea College, received his master's from Berea and an M.D. from the Louisville National Medical College. He organized and established The Standard Printing and Publishing Company in Lexington, and served as editor of its paper the *Lexington Standard*. He taught Latin and Mathematics at Berea College for ten years, then joined what was to become Kentucky State University as professor in 1893 and as President in 1900. While teaching at Berea, he served as Clerk of the Town of Berea. Dr. Hathaway died in Richmond, Kentucky in 1930.

Angus Augustus Burleigh

Angus Augustus Burleigh was for eleven years in the mainstream of American history. He was the son of Charles Burleigh, an English sea captain, and Charlotta De Dasco, and was born in 1848 aboard ship in the Atlantic Ocean. His mother was a woman of color. At his father's death, A.A. and his mother were abducted from their home in Virginia and sold into slavery in Kentucky. In 1864, A.A. escaped and made his way to Frankfort, Kentucky. At age 16, he joined the newly formed 12th U.S. Colored Heavy Artillery, Co. G. He was appointed a sergeant the next year. Mr. Burleigh mustered out in 1866. Rev. Fee invited him to attend the school at Berea. He graduated in 1875 and headed to Wilberforce University near Xenia, Ohio, where he married Louisa Shaffer on Thanksgiving Day. He taught and had ministries in Indiana, New York, Virginia, Wisconsin, Michigan, Minnesota, Iowa, and Illinois. After four decades in ministry and teaching, he was appointed in 1889 as Chaplain of the General Assembly of Illinois. Rev. Burleigh wrote a booklet entitled *John G. Fee: Founder of Berea College*. He died at the National Military Home in Los Angeles.

William Levant Dodge

Levant Dodge was born in Trumbull County, Ohio, in 1838, and died in Berea, Kentucky, in 1925. He married Lucinda Green in 1862. They lived in Michigan, where he taught school. His son Ernest Green Dodge was born in Michigan, after which the family moved to Berea. At Berea College, he served as professor of Greek and Mathematics. His wife died in 1895. He married Mary Helen Lamson in 1896. During the Civil War, he joined the 177th Ohio Infantry for one year and then the Second Cavalry, Company K in Wisconsin. After the war, he was affiliated with the Grand Army of the Republic. He was commander of the Berea Lodge, 1895, and Commanding General, GAR Department of Kentucky, 1906-07. Through strong political connections of Dodge, local Berea community leaders acquired a city charter in a relatively short time and Berea was incorporated April 4, 1890.

The Grand Army of the Republic (GAR) was a fraternal organization of Union army veterans, first formed in 1868, Decatur, Illinois, for mutual support, for relief of war widows and orphans, and for the promotion of patriotic ideals. The GAR was organized in Kentucky in 1883 with 222 posts, not all of which remained active. There were four posts in Madison County at Round Hill, Kirksville, Richmond, and Berea. The Berea post was named for Captain James West. James C. West had been a student at Berea College at the start of the Civil

War and possibly after the war finished. He enlisted in Company G of the 4th Kentucky Infantry and earned the highest rank of any person from Berea. Levant Dodge was one of eleven charter members of Captain James West Post 171, organized on May 24, 1890. A.J. Hanson was the first commander. In 1895, Dr. Levant Dodge was elected commander of the local post. In 1906 and 1907, he was elected the Commander of the GAR Department of Kentucky. He and his wife Mary regularly attended the annual national encampment. The Capt. James West Women's Relief Corps (WRC) #48 was formed in Berea in 1906. Mary Dodge headed the Kentucky WRC from 1910-12. The Women's Auxiliary worked with the GAR to perpetuate the memory of their dead, assist Union veterans in any way possible, to extend needful aid to their widows and orphans and to promote patriotism. Both groups ceased operation in 1939. G.A.R. information is from William Williams in *Heritage Highlights* of the Madison County Historical Society.

Burials of Former Civil War Soldiers in Berea

The first three persons buried in the Berea Cemetery were Union soldiers, now unknown, who were wounded in the August 1862 Battle of Richmond and taken to a farm in Berea, which served as a short-term hospital. They died there a few days later. Their graves are to the immediate right upon entering the cemetery.

Madison D. Alcorn, 11/3/1825, Indiana, - 11/6/1900, Berea., Company B, Kentucky 8th Infantry Regiment; private

Barton Potter Ambrose, 7/4/1846 – 5/26/1935, Company C, 47th Regiment, Kentucky Infantry Volunteers, employed by Berea College

John Lee Ballinger, born in Madison County

Robert E. Baugh, 1847 – 1926, U.S. Army, private, born in Berea

William Henry Bicknell, born in Estill County

George W. Bogie, 1839 – 1898, Company A, 11th Kentucky Cavalry, private, prisoner at Andersonville

Schuyler Browning, born in slavery in Madison County

William H. Burdett, 8/21/1843 – 3/31/1898, U.S. Army, private, prisoner at Andersonville

Thomas Bybee, born in Tennessee, 122nd U.S. Colored Infantry

James Marion Cain/Kain, born in Knox County
John R. Calloway, born in Washington County
Henry Calvin, captured at The Battle of The Wilderness
Jesse Chasteen, born in 1833, prisoner at Camp Ford, Tyler, Texas
Nicholas B. Chasteen, born in 1835, prisoner at Camp Ford, Tyler, Texas
Henry J. Clark, born in Clay County
Alvin Cooper, 6/1842 – 5/12/1920, Company D, 21st Kentucky Infantry
Tipton Cooper, 4/1840 – 4/16/1929, Company D, 21st Kentucky Infantry
William Henry Harrison Creech, Company D, Three Forks Battalion Regiment, Kentucky, private
Thomas Daugherty, 5/22/1836 – 3/17/1915, born in Lee County, Virginia
William LeVant Dodge, 5/8/1838 – 1925, 177th and 191st Regiments, Ohio Infantry, private, 2nd Wisconsin Cavalry
Lindsey C. Duncan, prisoner at Andersonville
Stephen Farris, born in Madison County
Abraham Fauler/Fowler, year of birth, about 1831, Company C, 8th Tennessee Cavalry, private
Robert Fish, year of birth, about 1845, Company C, 124th U.S. Colored Infantry, private
George William French, 11/15/1849 – 11/13/1932, Company F, 14th Regiment, Kentucky Cavalry, sergeant
Greenberry Gabbard, captured at Stones River, Tennessee
Lewis Cox Gabbard, 10/23/1841 – 1/17/1903, born in Estill County
Mathias J. Gabbard, Company D, 8th Kentucky Infantry, born in Owsley County
William Riley Gabbard, 9/23/1844 – 5/4/1922, 47th Infantry, private
Simpson Gentry, 10/15/1821 – 2/5/1905, born in Madison County, 121st U.S. Colored Infantry
Hardin Golden, 6/9/1839 – 7/8/1923, Company G, 4th Kentucky Mounted Infantry, private, born in Madison County
Joseph Grant, Company F, 3rd Kentucky Infantry, wounded August 31, 1862

Isaac Haley, 1841-1897, private, born in Rockcastle County, 114th U.S. Colored Infantry

Arthur J. Hanson, Berea Postmaster in 1875

William R. Harris, 5/2/1847 – 7/17/1933, Company E, 6th Kentucky Cavalry, private, born in Rockcastle County

William M. Hayes, 1846-1930, Company D, 49th Kentucky Infantry, born in Rockcastle County

Alexander Franklin Hays/Hayes, 4/6/1840 – 6/4/1924, 8th Infantry, born in Knox County

Samuel Hollandsworth/Hollingsworth, 1842-1928, 24th Regiment, Kentucky Infantry, private, born in Clay County

H.C.A. Hollinsworth, Company F, 101st U.S. Colored Infantry

Benjamin Johnson, Company B, 47th Kentucky Infantry

Robert Johnson (or Johnston), 3/10/1843 – 12/23/1911, Company I, 14th Kentucky Cavalry, private, born in Perry County

Curtis F. Kelley, 3/3/1843 – 12/22/1932, Company G, 8th Kentucky Infantry, private, born in Estill County, captured at Blue Springs, Tennessee

Harrison Kennedy, 1827 – 1880, Company C, 124th U.S. Colored Infantry

Levi G. Kimberlain, born in Wythe, Virginia

Charles Lester, born in New York City, lived in Berea

William Daniel Lewis, 6/25/1837 – 1/3/1926, Company B, 24th Infantry

John W. Lunsford, 1843 – 6/4/1911, Company B, 12th Kentucky Regiment, private, born in Clay County

Edward S. Marshall, born in Marshall County

Schuyler McKinney

William Moberly/Mobley

Alexander Moore, born in Madison County, captured near Monticello, Kentucky

William Morris, born in Jackson County

James Nugent, Company F, 137th Indiana Infantry, born in Pennsylvania, lived in Paint Lick

Archibald (Archie) Pettiford, Company E, 29th U.S. Colored Infantry, minister in the Christian Church

Pleasant J. Polley/Pauley, year of birth about 1846 in Knox County, Company G, 4th Kentucky Infantry

Morgan B. Ramsey, 1844 – 1930, Company D, 49th Kentucky Infantry, corporal, born in Rockcastle County

Robert George Ramsey, 5/10/1846 – 12/24/1920, Company G, 8th Kentucky Infantry, corporal

Jefferson Reed, 1/9/1823 – 1/29/1878, 12th U. S. Colored Heavy Artillery

Turner Reed, year of birth about 1850, Company D, 119th U. S. Colored Infantry, used the last name Todd after the Civil War

Henry Reynolds, Company D, 6th Kentucky Cavalry, born in Clay County

John S. Richardson, born in Estill County

William H. Robe, 1847 – 1905, Company C, 59th Ohio Infantry, private, born in Adams County, Ohio, instructor and Superintendent of Buildings at Berea College

Alfred E. Robinson (or Robertson), 1842 – 1926, 7th Regiment, Kentucky Infantry, private

He also participated in the Spanish-American War, enlisted as Alfred Robertson, mustered out as Alfred Robinson, born in Clay County

William Sexton, born in Green County, Tennessee

R. Y.

Henry West, 5/4/1843 – 12/5/1903

Chapter Six

Civil War Participants

American Indians in the Civil War

In the magazine *Cowboys and Indians*, Dr. Clarissa W. Confer writes, "In the midst of a war fought on land that once was theirs, over a nation that denied them citizenship, Native Americans found themselves faced with a dubious decision: Whose side should they be fighting for? In 1861 it seemed that America was coming apart. Secession, Confederate nationhood, the firing on Fort Sumter and a mesmeric rush to combat engulfed the nation."

She continues, "By the time the Civil War started, Indians in settled regions experienced the conflict as members of larger communities whose movements they did not control. Indians living on the edge of incorporated states were better able to retain tribal autonomy, yet they were still strongly influenced by national and state political discourse. Those groups well beyond the white frontier...generally lived with little concern for U.S. politics." Dr. Confer says few Anglos considered the American Indians living among them. East of the Mississippi, tribal lands were so diminished that most Indians did not live in powerful tribal units. These Natives were left to make individual choices about whether or not to engage in the conflict.

There were approximately 30,000 American Indians who fought in the U.S. Civil War. The number is difficult to determine but is officially listed at 28,693. Since removal earlier in the century, most Indians hid their identity, made easier by the fact that so many people in the removed tribes were mixed bloods. Indians were considered to be people of color. Many had been enslaved and listed on the plantation manifests as Negroes. When the Civil War began, it was a white man's war. It was only when man-power became scarce that greater numbers of non-whites, including Indians, were officially admitted into the armies. There had already been mix-blood natives fighting, but their appearance did not identify them as Indians.

Laurence M. Hauptman in the March 2015 magazine *Indian* (National Museum of the American Indian) states that Indians enlisted for a variety of reasons — past alliances, treaty obligations, and earlier military experiences. The overriding reason for enlistment in both Union and Confederate armies was to maintain their homelands. All Native peoples who participated hoped to save their communities from further land loss and removal. They were fighting to be left alone from intrusions and threats to their lives and land. Al Carroll, in *Medicine Bags and Dog Tags* says, that the majority of Cherokees were pro-Union.

The exception to early Indian involvement came from Confederate Brig. Gen. Albert Pike, who was appointed Confederate Commissioner of Indian Affairs, and was assigned to command Indian Territory. He promised funds, ammunition, artillery, arms, commissary supplies and clothing to Indians, but after the Battle of Pea Ridge, 1862, all supplies stopped at Fort Smith and Little Rock. Pike was a former teacher, newspaperman, lawyer and Mexican War officer. His contacts with Indian tribes enhanced his promotion as a Confederate officer.

General Pike also recruited Choctaws and Chickasaws. Those treaties covered sovereignty, citizenship and representation in the Confederate Congress. Battalions were formed but quickly evaporated when no arms, pay, tentage, clothing or garrison equipment were furnished. Gen. Pike did not have a high regard for Indians and did not think they would be useful outside of Indian Territory. There were eventually about fifty Confederate companies that were Indian to some extent. Cherokee, Choctaw, Creek, Seminole, and Catawba tribes were the only ones to fight on the Confederate side.

In addition for the Confederacy, Stand Watie (He Stands and Waits), Principal Chief of the Southern Cherokees, the Old Settlers who had voluntarily removed prior to 1835, organized the First Cherokee Mounted Rifles in 1861, later designated the Second Cherokee Rifles. Gen. Watie's troops were noted for covering the retreat of Confederate forces and for capturing federal artillery in the Union victory at Pea Ridge. Gen. Watie and Gen. Gano captured a federal wagon train in September 1864 with a million dollars worth of supplies in 300 wagons at Cabin Creek. Watie's forces also captured the steamboat *J.R. Williams* loaded with supplies for Fort Gibson. Watie's troops participated in twenty-seven major engagements. Stand Watie never really surrendered. On June 23, 1865, at his request, he signed a cease fire agreement with Union representatives in the Doaksville Masonic Lodge,

Choctaw Nation, signing as brigadier general, governor and principal chief of that part of the Cherokee Nation under his control. He was a Freemason. Stand Watie continued to serve as Principal Chief of the Southern Cherokees until his death in 1871. Civil unrest continued, and his tribe moved to Kentucky after he died. Settling in Henderson, Kentucky, for many years, the tribe also owns land in Manchester with an office in Frankfort.

The Cherokees were bitterly divided during the Civil War. The Confederate Congress promised the Cherokees a seat in the legislature. Elias Cornelius Boudinot, a nephew of Stand Watie, an engineer and lawyer, held the rank of colonel in the Confederate Army. He was selected for this office because he was Cherokee delegate to the Confederate House of Representatives.

East of the Mississippi River, notable Confederate Indians were in Thomas' Legion, organized by William Holland Thomas, a great-great-nephew of Lord Baltimore through his mother and a cousin of Zachary Taylor through his father. He was fluent in the Cherokee language, adopted by Chief Yonuguska and given the name Wil-Usdi (Little Will). Thomas served as Principal Chief of the Eastern Band Cherokees and was their agent in buying land called the Qualla Boundary, the 2,200-acre tract and other scattered farms. These Cherokees were not legal residents and could not purchase their own land. Thomas recognized that Indian neutrality was impossible. He organized 350-400 Cherokees and an equal number of Scottish-Irish highlanders, eventually operating in western North Carolina and east Tennessee, with a brief assignment in the Shenandoah Valley. Thomas' Legion was never defeated by Union troops. He entered Waynesville, N.C., on May 9, 1865, and was informed that Gen. Lee had surrendered the previous month. Thomas ceased hostilities the next day, sending his soldiers home.

Another Cherokee of note was Confederate Major Gen. George Washington Morgan. He was a descendant of John Sevier, first governor of Tennessee, and of Cherokee chief Oconostota. His father and the grandfather of John Hunt Morgan were brothers. He served initially in the Third Tennessee Infantry, fought in the 1861 Virginia battles at Winchester and Manassas, and was in the Second Kentucky Cavalry by 1862. Morgan formally mustered Cherokees into three-year Confederate military service. There were approximately 200 Cherokees in two companies, including major Cherokee figures Peter Greybeard and

Astoogatogeh, commissioned as lieutenants, and noncommissioned sergeants Enola and Swimmer.

In 1862 and 1863, Confederate Cherokee military service was focused on pacifying East Tennessee. The mountainous area was not fit for cotton agriculture. There were few slaves and residents were only lukewarm to the "peculiar institution." Union sentiment was strong in that section of Tennessee as well as Eastern Kentucky. Cherokees guarded the mountain passes, hunted down spies, disarmed citizens, enforced conscription, tracked down deserters, impressed crops and livestock, and obtained loyalty oaths from fiercely independent locals. On September 1, 1863, Union forces under General Ambrose Burnside captured Knoxville, forcing Thomas to withdraw from Strawberry Plains to the North Carolina side of the mountains near Clingman's Dome.

For the Union, the most notable Indian unit was Company K of the First Michigan Sharpshooters made up of Ottawa, Lenape, Huron, Oneida, Potawami, and Ojibwe men. These men were afraid of the Confederate cause, having been warned by their leaders that Confederates would make slave-dogs of them and take away everything they owned. Rejected for service at first, they were eventually assigned to guard prisoners. Their first combat encounter was in the Battle of the Wilderness. They fought at Spotsylvania and Petersburg, and later gained prominence in The Crater. Once they were accepted for service as sharpshooters and despite continuing discrimination, they received extra training, enjoyed high morale and used their Sharps breechloaders with devastating effect. Of the 1,300 men who had enlisted, only twenty-three officers and 386 enlisted men returned. The Union also formed Indians into home guard units in Indian Territory. These units were the only reason Indians were able to retain any land after the Civil War.

In Virginia and North Carolina, the Pamunkey and Lumbee chose to serve the Union. Pamunkey served as civilian and naval pilots for Union warships and transports. Lumbee acted as guerrillas. Iroquois joined Company K, 5th Pennsylvania Volunteer Infantry. Powhatan served as land guides, river pilots, and spies for the Army of the Potomac. Many Pequot served in the 31st US Colored Infantry in the Army of the Potomac. In the West, Lenape (Delaware) cavalry killed five Confederate agents and captured 100 ponies in a major Union victory. Confederate Second Cherokee Mounted Rifles led by Col John Drew, defected to the Union forces in Kansas joining the Indian Home

Guard. Tribes fighting for the Union were Lenape, Creek, Cherokee, Seminole, Kickapoo, Seneca, Osage, Shawnee, Choctaw, Lumbee, Chickasaw, Iroquois nations, Powhatan, Pequot, Ojibwe (Chippewa), Huron, Odawa, Potawatomi, Menominee, Catawba, and Pamunkey.

In both the Southern and Northern armies, Indians were issued little military clothing, probably only a frock coat. Cherokee men usually wore two belts, an under-belt to which leggings were attached, and a fancier over-belt to which a knife might be attached. The shirt might have been a cotton print or off-white muslin, or a Cherokee long shirt, coming down almost to the knees. Boots might have been worn, but moccasins were preferred. Indians were generally expected to use weapons brought from home.

Weapons used were rifles, and many Indians carried knives and tomahawks. Muzzle loaders were still in use, but Indians favored the Winchester rifle. Bows and arrows were very rarely used. There is evidence they were used in the Battle of Chustenahlah, Osage country, in the Indian Territory, Dec. 26, 1862. At Pea Ridge or the Battle of Elkhorn Tavern, Arkansas, fought March 6-8, 1862, Laurence Hauptman notes in *Between Two Fires* that many of the Indians were armed with only traditional weapons. This was the first battle in which Union Indian troops encountered Confederate Indian troops. This was only a few miles from Indian homeland. Confederate native units present were the First and Second Cherokee Mounted Rifles under Stand Watie, Col. Tandy Walker's Choctaw and Chickasaw Mounted Rifles, the First Chickasaw Infantry, Shecoe's Chickasaw Battalion and the First Battalion of Chickasaw Cavalry. Also present was Col. John Drew's Second Cherokee Mounted Rifles. Drew had lost many of his unit in December 1861, when they refused to fight Creek Chief Opothleyahola's Union forces. After Pea Ridge, Drew's forces defected to the Union side. There was also use of traditional weapons at the Battle of Honey Springs, a fight for control of Fort Blount, also known as the Affair at Elk Creek, July 7, 1863, Indian Territory, in what would eventually be called Oklahoma. By this time, arrows used were made of steel and were often commercially produced with brand names stamped on them. Knapping was becoming a lost art. Handmade arrow points might be fashioned from iron wagon wheel rims.

While many Indians fought in battles, they were also commonly employed as scouts. One of the most noted was a Lenape called Black

Beaver (Suck-tum-mah-kway), who was recognized as one of the most accomplished scouts in North America. He was born in Belleville, Illinois, in 1806, the son of a chief. From 1824 onward, his name appears frequently in historical records. In the era of mountain men, Black Beaver visited nearly every part of the newly acquired American territory. In April 1861, when he was in his fifties and was leading a respected and comfortable life on his farm near Fort Arbuckle, Black Beaver guided Union troops out of Arkansas and away from William W. Averell's Texas Mounted Rifles. He served the Union throughout the war as a valuable scout. Confederates seized his cattle, horses and crops, destroying his farm. He died in 1880 without having been compensated for his losses during the war.

One Union Indian who appeared in full uniform was Ely (rhymes with freely) Samuel Parker, a Seneca sachem (paramount chief), attorney, engineer, and tribal diplomat. Commissioned a lieutenant colonel, he served as adjutant to General Grant. Later he rose to Brevet Brigadier General, and after the war was appointed U.S. Commissioner of Indian Affairs by President Grant. Parker wrote the final draft of the Confederate surrender terms at Appomattox Court House. (Brevet was a promotion without a higher pay grade.)

His brother, Isaac Newton Parker, called Newt, was a noncommissioned officer, promoted to Third Sergeant and Color Bearer of D Company, 132nd New York State Volunteer Infantry. From 1863-65, he was stationed in New Bern, North Carolina, guarding the rails at this major transportation hub. He served with twenty-four other Iroquois in an integrated unit popularly called "the Tuscarora Company." The two Parkers were sons of Chief William Parker, Jo-no-es-sto-wa, who had been wounded in American service during the War of 1812.

At the Battle of Richmond, two Confederate units had a sufficient number of American Indian members to warrant adding red stars representing the tribes to their unit flags. These were the Tenth Texas Cavalry and the First Arkansas Mounted Rifles.

Clarissa Confer writes, "For many Natives, the irony of the Civil War was that they were inexorably involved whether they chose sides or not. The repercussions of the enormous conflict entangled Native peoples living both within and without the borders of the Union and Confederate states. Not desired as participants at the start, their value as recruits grew as the war dragged on, as more and more white men died."

The Civil War reduced Indian country to rubble, as was the case everywhere battles were fought. Homes were burned, crops destroyed, and livestock killed. Citizenship had been promised but did not materialize. Indians were not recognized as persons until the court case of Standing Bear v. Crook, 1871. Standing Bear was an elderly Ponca imprisoned for leaving the reservation. This was the first successful challenge to the government's ability to impose reservations on Native people. Many Indians did not receive citizenship until 1924 in the Snyder Act, which seemed to be a response to the military service of Natives in the First World War, and the right to vote was not acquired in seven states until 1948, a response to their distinguished service in the Second World War.

Foreign Soldiers in the Civil War

Of the 2,000,000 or so Union soldiers who served in the American Civil War, a third were foreign born. Of these, 200,000 were German, 170,000 were Irish, 40,000 were from Scotland and Wales, 10,000 were English, 50,000 were Canadians and 75,000 others were mostly European. The number of German speaking troops was particularly large from Austria, Switzerland, and Alsace-Lorraine mainly because of the economic and political troubles, which culminated in the revolution of 1848.

1848 was a year of upheaval in Europe. Revolutionary movements broke out spontaneously from Copenhagen to Palermo and from Paris to Budapest. Revolutions succumbed to military repression. New European governments were hostile to revolution but were strong on national unification and constitutional government with limited representation. 1848 left a legacy of class fears and class conflict. Louis Napoleon Bonaparte was elected president of the French Republic in 1848, and in 1852 assumed the title of Emperor Napoleon III. He ruined himself by war. He was fighting in Italy in 1859 and in Mexico from 1862-67. Another major conflict was the Crimean War of 1854-56, with Russia making demands on the Ottoman Empire. From 1859 to 1867 with extensive fighting, Italy was unified under Victor Emmanuel II as King of Italy in 1861 through the work of the brilliant politician Camillo di Cavour and Giuseppe Garibaldi. In Germany from 1862-66 with Otto von Bismarck serving as prime minister enlarged, reorganized, retrained, and re-equipped the army. The Danes engaged in national consolidation beginning in 1863. The Germans were concerned about losing Schleswig and Holstein. In 1864, Bismarck persuaded Prussia and Austria to go to war with Denmark.

Officers and aristocrats, seasoned by war in Europe, came to America anticipating the opportunities offered in this Civil War, and perhaps to avoid government intrigues in Europe. Common people came here to escape repression and to gain freedom from their situations in the home country. They were most often opposed to slavery. There might be Civil War in the United States, but America was still a land of opportunity. Here they could find land that did not belong to some Duke or Prince.

These new recruits had not been here long enough to become assimilated and they often retained their language and customs. Gen. McClellan allowed the formation of Louis Blenker's German Division of New York and Pennsylvania units in the Army of the Potomac. The 9th Ohio, 74th Pennsylvania, 32nd Indiana and the 9th Wisconsin Infantry consisted entirely of Germans. The Garibaldi Guards (39th New York Volunteer Infantry) was part of the Blenker Division. It was composed, however, of Germans and Italians, with a mixture of real Zouaves from Algiers, foreign legionnaires, Cossacks, Indian Sepoys, Turks, Slavs, Swiss, Spaniards, and Austrians. Its commander was Col. Frederick D'Utassy, a Hungarian. Also serving with him were his brothers Carl and Anton. Other Hungarians were Maj. Gen. Alexander Asboth, Maj. Gen. Julius Stahel Szamwald, and four brigadiers: Eugene A. Koslay, Frederick Knefler, Nicholas Perczel and Gabriel DeKorponay. Colonels Bela Estvan and Charles Vidor served the South.

Irish formed units in both Northern and Southern armies. The most celebrated was an Irish Brigade organized by Thomas Francis Meagher, New York, composed of the Fighting 69th New York Infantry Regiment, the 63rd, the 88th New York, the 28th Massachusetts and later the 116th Pennsylvania. Large numbers of Norwegians and Swedes served in the Western campaigns. The most famous was the 15th Wisconsin, whose commander Col. Hans Christian Heg died at Chickamauga.

The 55th New York Volunteer Infantry (the Lafayette Guard) organized by Count de Trobriand was composed of French residents from New York. The 58th New York (Pulaski Guard) contained many German speaking Poles from the Prussian and Austrian ruled sections of

Poland. The 79th New York "Highlanders" was composed principally of men of Scottish birth. They wore kilts, bonnets and were accompanied by the bagpipes.

Dutch immigrants were deeply committed to the cause of liberty. When a call for volunteers was issued in 1862, they were among the first to respond. One of their leaders was Dr. H.P. Scholte of Iowa, who had served as vice president of the Republican National Convention when Lincoln was nominated for the presidency. Men from the Netherlands formed the 25th Michigan Volunteer Regiment. Many of these men had been in this country only a few years and spoke only a few words of English.

Russian soldiers also served in the Union Army. Russian immigrant Peter Petroff so highly impressed his commanders with his military dedication that he was promoted to corporal despite the fact that he could not speak any English. Vladimir Magazinoff had deserted the army of Tsar Alexander II, then jumped ship in New York to enlist in a Union artillery regiment. Prince Alexander Eristoff arrived in New York in 1862 and fought for the principles of progress and freedom of the North. The most famous Russian-born soldier was Ivan Vasilyevich Turchaninov, better known as John Basil Turchin, a veteran of the Crimean War, who immigrated to Chicago in 1856. He was commissioned a colonel in 1861. Turchin's Russian methods combined with American patriotism were so impressive that a fourth regiment of the 19th Illinois was put under his command.

Because of the number of soldiers who did not speak English, communication was always a problem. One regiment was under the command of Maj. Gen. Franz Sigel, who had officers and soldiers from fifteen different nations. His orders were translated from his native German to Hungarian for his officers, then into seven other languages, then to English and back into German.

His regiment may have included soldiers from the Middle East: Turkish, Arabic or Persian areas and African, either Sub-Sahara or the Maghreb—Berber states of North Africa. Research suggests 292 persons from Africa or the Ottoman Empire who fought in the Civil War, with ten of these in the Confederate military. Most of these soldiers were probably Muslim, but a small number might have been Maronite, Coptic or Orthodox. There were two Mahomets, two Hasans, three Alis, seventeen Saids and fifty-eight Hassans who fought in the Civil

War. A Civil War magazine stated, "Senegal-born slave Ayuba Suleiman Diallo (...Job Ben Soloman) played a major role in exposing the horrors of slavery in his many slave narratives."

Hajji Ali (or Hadj Philip Tedro), Syrian-Greek, was recruited by Jefferson Davis as U.S. Secretary of War for the U.S. Camel Corps in 1856. The United States had purchased thirty-three camels for this army unit that lasted until 1864. The project was an attempt to establish transportation from Texas to California during the Gold Rush. Ali, known as Hi Jolly, lived until 1902. Private Mohammed Kahn was born in Persia and raised in Afghanistan. Sergeant Max Hassan, born in Africa, served in the 14th Heavy Artillery Regiment. The highest rank of any Muslim was achieved by Capt. Moses Osman of the 104th Illinois Infantry. There is disagreement on his origin and religion. The name would suggest that he was Osmanli Turk or West African, but it could also be traced to the Norman Conquest.

Mohammed Ali ben Said (long i, long e), known as Sergeant Nicholas Said, born in 1831, was the son of a general in the Bornu army, Central Africa. After his father was killed, he was captured by Tuaregs and sold several times in Turkey and Libya. Said was taken on a hajj pilgrimage to Mecca and then sent to Turkey where he was again sold. He became the slave of Russian Prince Mentchikoff in Odessa and then of Prince Troubetzkoy in St. Petersburg, with whom he took a grand tour of Europe. He learned seven languages. He asked the prince for permission to visit his homeland, and in 1857 Said escaped slavery and became the servant of De Sanddrost I.J. Rochussen of Suriname (Dutch Guiana). They visited the Bahamas, Haiti, and Canadian cities. Then Said came to New York. He had no money. A pastor loaned him ten dollars and suggested he go to Detroit or Buffalo to find work. Said became a teacher in Detroit. In 1863, Said enlisted in the 55th Massachusetts Colored Infantry. His autobiography published in 1873, is considered to be a rare historic treasure. It was rediscovered and again published in 2001. Said died in 1882.

Only nine per cent of the Southern Army of perhaps a million soldiers was composed of foreigners. There were Irish regiments and the Polish Legion, as well as several German and Mexican divisions. The 33rd Texas Cavalry was Hispanic. The most notable volunteer division was formed from various European countries in Louisiana under the command of Maj. Gen. Count Camille Armand Jules Marie, Prince de Polignac, from France. Soldiers who could not pronounce his name often called him Prince Polecat. Polignac saw action at the Battle of Richmond. The largest number of foreign born soldiers in the Confederate Army were Irish, followed by Germans, French, Mexicans, and British. A noted foreign born officer was Patrick Cleburne from Ireland, who fought at Richmond and was wounded early in the battle at Mt. Zion Church. One Cuban served as a Confederate general, Ambrosio Jose Gonzales.

Two Hispanics were brigadier generals in the Union Army, Diego Archuleta from Mexico, and Henry Clay Pleasants from Argentina. Approximately 3,500 Mexicans, Puerto Ricans, and Cubans were engaged early in the war, mostly for the Confederacy. By the conclusion of the Civil War, 10,000 Hispanics were involved. Union units included the First, Second, and Third New Mexico Volunteer Infantry. The Garibaldi Guard Company D was called the Spanish Company. Confederate units were the 5th Regiment, Spanish Regiment, the Cazadores Espanoles Regiment, the Louisiana Tigers, the Spanish Guards, 55th Infantry, and 2nd Infantry. Three Hispanics were awarded the Medal of Honor, including Seaman Philip Bazaar, from Chile, assigned to the USS *Santiago de Cuba*, for his heroic actions in the assault on the port of Wilmington, North Carolina.

David Glasgow Farragut, Union Vice Admiral in 1864 and full Admiral in 1866, was from Spain. His Spanish name was Jordi Farragut Mesquida. He had been adopted by David and Evalina Porter. Farragut's greatest victory was the Battle of Mobile Bay. When the USS *Tecumseh* struck a mine and sank, he shouted through a trumpet, "What's the trouble?" The reply was "torpedoes!" to which he replied, "Damn the torpedoes! Full speed ahead!" Farragut's foster brother was David Dixon Porter whose great friend Gen. Sherman called the "Lord High Admiral." Gen. Grant said Admiral Porter was the equal of Lord Horatio Nelson, who had been famous for his superb grasp of strategy and tactics during the Napoleonic Wars.

Six generals who fought for the Union were Germans born in Prussia. Karl Leopold Matthies was involved in charging Missionary Ridge in Chattanooga and was wounded. Alexander Schimmelfennig avoided capture for two days at the Battle of Gettysburg by hiding in a pigsty. Peter J. Osterhaus assisted Gen. Sherman on his march through Georgia. August Willich was captured at the Battle of Stones River and wounded at the Battle of Resaca. Others were Brig. Gen. Carl Schurz

Chapter One

Edmund Kirby Smith was born in St. Augustine, Florida, in 1824. He died in Sewanee, Tennessee, in 1893 and is buried there. Kirby Smith graduated from West Point in 1845 and served with his brother Ephraim Kirby Smith, West Point, 1826, in the Mexican War. Edmund surrendered his Confederate army at Galveston, Texas, June 2, 1865. He served as President of the Atlantic and Pacific Telegraph from 1866-1868 and was President of the University of Nashville from 1870-1875. He became Professor of Mathematics and Botany, University of the South, Sewanee, Tennessee, 1875-1893, and is credited with discovering several species of plants in Tennessee and Florida.

Mahlon D. Manson (pronounced May' lun). Following the war, he served in Congress as Indiana State Auditor and as the state's lieutenant governor.

Charles Cruft, wounded at the Battle of Richmond, September 29, 1862.

William "Bull" Nelson, killed at the Galt House in Louisville, Kentucky in September 1862.

Henry Heth. His forces marching from Barbourville to Richmond, arrived after the battle.

Leonidas Metcalfe, son of the tenth governor of Kentucky, commanded the newly formed Union 7th Kentucky Cavalry.

Old poster from Big Hill looking toward Richmond. This is the view the Confederate Army would have had. Kentucky Digital Library

Major Green Clay, aide to General Nelson and son of Cassius M. Clay, served as his father's aide in Russia after the Civil War. He took wounded General Nelson to Jessamine County.

Camille Armand Jules Marie, Prince de Polignac. He was the last Confederate Major General.

Col. John S. Scott, commanding the Kirby Smith Brigade of Cavalry, comprised of 1st Louisiana Cavalry, 1st Georgia Cavalry, 1st Louisiana Mountain Howitzers, and Buckner Guard.

Dr. Alexander H. Darnes, 1840-1894, half-brother of Edmund Kirby smith and his servant during the Battle of Richmond. He practiced medicine in Jacksonville, Florida, after the war.

Joe Lick Knob from the porch of Pleasant View at Battlefield Park. This is the pleasant view for which the house and farm were named. Bill Robinson photo, used with permission

Kentucky River at Boonesborough in Madison County. Many soldiers escaped after the Battle of Richmond by fording the river, low from drought, in this area.

Chapter Two

Boone's Trace

Merritt Jones Tavern at the foot of Big Hill. Madison County Historical Society photo

Interior rooms of Merritt Jones Tavern.

Interior rooms of Merritt Jones Tavern.

Two chimneys remain of the tavern. Courtesy of civilwaralbum.com, Trooper Bruce Schulze (ret), webmaster.

Thirteen Confederate graves lie near the tavern. Courtesy of civilwaralbum.com, Trooper Bruce Schulze (ret), webmaster.

This home on the battlefield served as a hospital. It was reported that a porch and one room were destroyed by Confederate cannon fire. It is now the pro shop of the Battlefield Golf Course.

Squire Boone Rock inside the Madison County Courthouse.

The Rogers House, later designated Quarters 29, served as the commander's home, Blue Grass Army Depot. It is now the Visitors Center for Battlefield Park.

Battlefield Park Visitor's Center.

Chapter Three

Dr. Alexander Thomas Augusta

Dr. Bernard J.D. Irwin

Dr. Bernard J.D. Irwin wearing the Medal of Honor

Dr. Luke P. Blackburn, first person to implement a yellow fever quarantine, created the first well-organized system of treament of wounded in Bermuda who contracted yellow fever; 28th Governor of Kentucky.

Dr. Jonathan Letterman, Medical Director of the Army of the Potomac; in 1848, Confederate agent for Kentucky and Mississippi; aided blockade runners on the battlefield followed by rapid transit of wounded to hospitals.

Dr. William A. Hammond, 11th Surgeon General of the U.S. Army, founded the part of the University of Virgnia to specialize in neurology.

Dr. Hunter H. McGuire founded schools and hospitals that became American Medical Museum; first physician promoted to Chief Surgeon of the Army of Northern Virginia.

Dr. William Whelan, U.S. Navy surgeon, 1837-1865, Chief, U.S. Bureau of Medicine and Surgery, 1861-1865.

USS Red Rover, first U.S. Navy hospital ship, Mississippi River Squadron.

Madison Female Institute was used as a hospital during the Battle of Richmond and was the main facility used by the Sisters of Charity.

Dr. James McCune Smith, 1813-1865, physician (surgeon), apothecary, abolitionist, and author. Born in slavery in New York, he was the first African American man to receive a medical degree from a medical college, graduating top of his class from the University of Glasgow, Scotland, in 1837.

Dr. David Jones Beck

Sister Anthony O'Connell (Mary Ellen O'Connell)

Sister Anthony's medical bag

Dr. Elizabeth Blackwell

Dr. Rebecca Lee Crumpler

Dr. Esther Hill Hawks

Dr. Orianna Moon Andrews

Dr. Mary Edwards Walker wearing the Medal of Honor

Dr. Susan La Flesche Picotte, Omaha Nation, 1865-1915, valedictorian of her class, Women's Medical College of Pennsylvania. She was the first Native American to become a physician and was employed by the U.S. Government as physician for the Omaha Agency Indiana School.

Dr. Mary Ellen Britton, 1855-1925, graduate of Berea College and the first black woman licensed as a physician in Lexington, Kentucky.

Eliza Clinedinst Crim nursed New Market Cadets

Susie King Taylor, first black woman to serve as a U.S. Army nurse

Augusta Jane Evans, Confederate nurse, author, and first woman to earn $100,000 from writing.

Dorothea Dix

Sarah Emma Edmonds

Harriet Tubman

Florence Nightingale

Sarah Edmonds

Chapter Four

John Malcolm Miller

William Joel Stone, Governor of Missouri

David Rowland Francis, Governor of Missouri, Ambassador to Russia

Rev. Dr. Madison Campbell, 1823-1897.

General Green Clay, soldier, land surveyor, businessman, and politician, buried with Masonic Rites in Richmond, Kentucky, 1828.

Cassius Marcellus Clay

Aerial view of White Hall. Built in 1798-99, the home was remodled by Cassius and Mary Jane Warfield Clay while he was minister to Russia and was renamed White Hall. This Georgian-Italianate home has forty-four rooms.

Laura Clay

The front of Green Clay's home, Clermont.

Mary Barr Clay

Chapter Five

Alfred Ellis Robinson wearing the badge of the Capt. James West Post 171, GAR, Berea, Kentucky, great-grandfather of Paul Rominger.

Freedman's Bell, Old Bell Tower, First Christian Church. Berea College Archives

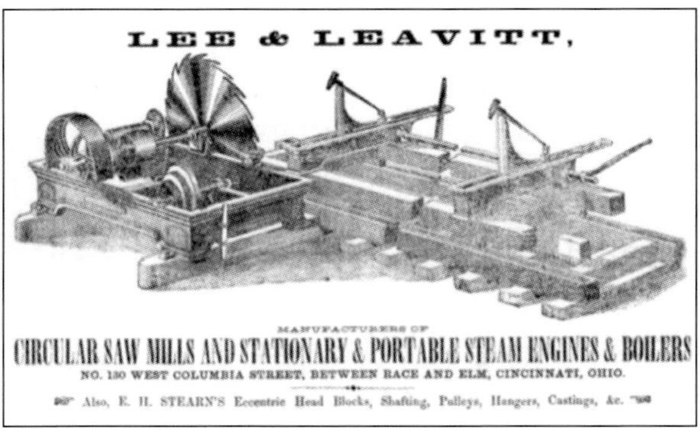

Advertisement for Lee & Leavitt circular saw mills, stationary, portable steam engines, and boilers.

First Berea College building

James Shelton Hathaway

Angus Augustus Burleigh. Hutchins Library, Berea College archive photographs

Levant Dodge

Captain James West

The Captain James West Post G.A.R. #171 and Women's Relief Corps #48, Berea, Kentucky, date unknown. Berea College Special Collections Archives

1862 Union graves, Berea Cemetery. Photo by Sharon Farthing Grave

Chapter Six

Black Beaver, Delaware, one of the most accomplished Indian scouts in North America. Credited with establishing the California and Chisholm Trails, he was fluent in English, Lenni Lenape, and several other European and Native languages.

Payson Wolfe, Odawa Nation (Ottawa), First Michigan Sharpshooters, Company K

Syrenius Welch, Brothertown Indian, Second Wisconsin Volunteer Cavalry

1st Louisiana Native Guard, 1861

Walter Thompson Adair, Surgeon, First Cherokee Rifles. The green sash indicates Medical Corps.

Flag of Stand Watie

Opothlayehola, Muscogee Creek, brilliant orator, speaker of the Upper Creek Council

Dr. Carlos Montezuma, 1865/66 - 1923, Yavapal Apache, University of Illinois (age 14), Chicago Medical College of Northwestern University

Mexican Texans in the Civil War

Mohammed Ali ben Said

Dr. Charles Eastman, 1858-1939, Santee Dakota, Dartmouth College, Boster University

Dr. William W. Mayo

Hajji Ali and Gertrudis Sema

Dr. Anderson R. Abbott, first black Canadian physician, 1861, U.S. Army surgeon

Calixa Lavallee, composed the national anthem "O Canada"

Edward P. Doherty led the detachment of troops that captured and killed John Wilkes Booth

Wlodzimierz Bonawentura Krzyzanowski

Antonio F. Gomez (Anthony), Punjab (Conjee Rustumjee Cohoujee Bey)

Felix Cornelius Balderry, Filipino

CSS Shenandoah, on which many Asian, Hawaiian, and Austrailian sailors served. It was iron-framed, teak-planked, and fully rigged with auxiliary steam power. Capturing thirty-eight vessels, it fired the last shot of the Civil War on June 22, 1865 across the bow of a whaler off the Aleutian Islands.

English officers in the Civil War

SS Rob Roy, Confederate blockade runner to Bermuda, Bahamas, and Cuba, Captain William Watson, Scotland.

The sloop of war CSS Alabama, 19th century painting by Samuel Walters, United Kingdom.

Patrick Ronayne Cleburne

Henry Ho'olulu Pitman

79th New York Volunteer Infantry Regiment

Prince Philippe of Orleans, Count of Paris, Prince Royal

Powhaten Beaty

Russian sailors sent to aid the Union

Flag of the Black Brigade of Cincinnati, 1962. Ohio Historical Society

Sgt. Maj. Christian A. Fleetwood, 4th U.S.C.T., Medal of Honor

Sgt. William Carney Jr., Medal of Honor

1st Sgt. Robert A. Pinn, Ohio 5th U.S. Colored Troops, Medal of Honor

John Lawson, Pennsylvania, USS Hartford, Medal of Honor

4th United States Colored Troops, Company E, Fort Lincoln, Washington, D.C.

29th Connecticut Volunteer Infantry

Captain William D. Matthews, commanding Company D, First Kansas Colored Volunteer Infantry Regiment, State Unit organized in August 1862.

Nicholas Biddle, Pennsylvania, first soldier to be wounded in the Civil War

Sgt. Maj. Lewis H. Douglass, son of Frederick Douglass, 54th Massachusetts

George Commodore, Union Navy, sailor with the USS New Hampshire

Elijah P. Marrs, 1840-1910. Born into slavery in Shelby County, Kentucky, he escaped in 1864, formed a company of twenty-seven men who marched to Louisville and joined the U.S. Army. He was made sergeant in Company L, 12th Regiment Heavy Artillery, U.S. Colored Troops.

Double slave cabin

Slave housing at Rose Hill, Lexington

Cpl. Andrew J. Smith, 55th Massachusetts, from Kentucky, awarded the Medal of Honor in 1864, issued in 2000.

Maj. Martin R. Delaney, first African American with field command rank in the Civil War.

Slave cabin

Louis Napoleon Nelson, rifleman, 7th Tennessee Cavalry, Co. M, Army of Tennessee, Gen. Nathan Bedford Forrest, commanding.

Restored slave cabin

Recruitment poster

Confederate Infantry, probably a drummer

Private Edwin Francis Jemison

Robert H. Undershot

Young Confederate soldier, one of many unidentified

Edward Black, age 8, youngest Union soldier

Cadet Private William H. McDowell, Virginia Military Institute, Class of 1867, killed at the Battle of New Market

Orion Perseus Howe, 1848-1930

Drummer Jackson of the 79th U.S.C.T.

Medal of Honor

Alexander H. Johnson after the war. Johnson enlisted as a drummer at age 16 with the 54th Massachusetts Infantry.

Powder Monkey, USS New Hampshire

John Lincoln Clem, 1851-1937. This photo was probably taken in 1871 at his appointment by President Grant to Second Lieutenant, 24th U.S. Infantry, or possibly 1874 at his promotion to First Lieutenant.

Robert Walker, First Class Boy

In 1860, Col. Lewis Wallace organized the Crawfordsville Guards Independent Militia, Indiana Zouaves, as Maj. Gen. Wallace commanded the successful 1862 defense of Cincinnati.

Young unidentified Union soldier

Pvt. Francis E. Brownell was the first soldier to earn Medal of Honor for Civil War action in 1861, awarded in 1877.

Soldiers in Zouave uniform

146th Pennsylvania Infantry, 1863, tinted. Pictured include David W. Allen, Chauncey B. Smith, Jesse C. Johnson, and John Duckworth.

114th Pennsylvania Zouaves

Boys in Zouave uniforms

Prince Phillip of Orleans, Count of Paris, Prince Royal

David Wood, age 10, 6th Missouri Cavalry, aide to the colonel, his father

Elisha Stockwell Jr., 14th Wisconsin Infantry, Co. I

Joseph Pierce, from Guangzhou, China

Mohican Stockbridge Munsee, Native troops being sworn into the United States Army

The Russian Imperial frigate Osliaba, one of six Russian ships sent as a show of support to the Union in 1863.

Sailor with the USS New Hampshire

Waite and Parker

Chapter Seven

Adams Cottage Printing Press

Madison County Courthouse, Richmond, built in 1848. A large fence surrounding the courthouse was used to hold Union prisoners while they awaited parole.

Louisville Military Prison at 10th and Broadway, across from the L&N Depot. This Federal facility began receiving prisoners in October 1862.

Playing cards

Boxing match

Reading newspapers

Fishing

Clay marbles

Early baseball

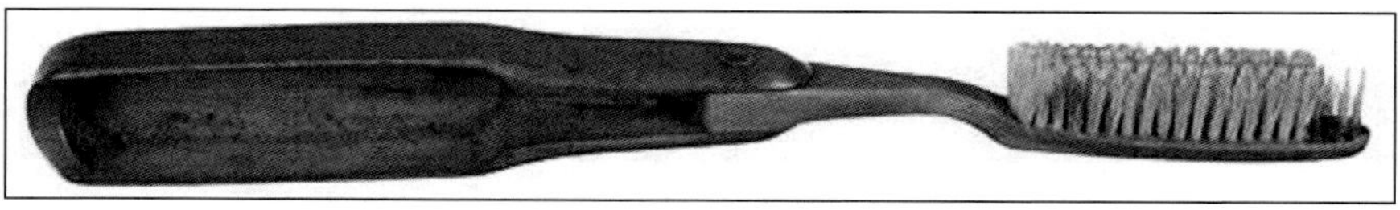

Travel toothbrush

Asteroid, unbeaten in twelve starts

Artillery with cavalry and horses

Isaac Burns Murphy, 1861-1896. Born in Frankfort, Kentucky and died in Lexington, Kentucky, he won three Kentucky Derbys, four American Derbys, and five Latonia Derbys, with 628 total wins of 1,412 to 1,538 mounts.

Springhouse trough found on the farm of Sylvester F. and Catharine Pickering Storrs on Guynn Road near Berea. This trough was given to Berea Tourism by Paul Rominger, great-great-grandson of Mr. and Mrs. Storrs. It is displayed in the Jon Carloftis Garden at Berea Tourism on Broadway in Berea. Photo by Scharme Brunner Price

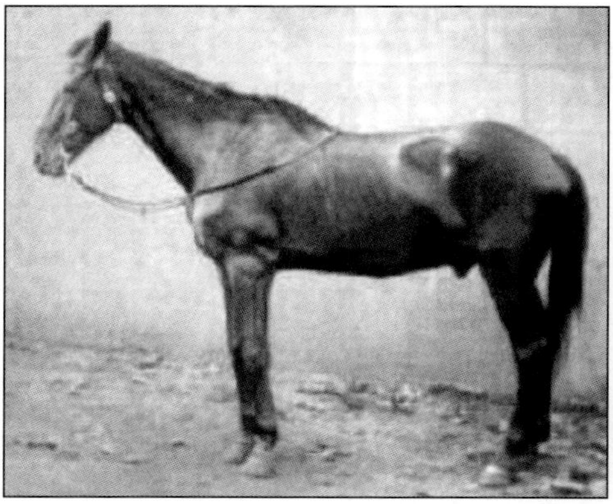

Little Sorrel, Morgan horse of Gen. Thomas J. Jackson

Black Allan, major Tennessee Walker sire after the Civil War

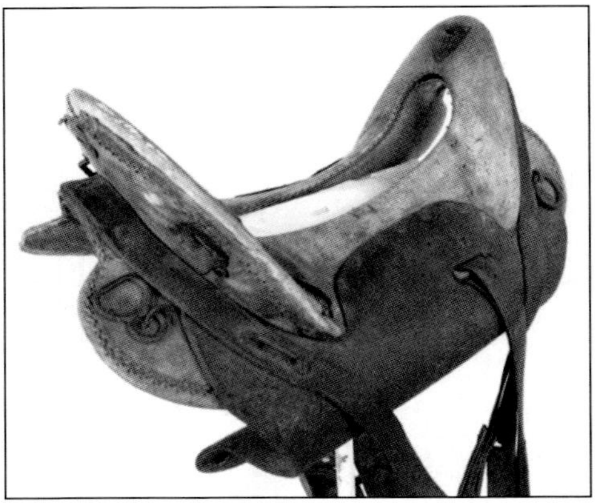

McClellan saddle

Gen. R.E. Lee and Traveller, American Saddlebred

Salisbury Prison Yard

Chapter Eight

1828 Tennessee hog rifle, modified from flintlock to percussion about 1860, owned by W.W. Rominger, grandfather of Paul Rominger. Photo by Sherman Rominger

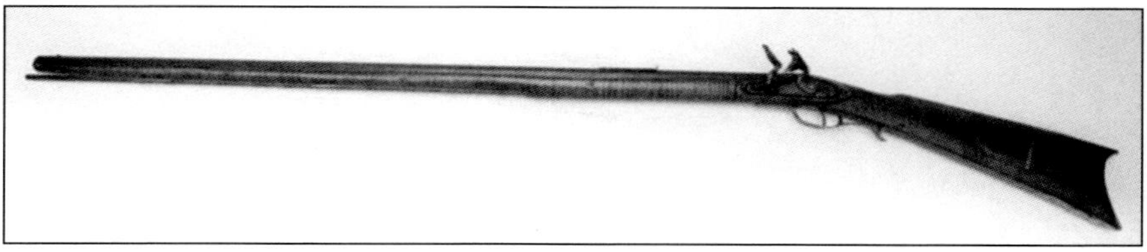

J. Dixon left-handed long rifle

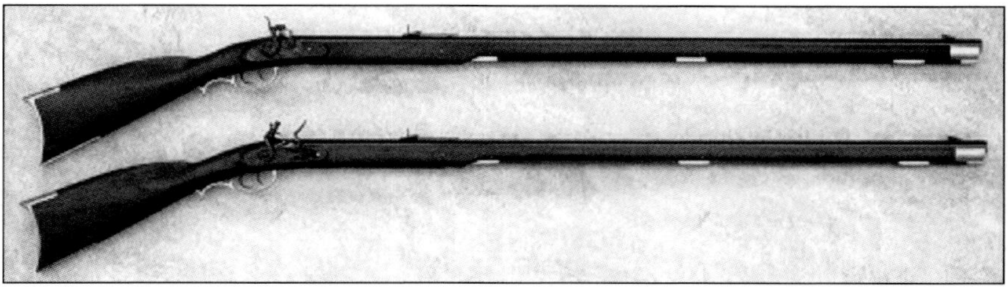

Two long rifles; one is percussion and the other is flintlock

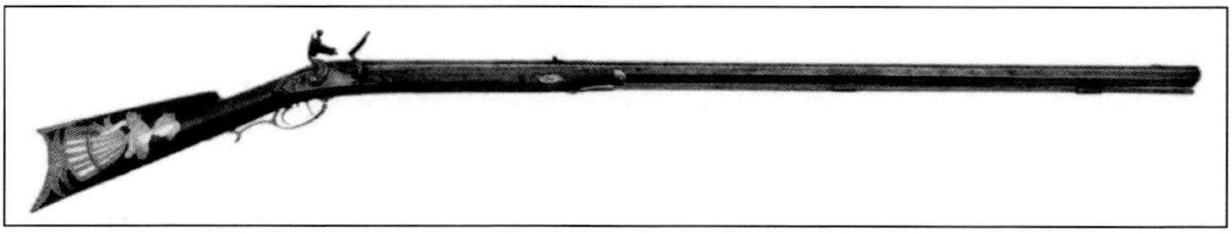

Southern Belle long rifle, made in Macon, Georgia, .36 caliber, seven helical grooves of rifling, metallic lady patch cover

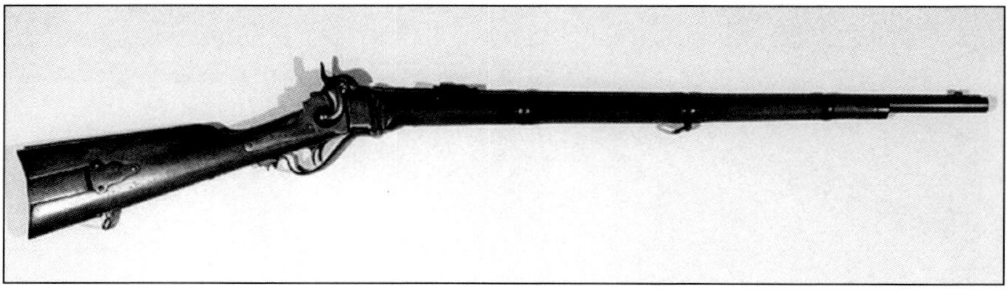

Sharps single shot, large caliber, breech loading. One of the finest rifles ever made.

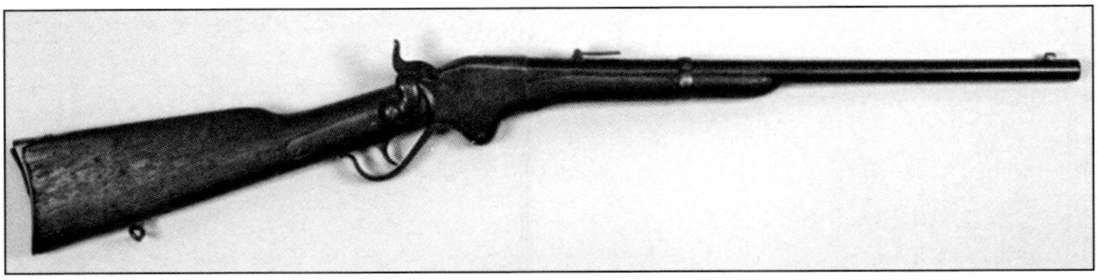

Spencer Model 1860. Designed by Christopher Spencer, it was the most advanced rifles of the Civil War. It had a seven-shot magazine, lever fed, the first repeater to use metal cartridges.

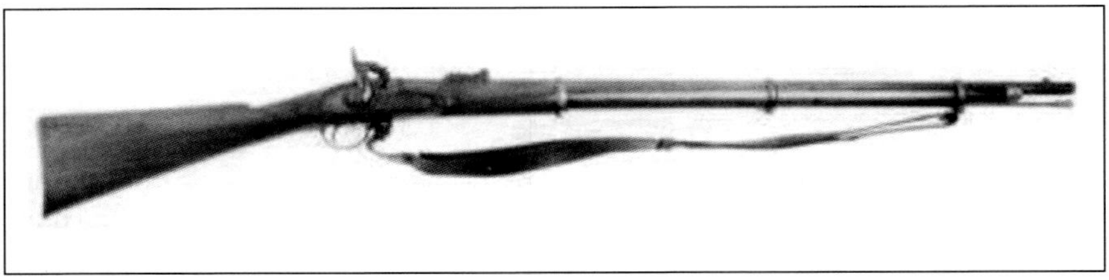

Pattern 1853 Enfield

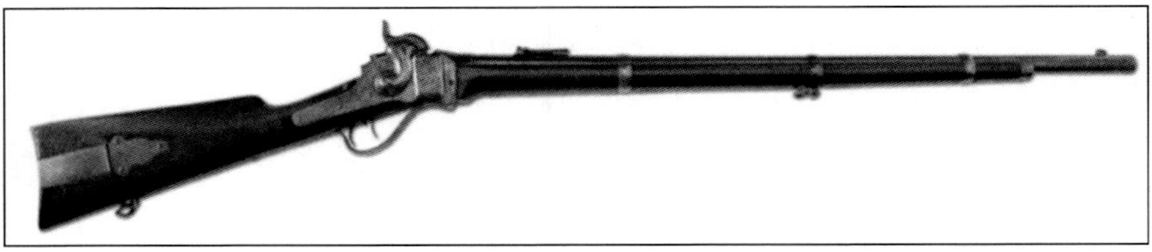

1859 Sharps, Berdan special order preferred by Union sharpshooters

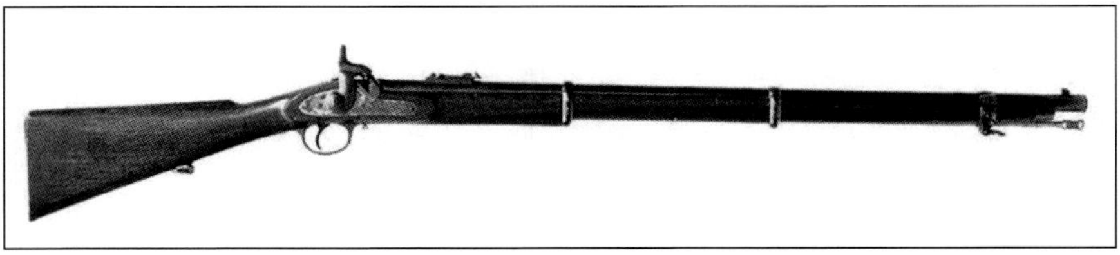

Whitworth used by Confederate sharpshooters

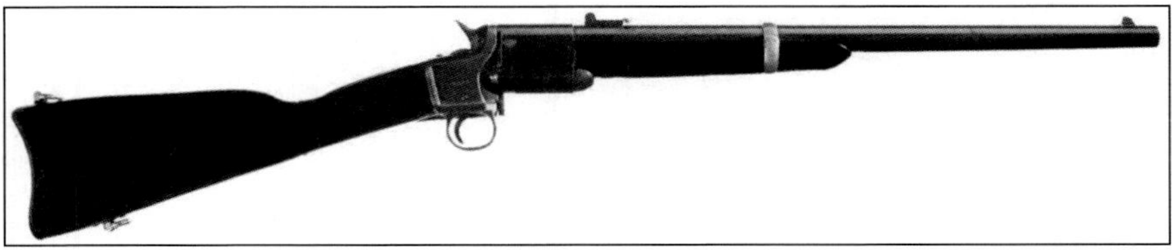

Triplett and Scott repeater carbine produced in Columbia, Kentucky, for Kentucky Home Guard units to protect Union supply lines, .50 caliber, rim fire, only 5,000 were made.

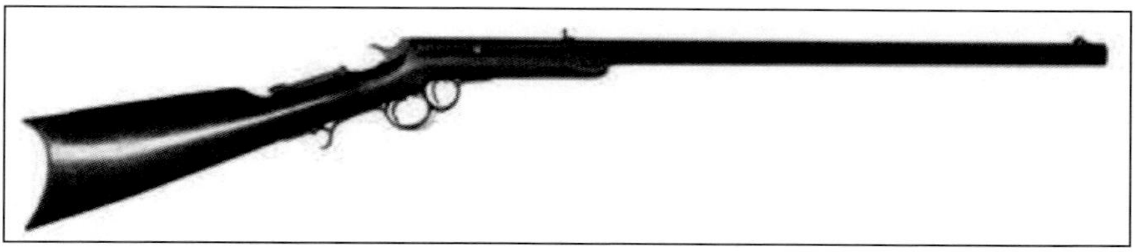

Frank Wesson two trigger carbine manufactured in three calibers: .22, .32, and .44 caliber military model. The Commonwealth of Kentucky purchased 1,344 of these through Benjamin Kittredge of Cincinnati. This carbine was first used by Col. Metcalfe's cavalry in the Battle of Big Hill.

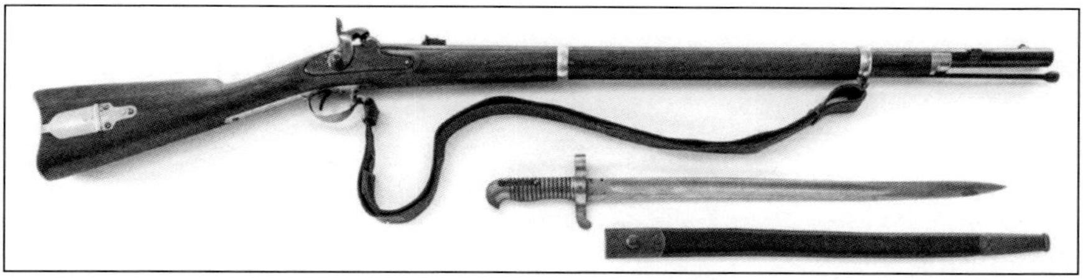

Remington Model 1863, .58 caliber muzzle loading rifle. Called the Zouave rifle, 12,501 of these were made. The rifle was maneuverable, with a barrel length at 33 inches. The rifle was intended for the U.S. Artillery Department, but it was never distributed to any Army division.

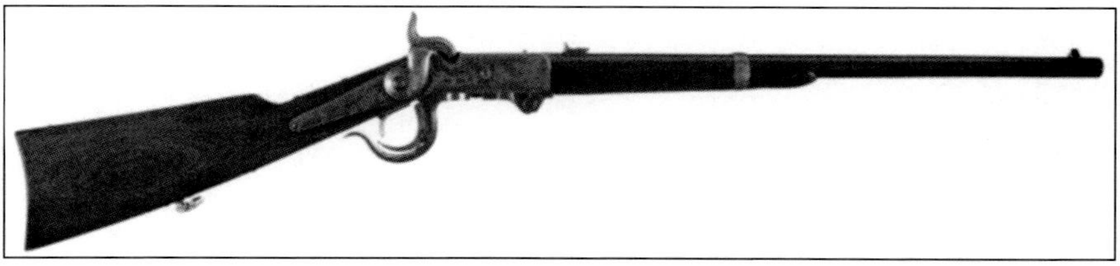

Burnside carbine, first to use metallic cartridges. Models 2, 3, 4, and particularly 5 were used in the Civil War.

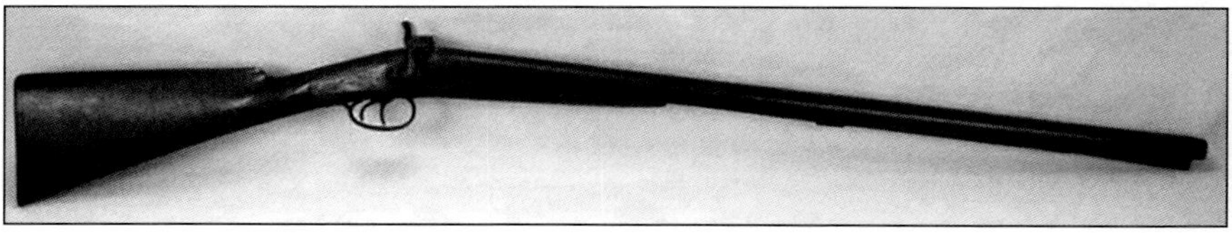

Civil War double barrel percussion shotgun

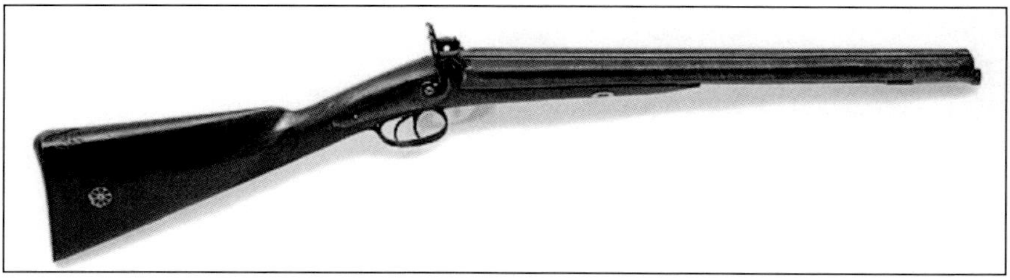

Perkins sawed off double barrel Civil War shotgun

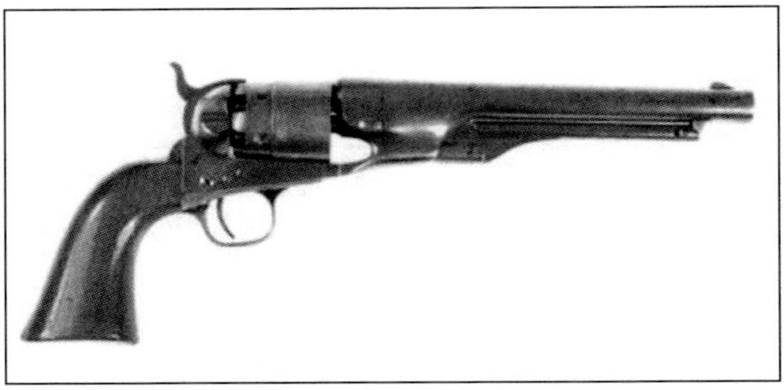

Gen. Nelson's Colt Army Model 1860.

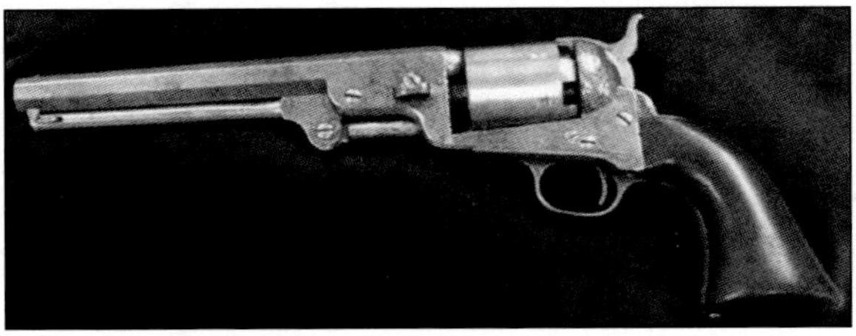

Gen. Cleburne's Colt Navy Model 1851.

Confederate cavalryman with shotgun.

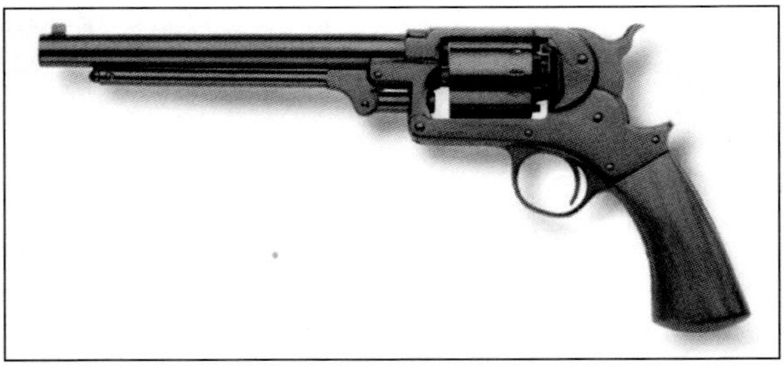

Starr Model 1848

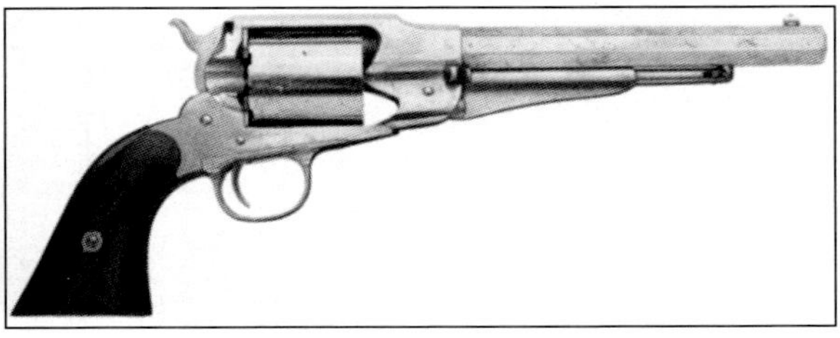

Remington New Model

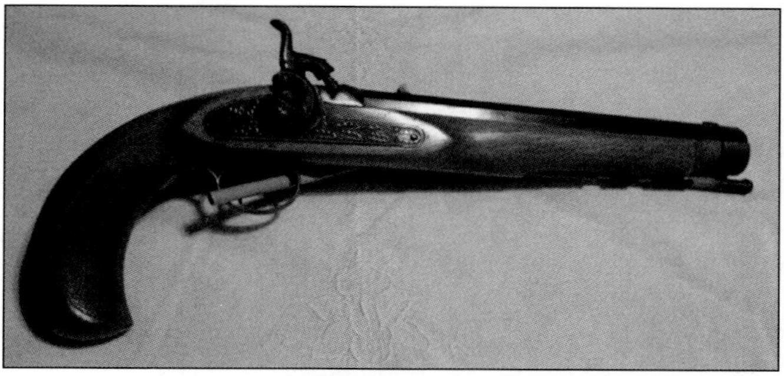

1841 Kentucky Pistol. Photo by Sherman Rominger

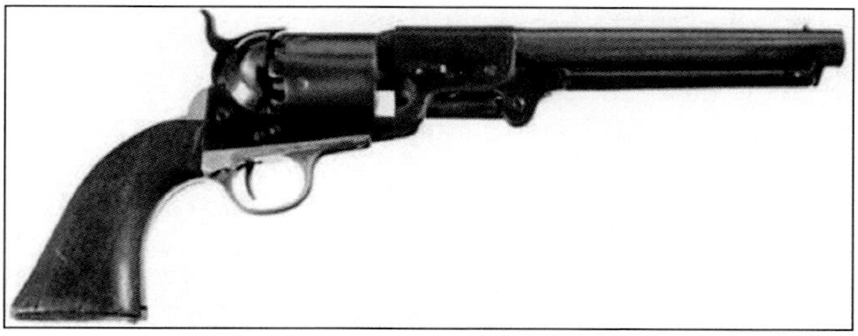

Leech and Rigdon

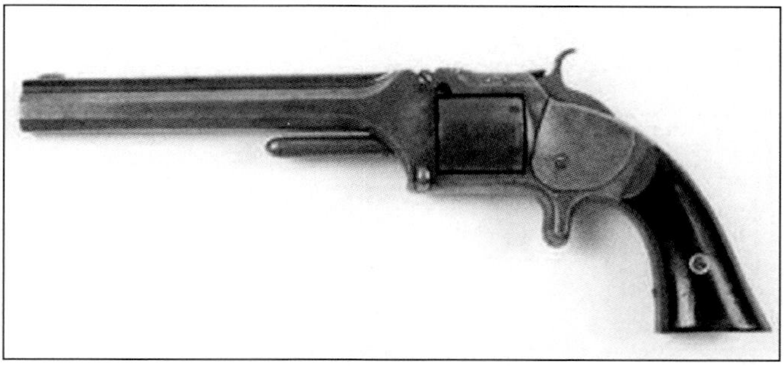

Smith and Wesson Number 2, .32 caliber rim fire; 816 of these were purchased by the Commonwealth from Benjamin Kittredge of Cincinnati in early 1862.

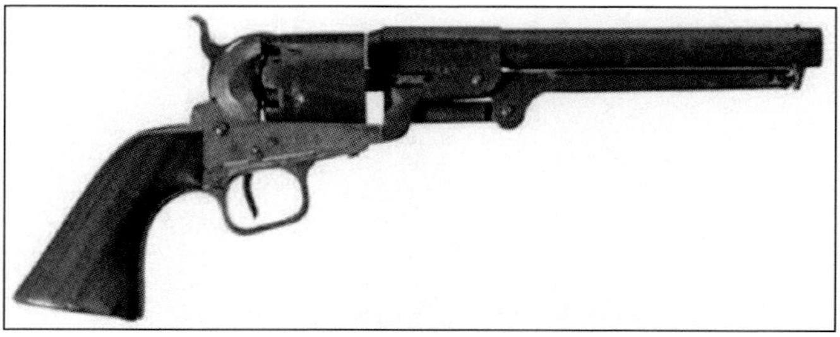

Griswold and Gunnison revolver, manufactured in Georgia for Confederate use, similar to a Colt Navy Model 1851 percussion revolver, brass framed, .36 caliber with a cylinder holding six shots.

Minie balls calcified from being in the ground.

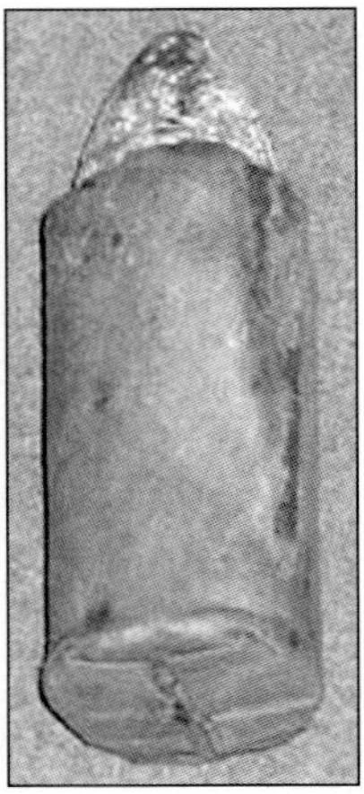

Paper cartridge

Buck and ball

Shaler

Wooden ammunition box

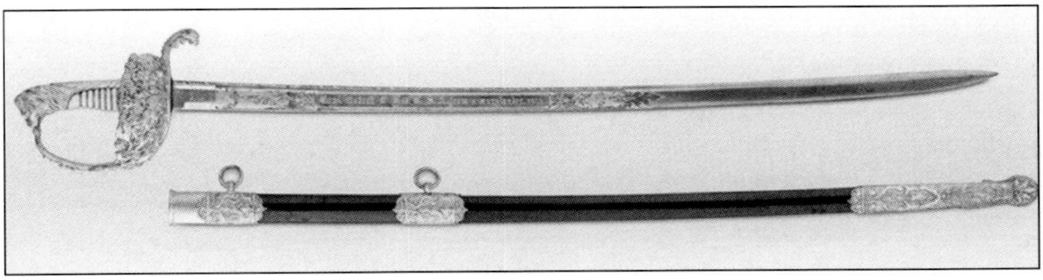

General Lee's ceremonial saber

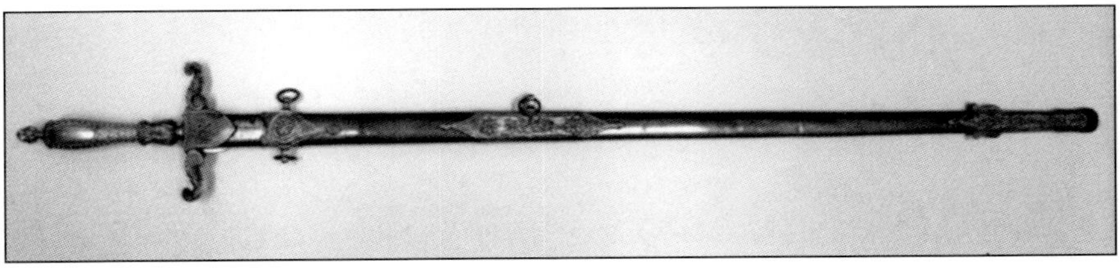

Civil War surgeon's sword

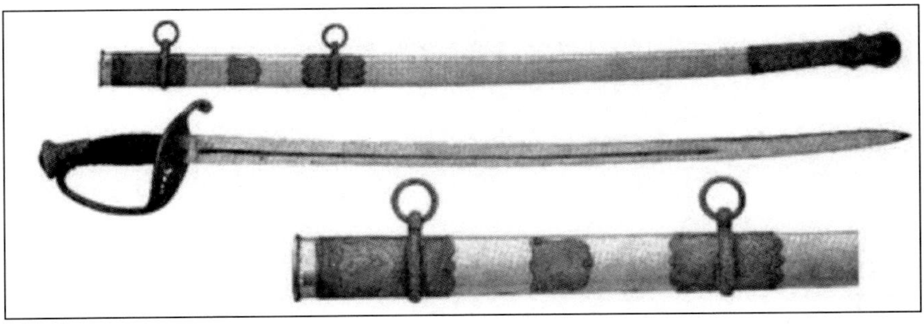

General Cleburne's sword and scabbard

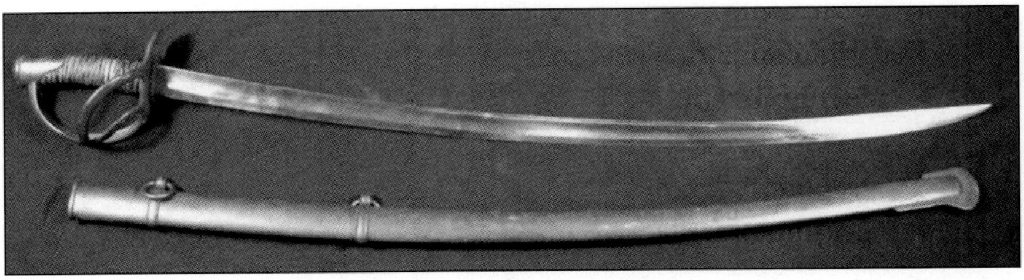

Cavalry saber, Model 1840

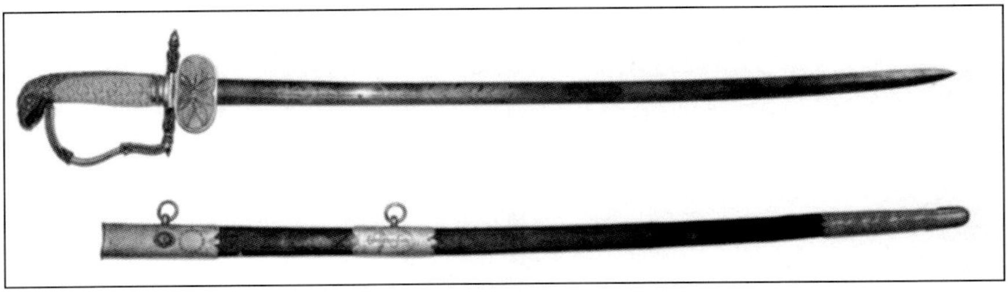

Joseph Rodgers and Sons, U.S. Navy

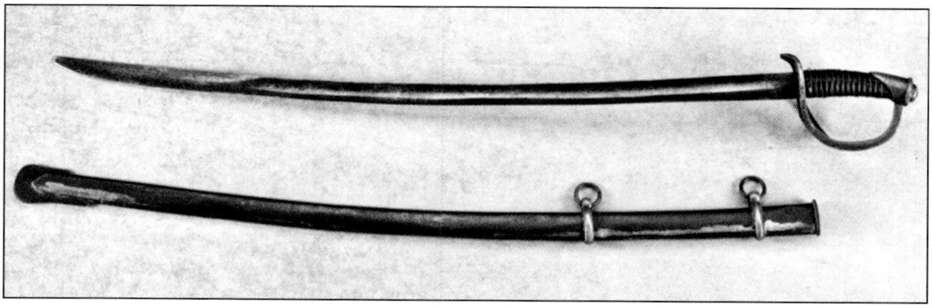

Confederate cavalry sword

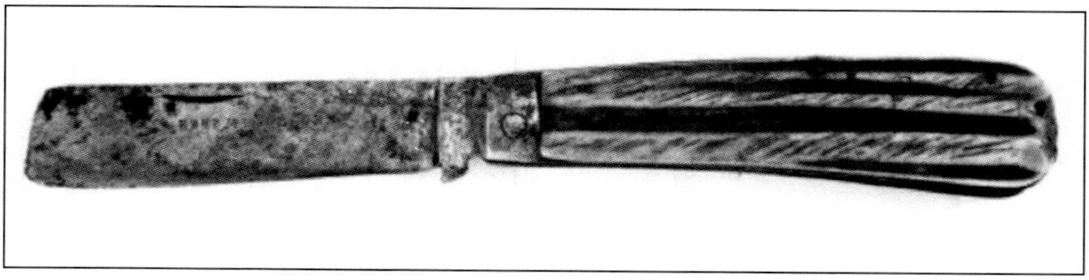

Jack knife used by a Civil War sailor

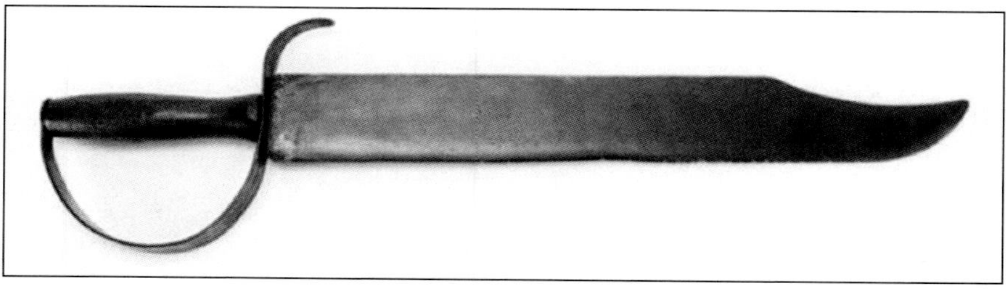

Confederate D-guard bowie

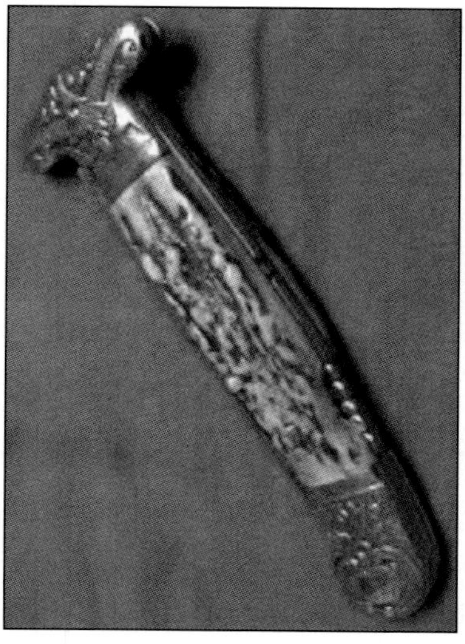

Folding bowie

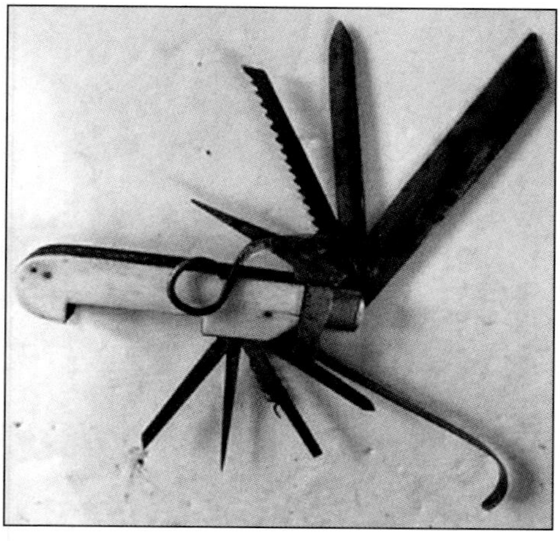

Hand-made farrier's multi-tool. A farrier was a person who specialized in trimming and balancing horse shoes.

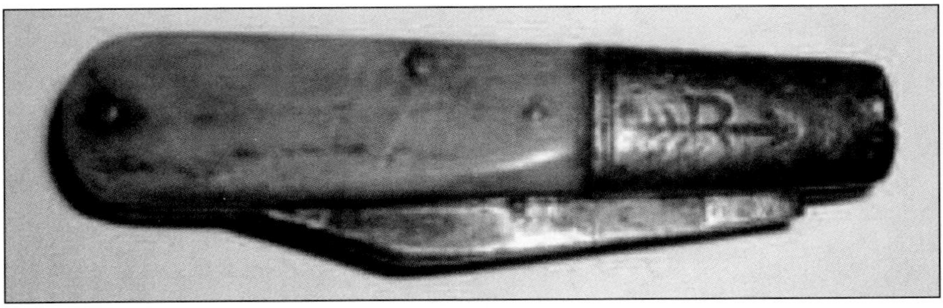

Barlow knife, very common in early America. The first barlow maker in the United States was John Russell of Massachusetts in 1834.

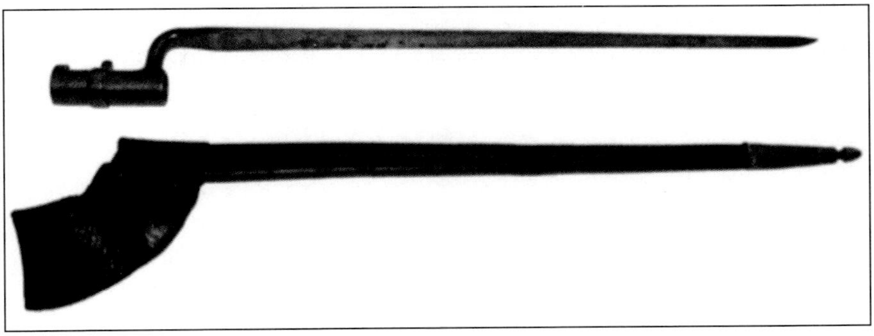

Model 1855 socket bayonet with scabbard

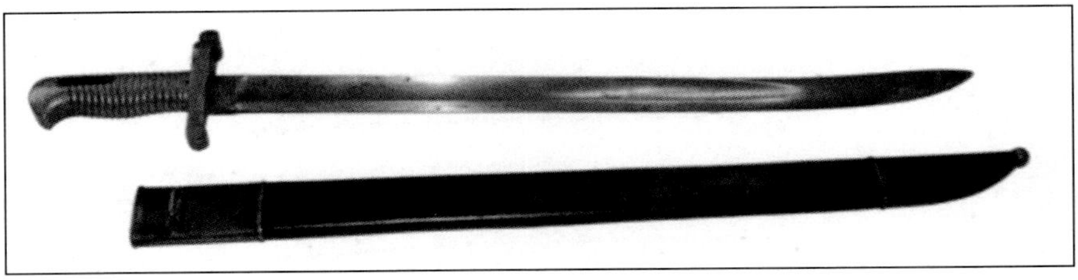

Model 1855 saber bayonet with scabbard

Dahlgren Navy bayonet with scabbard

Napoleon

Three-inch Ordnance rifle

Parrott Rifle

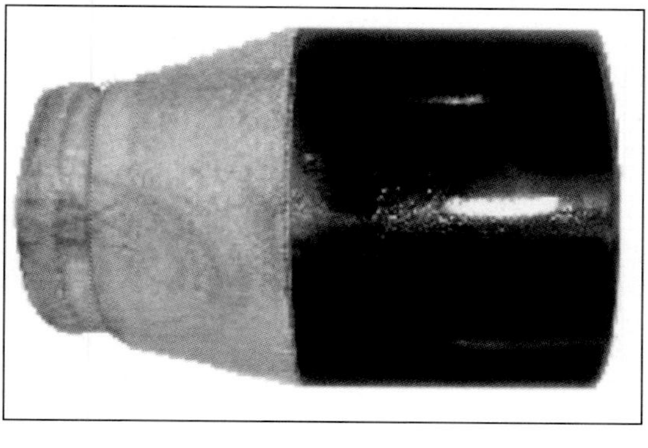

Canister, which consisted of 148 .69 caliber lead balls packed in sawdust and placed in a tin-plated iron cylinder. This had the same effect as a huge shotgun or scattergun with a range of up to 400 yards.

Solid shot, which consisted of a solid "ball" attached with two straps to a wood sabot. The powder was attached to the groove in the sabot with a string.

Tinted photo of howitzers

Shell, which consisted of a "ball" attached with two straps to a wood sabot. Typically a Bormann fuse was used to set off the shell.

1862 Gatling gun, designed by Dr. Richard J. Gatling, North Carolina, 1861.

USS Lafayette

Typical cannon used at the Battle of Richmond.

USS Lexington

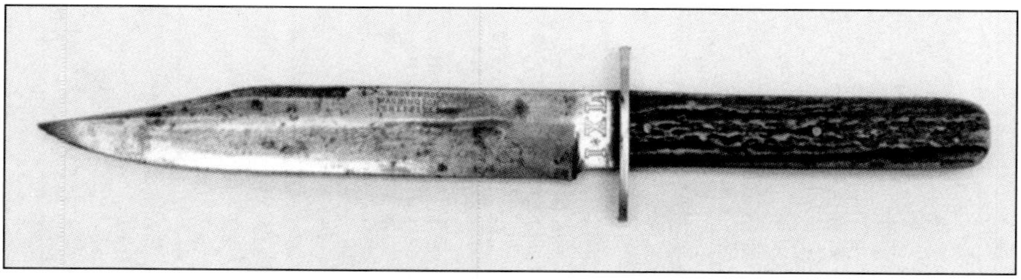

George Wostenholm Civil War knives

Sword presented to U.S. Grant at General-in-Chief in 1864. The sword was crafted by St. Louis silversmith and jeweler Henry Folsom and presented to Gen. Grant by the citizens of the Commonwealth of Kentucky. It has pure silver, gold, an amethyst, and twenty-six diamonds in his monogram U.S.G. Tharpe Collection of American Military History.

Chapter Nine

12th Regiment Heavy Artillery U.S.C.T.

Abraham Lincoln statue, capitol rotunda, Frankfort, Kentucky

Alpheus Lewis, field physician, Sixth Ohio Volunteer Infantry, treating a wounded soldiers, Wayne Peters.

Bas Relief of Slaves Being Sold South, Waterfront Park, Louisville.

Battle of Richmond annual reenactment

Battle of Richmond annual reenactment

Battle of Richmond annual reenactment, drone photo courtesy of Richmond Tourism.

Cheapside Slave Auction Block in Lexington.

Confederate First National Flag. This would have been at the Battle of Richmond.

Colored Soldiers Monument, Greenhill Cemetery, Frankfort, Kentucky

Confederate monument formerly in Louisville, moved to Brandenburg

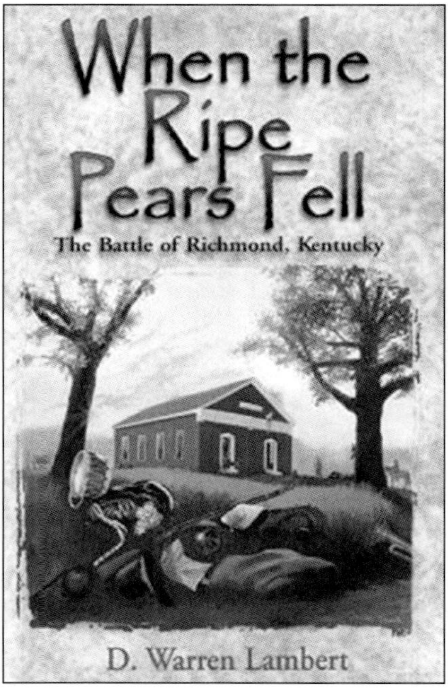

Cover for the book, When the Ripe Pears Fell

Elizabeth Freeman aka Mumbet, Bett, Mum Bett, 1744-1829, Berkshire County, Massachusetts. She filed and won a lawsuit, Brom and Bett v. Ashley, 1781, on which the Massachusetts Supreme Judicial Court ruled that slavery was inconsistent with the Massachusetts State Constitution of 1780. It implicitly ended slavery in Massachusetts. She won her freedom plus thirty shillings in damages.

Henry Walton Bibb, 1815-1854

Jefferson Davis monument, rotunda, removed

John C. Breckenridge monument, Lexington, removed

Monument to the Black Brigade of Cincinnati, Smale Riverfront Park

Lewis C. Robards owned this building in Lexington, which he used as a jail for "fancy women" and other choice stock of slaves for sale.

Major General George H. Thomas never lost a battle but was disparaged by Gen. Grant and Gen. Sherman and their allies, Gen. Sheridan and Gen. Schfield. President Lincoln distrusted him because Thomas was from Virginia.

Rev. Dr. William Eleazar Barton, 1861-1930, scholar, prolific author and lecturer on Abraham Lincoln. A cousin of Clara Barton, he was a Berea College graduate.

GENERAL LAMBERT WITH STAFF AND ESCORT—Left to right, Sgt. Billy R. Browning, orderly, Company C, 7th Kentucky Volunteer Cavalry Regiment; Pvt. William Ray Hudson, dispatch rider, same company; Capt. M. Douglas Hazelwood, commanding company, currently assigned as Gen. Lambert's headquarters escort; Maj. Gen. Murray M. Shearard, commanding First Division, XIII Corps; Lt. Gen. Lambert, commanding XIII Corps and acting commander, Military Department of the West, C. S. A.; Brig. Gen. Lyle Ray, adjutant, XIII Corps, and Maj. Gen. Auguston E. Kilgore, commanding 3rd Reserve Division, XIII Corps. Not present when picture was made, Maj. Gen. Robert W. Pollard, commanding 2nd Division, XIII Corps, and Brig. Gen. Jerome S. Fish, adjutant and inspector general, Department of the West.

Photo by Ruby R. Ford (aunt of Paul Rominger), courtesy of Ron Garrison, Photo Director, Lexington Herald-Leader, Kentucky Photo Archive

Rectangle flag, Army of Tennessee, Nov. 20, 1862-April 26, 1865.

Reflections, by Berea artist Timothy Pack.

Robert Bell, 12th Regiment Heavy Artillery U.S.C.T., Lexington Herald-Leader archives, used with permission

Saturday night firing of cannons, twelve pound cannon with a double powder load. Photo by Sherman Rominger

Square flag, Army of Northern Virginia

Confederate Topographic Engineers

Union cavalry surrounded the lone Confederate first sergeant. He had no horse and his clothes were dirty and tattered. A Union officer said to him that it was obvious he had no wealth and no means to own slaves. "Why are you fighting this war?" the officer asked. The Confederate officer answered, "Because you are here."

Monument

Discarded Painting

and Brig. Gen. Frederick Salomon. Another Prussian, Col. Hermann Korff fought in the Battle of Richmond.

Wlodzimierz Bonawentura Krzyzanowski (shiz enuf skee) was a Polish noble engineer, politician, and military leader who took part in the 1848 uprising against Prussia. When it was suppressed, he left Poland and in early 1861 he enlisted in the Union Army. He recruited a company of Polish immigrants and became a colonel of the 58th New York Volunteer Infantry Regiment, the "Polish Legion." In 1862, he was promoted to brigadier general. Another Polish national was Union Brig. Gen. Albin Francisco Schoepf.

Ireland contributed more generals to the Civil War than any other foreign country, with the highest rank in the Union Army by a foreigner was first held by Maj. Gen. Michael Lawler. The best known and one of the most competent Confederate commanders was Brig. Gen. Patrick Ronayne Cleburne (RUN ane, as in pane), a veteran of Richmond in 1862. As a major general, he was killed on Nov. 30, 1864, at the disastrous Battle of Franklin. The remaining Irish generals were brigadiers. The Union had nine: Richard Busteed, Patrick Conner, Michael Corcoran, Richard Jackson, Patrick Jones, James Kiernan, James Shields and Thomas Sweeny. The Confederacy had four—Joseph Finegan, James Hagan, Walter Lane and Patrick Moore.

Notable English officers were Union Cavalry Commander Sir Percy Wyndham and Confederate Brig. Gen. Collett Leventhorpe. Lieutenant Colonel Sir Arthur James Lyon Fremantle, British Coldstream Guards, was an observer of many battles. Dr. William Worrall Mayo had a private medical practice that evolved into the Mayo Clinics. He volunteered as a Union surgeon and was second in command of the medical corps at Vicksburg. Henry Morton Stanley, a Welch immigrant, joined the Dixie Grays. He was captured at Shiloh. Stanley later served in the U.S. Navy as record keeper for USS *Minnesota*. This led him into journalism and exploration. He is noted for finding Dr. Livingstone near Lake Tanganyika in what is now Tanzania in 1871. Many British citizens from the Colony of Bermuda fought for the Union, including Robert Tappan in the U.S. Navy. The best known Bermudan was First Sergeant Robert John Simmons of the 54th Massachusetts Infantry Regiment. He died from wounds at Fort Wagner.

From France, in addition to Prince de Polignac, other French nobles serving for the Union were Prince de Joinville, third son of the Duke d'Orleans and an admiral of the French Navy, and Prince Philippe, Comte de Paris and Prince Royal, heir to the French throne, with his younger brother, Prince Robert, Duke de Chartres. Brig. Gen. Phillippe Regis Denis de Keredern de Trobriand served in the Union Army. Brig. Gen. Raleigh Edward Colston served in the Confederate Army.

Asians and Pacific Islanders and the Civil War, an Official National Parks Service Handbook, states that the U.S. population in the 1860 census was 31,443,321. In the West, men outnumbered women ten to one. The Chinese population in California at that time was 34,933 men and 2006 women. East of the Mississippi, there were approximately 200 Chinese, Japanese, Filipinos, Indians from the Subcontinent, Thais, and Malays had a total U.S. population of only about 500. Numbers could vary on these. Some persons had taken names more common in America. Immigrants' names were often simplified or invented when an official could not understand or spell original given names.

From the Kingdom of Hawaii, more than 100 people fought on both sides. One was Henry Ho'olulu Pitman, the son of the last high chiefess of Hilo. He was captured and held in Libby Prison. Spencer's Invincibles was a drill team of forty Hawaiians raised to support Pres. Lincoln should he need them. A few dozen students from the Punahou School enlisted in the US army, and five were killed. Twelve Hawaiian sailors served on the CSS *Shenandoah*. Forty Australians also served on the CSS *Shenandoah*. Fifty South Asians from the Indian Subcontinent served on sixteen ships in the US navy and in the cavalry, infantry, and artillery. And at least fifty-eight Chinese officially served in the forces of both sides. This number of Chinese and other Asians is increasing, as soldiers and sailors are identified whose English names did not indicate their national identity. Prior to the war, 150 Chinese were serving the U.S. Navy in various capacities.

A prince from India served in the U.S. Navy. Taking the name of Antonio F. Gomez (Anthony Gomez), Conjee Rustumjee Cohoujee Bey, from the royal family of Punjab, joined the Navy in 1862 and served for forty-four years. With a British education, he had been befriended by the Beecher Family and Henry Ward Beecher served as his mentor. Gomez served in succession on the USS *North Carolina*, the steam sloop USS *Dacotah*, the sloop of war USS *Iroquois* when she was involved in the capture of New Orleans, and was on the USS *Niagara* when the American flag was again raised at Fort Sumter.

Woo Hong Neok was born in 1834 in the small settlement of Antowston, near Zhangshou in the Province of Fujian. When he was thirteen, he was enrolled in a Shanghai boarding school run by Bishop William Jones Boone. In 1854, Woo met sailors from the USS *Susquehanna*, commanded by Commodore Matthew C. Perry, and expressed an interest in visiting American. He served on the *Susquehanna* as cabin boy and aid to the ship's surgeon John Messersmith. After their arrival in Philadelphia, Woo went with Messersmith to Lancaster, Pennsylvania. He lived there for nine years and worked in a newspaper, eventually becoming a pressman. He joined the U.S. Army in 1863, where he served until he returned to China. He was ordained an Episcopal deacon in 1867, and a priest in 1880. Dzau Tsz-zeh took the name of a Methodist lay preacher, Charles K. Marshall, whom he had met at a Methodist Episcopal school in China. Ah Yee Way took the name Thomas Sylvanus, adding Duvall which he dropped later. Christopher Bunker was the son of Chang and Adelaide Yates Bunker. Chang and his brother Eng, who married Sarah Yates, were the original Siamese Twins. They were well educated and skilled farmers in North Carolina, and were among the first to grow Bright Leaf tobacco. Christopher Bunker served in the Confederate cavalry under Brig. Gen. John McCausland when his cavalry took Chambersburg and was captured at Moorefield, West Virginia. Many Chinese served in the U.S. Navy as sailors, stewards, and cooks, but service records were not maintained, making research difficult.

Thirty-one Filipinos served in both Confederate and Union forces, most serving in the Union Navy. They served on several ships, but most notably the USS *Little Ada* and the USS *Conemaugh*. Most Filipinos had English or Spanish names. Felix Cornelius Balderry was a Filipino who served in Company A, 11th Michigan Volunteers. Prince Romulus served in the 5th Massachusetts Cavalry (colored). Some Filipinos served in the Confederate Navy with at least one aboard the CSS *Alabama* and in Louisiana, mainly with the Louisiana Zouaves. Filipinos had also fought in the Battle of New Orleans, War of 1812. General Jackson referred to them as the Manila Men.

"Every man should endeavor to understand the meaning of subjugation before it is too late...It means the history of this heroic struggle will be written by the enemy; that our youth will be trained

by Northern schoolteachers; will learn from Northern school books their version of the war; will be impressed by the influences of history and education to regard our gallant dead as traitors, and our maimed veterans as fit objects for derision..." Maj. Gen Patrick R. Cleburne, CSA January, 1864

The Black Brigade of Cincinnati

The Black Brigade was a military unit organized when Cincinnati was in danger of being attacked by Confederates after the Battle of Richmond. On September 2, 1862, many black males were rounded up by police and impressed into service to help construct emergency fortifications around the city. There was one fatality, Joseph Johns, killed in an accident Sept. 17. The Black Brigade consisted of 706 men. While the unit was not designated an official military organization at that time, it marched under a flag bearing the name "The Black Brigade of Cincinnati." In addition to fortifications, work involved military roads, trenches, and rifle pits. The brigade played a significant role in the defense of Cincinnati. Gen. Lewis Wallace said in a speech that it was the fortifications built by these men that saved the city.

The unit was disbanded September 20 after the threat of attack receded. They presented their commander, Col. William Martin Dickson, a ceremonial sword, and thanked him for his leadership and kindness. He was a thirty-four-year-old lawyer and judge of the Court of Common Pleas who had treated them well. Col. Dickson was a graduate of Miami University, Oxford, Ohio, an alumnus of Harvard Graduate School and a founder of the Republican Party. He participated in the framing of Emancipation Proclamation. Dickson accepted the gift and led the Black Brigade through the streets of Cincinnati with music playing and banners flying. After service in this brigade, many of the men became members of other US army units.

Powhatan Beaty, formerly of the Black Brigade, received the Medal of Honor for his service and bravery during the Civil War. Beaty was First Sergeant, Company G, 5th U.S. Colored Troops. He was twenty-four and a farmer when he enlisted on June 7, 1863. Two days later he was promoted to sergeant. He was honored for taking command of his company at Clafflin's Farm when all officers had been killed. He led his company on a second charge through the Confederate lines, and successfully drove them from their fortified positions with fifty percent casualties of his company. The medal was awarded April 6, 1864. Beaty eventually participated in thirteen battles and numerous skirmishes and received a brevet promotion to lieutenant.

Powhatan Beaty was born in Virginia as a slave in 1839. He moved to Cincinnati in 1849 where he received an education. In school, he developed an interest in acting and oratory. On September 5, 1862, he reported for service with the Black Brigade, and was assigned to Company Number 1 of the Third Regiment. Their duty was to build defenses near the Licking River in Kentucky. For fifteen days, they cleared forests, constructed forts, magazines, roads and dug trenches and rifle pits.

After the war, Beaty returned to Cincinnati. He became well-known for acting, readings, and elocution. He wrote one play "Delmar or Scenes in Southland," which was performed in 1881. When Henrietta Vinton Davis, a prominent African-American actress, was in Cincinnati, he joined her in a very successful musical and dramatic festival in Melodeon Hall. The *Cincinnati Commercial* wrote that Beaty "threw himself into his part with masterly energy and power." As a result, he was invited to perform as a principal actor in a Washington, D.C., Shakesperean production at Ford's Theater. The production was praised by the *Washington Post*. Beaty toured with Davis, performing also in Philadelphia.

Powhatan Beaty served as assistant engineer at the Cincinnati Water Works. He helped form the city's Literary and Dramatic Club. Beaty's son, A. Lee Beaty, became an Ohio state legislator and an assistant U.S. District Attorney for southern Ohio. Beaty died on December 6, 1916, and is buried in Cincinnati at Union Baptist Cemetery.

There were approximately 100 black commissioned officers who served in the Union Army, of 7,122 African Americans who served as officers, and 178,975 who were soldiers or sailors. Stephen A. Swails had served as a sergeant and became a second lieutenant. He was born in Pennsylvania to a black father and a white mother in 1832. He could have easily passed as white. While some light-skinned African-Americans had joined the army before Emancipation Proclamation, Swails enlisted on April 23, 1863, into Company F of the 54th Massachusetts Volunteer Infantry Regiment. He was an exemplary soldier, and was appointed sergeant before the famous July 18, 1863, assault on Fort Wagner. Swails was one of a group of soldiers who crested the fort's parapet before being forced back under Confederate fire. At Olustee, Florida, February 1864, he received a severe but not mortal head wound. After the Battle of Olustee, the 54th's commissioned officer ranks were thin. Swails had demonstrated "coolness, bravery, and efficiency" in battle, according to Col. Edward N. Hallowell, who recommended to Massachusetts Gov. John A. Andrew that Swails be promoted to second lieutenant.

To this point, the War Department had only approved commissions for a handful of African-American recruiters who would not see the theatre of war and about two dozen African-American chaplains and surgeons. It took ten months for Swails' commission to be approved. In the interim, he executed the duties of a second lieutenant under difficult circumstances. On January 15, 1865, Sergeant Swails was discharged from the 54th Massachusetts and immediately mustered into service as an officer. His commission was the only one that brought with it the possibility of giving orders to white soldiers.

The issues of emancipation and military service were intertwined following the news of Fort Sumter. There was a rush of free black men to enlist in U.S. military units, but they were turned away. African-Americans had served in the Revolutionary War and in the War of 1812. It is believed that the first Colonial killed in the Boston Massacre of 1770 was Crispus Attucks, a free man of color. There were eventually 9,000 black Patriot soldiers and sailors in the Continental army and navy and in state militia units. At Lexington and Concord, blacks were part of the Patriot forces, and were present at Bunker Hill. When Rhode Island was having trouble meeting a recruiting quota, the number was reached with free blacks and former slaves. In the siege of Yorktown in 1781, Baron Ludwig von Closen, a German officer of the French Royal Deus-Ponts Regiment, estimated that one fourth of the American army there was black. Unlike the Continental army, the navy recruited both free and enslaved blacks from the beginning of the war. One of the most famous black seamen was James Forten, who enlisted at age fifteen in the Continental navy. He served on the *Royal Louis*, a three-deck, twenty-two gun privateer commanded by Stephen Decatur, Sr. James Forten was captured along with the rest of the crew and spent time on a British prison barge before being released in a prisoner exchange.

After the war, Forten apprenticed as a sail-maker and eventually bought the business. James Forten was a self-made wealthy businessman in Philadelphia, born free in that city, who used his wealth and standing in the community to promote abolition of slavery, civil rights, education, and temperance for African-Americans locally and nationally. He financially supported William Lloyd Garrison's paper *The Liberator*.

Black Americans made up at least fifteen percent of the U.S. naval corps in the War of 1812. In the Battle of Lake Erie, Captain Oliver Hazard Perry's black sailors performed so well in thwarting the British that he wrote the Secretary of the Navy praising their courage. President Lincoln's Emancipation Proclamation, effective January 1, 1863, made it possible for Black Americans to enlist in the Union military forces. Lincoln was concerned, however, that if he authorized the enlistment of black troops, the border states might secede from the Union. Following the attack on Fort Sumter, public opinion in Kentucky, Missouri, and Maryland was sharply divided and allegiance uncertain. On September 22, 1861, he wrote to O.H. Browning, "I think to lose Kentucky is nearly the same as to lose the whole game. Kentucky gone, we cannot hold Missouri, nor, as I think Maryland. These all against us, and the job on our hands is too large for us. We would as well consent to separation at once, including the surrender of this capitol." In spite of the delay in enlistment, the many hardships and discrimination that black soldiers endured, they distinguished themselves through many battles in service to their country. After the September 1864, Battle of Clafflin's Farm, Virginia, which was part of the Siege of Petersburg, 13 Black Americans received the Medal of Honor. In total, twenty-five Black Americans received the Medal of Honor from actions during the Civil War. Of these, fifteen were members of USCT, seven were Navy and three were from other state units.

General Order 143, May 22, 1863, authorized the United States Colored Troops. There were eventually 175 USCT regiments, including 138 infantry, six cavalry, fifteen heavy artillery and ten light artillery. Heavy and Light are not opposites in classification. Heavy artillery is used in military attacks on fortified positions. Light artillery supports infantry and cavalry in the field. It does not include siege artillery, fixed fortification artillery, coastal and naval artillery. The U.S. Colored Troops were disbanded in 1865. Two years later, ten regiments of cavalry and forty-five regiments of infantry from the former USCT were added to Regular Army for use in the Indian Wars. On the plains, Natives referred to these regiments as Buffalo Soldiers.

The first authorized black regiments consisted of recruits from Massachusetts, Tennessee, and South Carolina, in areas under Union control. The Corps d'Afrique was formed May 1863, in Louisiana by Union Maj. Gen. Nathanial Banks. Black Union soldiers did not receive equal pay or equal treatment as did white soldiers, and they had to pay for their clothing, while white soldiers had no deductions in pay for clothing. Black units had white commissioned officers and black non-commissioned officers.

From Kentucky, 23,702 African-Americans served in the Civil War. Camp Nelson, located in Jessamine County, which borders Madison County, was the third largest Union recruiting and training facility for black troops in the country. Leading recruiting camps were in Boston and New Orleans. Camp Nelson was named for Maj. Gen. William "Bull" Nelson, Union commander at Richmond, killed in Louisville a month after the Battle of Richmond. Its initial purpose was to supply invasions into Tennessee. It quickly became a site for training recruits. Large numbers of free persons of color and former slaves came to Camp Nelson with their families who considered the place to be a refuge. Rev. John Fee of Berea served as preacher and teacher at Camp Nelson. The Freedman's Bell, which he used to announce services, now hangs in the bell tower of First Christian Church, Chestnut Street in Berea.

Angus Augustus Burleigh was born free in 1848, but after his father's death, he was forced into slavery, first in Virginia, then in Kentucky. Burleigh joined the 12th U.S. Colored Heavy Artillery at Camp Nelson when he was sixteen years old. At the conclusion of the war, John Fee persuaded A.A. Burleigh to attend Berea College, where he eventually became the first black graduate, and entered the ministry. Rev. Burleigh served as an African Methodist Episcopal pastor, U.S. army chaplain from 1874-1906, and was appointed chaplain of the General Assembly of Illinois. Rev. Burleigh moved to California where he died in 1938 at the National Military Home in Los Angeles. He wrote *John G. Fee, Founder of Berea College*. There is a copy of this book in Hutchins Special Collections and Archives.

Archie Pettiford, born in North Carolina, moved to Berea and was a great-grandson of Fanny Pettiford listed on the 1790 Kentucky census as a free woman of color. He joined the 29th U.S. Colored Infantry in

Illinois. His unit was involved in the Richmond-Petersburg and Appomattox campaigns. After the war, he returned to farming in Berea and followed the Christian Church teachings of John Fee, becoming a minister. Rev. Pettiford organized churches in the central Kentucky area, often buying the land, felling and dressing timber and assisting in construction. Rev. Pettiford died in 1906 and is buried in the Berea Cemetery.

In June 1863, the 4th US Colored Field Artillery (Heavy) was the first to organize with African-Americans from Kentucky and Tennessee. The last to organize was the 125th US Colored Infantry Regiment at Louisville, June 1865. Kentucky's 114th, 116th, and 117th USC Infantry regiments fought at Appomattox and Petersburg.

African-American units played a major role at the Battle of the Crater during the siege of Petersburg, and they were a major part of the Union force during the Battle of Nashville. At the Crater, one black sergeant wrote to a friend, "If I fall in the battle anticipated, remember I fall in defense of my race and my country." After the Battle of Fort Pillow, Tennessee, April 12, 1864, Confederate cavalry attacked a Union force of 500, about half of whom were black. Union casualties were high, but after the Union force surrendered, a number of unarmed soldiers and officers, both black and white, were killed. This was called the Fort Pillow Massacre, and "Remember Fort Pillow" became a battle cry for African-American soldiers. In the disastrous Battle of Olustee, Florida, on February 20, 1864, the unit that redeemed the day was the 54th Massachusetts. It was hurried into action at the very crisis of the battle and checked the onward sweep of the victorious Confederates and successfully covered the Union retreat toward Jacksonville. In this battle, the 8th U.S. Colored Infantry lost 310 killed, wounded or missing.

In the Battle of Milliken's Bend, Louisiana, one of the bloodiest battles of the war, African-American troops from the 9th Louisiana Infantry, the 1st Mississippi Infantry and the 13th Louisiana Infantry fought alongside white troops from the 10th Illinois Cavalry and the 23rd Iowa Infantry. The 41st USCT was present at Appomattox Court House. The 54th Massachusetts was made famous for its attack on Fort Wagner, an island stronghold that protected the harbor of Charleston, South Carolina. The unit was led by Robert Gould Shaw who volunteered his men to lead the attack on Fort Wagner after the first Union assault ended in failure. Shaw, a member of a prominent abolitionist family, was killed in the Second Battle of Fort Wagner. Two sons of abolitionist leader Frederick Douglass were in the regiment, as was a grandson of Sojourner Truth. (Battlefield Park has an original belt buckle on display from the 54th Massachusetts.)

The first piece of public art commissioned for the Smale Riverfront Park in Cincinnati honors The Black Brigade (Smale rhymes with mail). It has been installed south of Mehring Way in the park's East Tree Grove. It includes the names of all members of the unit. After the war, the Black Brigade was recognized as the first African-American unit to serve in the Civil War. By the time the war ended, over 186,000 black men had served in the Union armed services, ten per cent of the total, with 20,000 in the Union navy. Future analysis may increase this number. Approximately 40,000 African-American soldiers and sailors died as a result of the Civil War.

Slavery and General Orders, Number 14

The census of 1860 indicated a U.S. population of nearly 27 million whites, with approximately 8 million of these in the southern states, and 4.5 million blacks, with just under 4 million of these in the southern states. Of these 4 million in the South, 261,988 were free persons of color. Fewer than 385,000 of the American population owned slaves. This is 1.4 per cent of all whites, or 4.8 per cent of southern whites. There were 10,689 Creoles, free persons of color in New Orleans, twenty-eight per cent of whom owned slaves, and at least six who owned sixty-five or more slaves. Antoine Dubuclet, a black creole sugar planter in Louisiana, owned over one hundred slaves and had an estate in 1860 valued at $264,000. There were free blacks throughout the South who owned slaves. By 1860, 125 free blacks owned slaves in South Carolina. William Ellison held forty slaves and 1,000 acres of land. In North Carolina, sixty-nine free persons of color owned slaves. American Indians were also slave owners. A minority of Cherokees, Choctaws, Chickasaws, Creeks and just a few Seminoles were slave owners. Slavery was never widespread in the North, but many of the region's businessmen grew rich on the slave trade and investments in southern plantations.

From the University of Kentucky Libraries, there is information on a 1924 study starting with the 1830 Federal Census. It listed twenty-nine Kentucky counties in which there were approximately a total of

100 free persons of color who owned slaves. This included thirteen owners in Fayette County and fifteen more in Lexington, two in Clark County, one in Rockcastle County, three in Jessamine County and one in Madison County. Other counties of note not bordering on Madison were Bourbon County, Mason County, and Mercer County where nine free persons of color in each county owned slaves, Woodford County, where thirteen owned slaves, Franklin County, six, and Jefferson County, five. The Madison family with ties to northern and southern sections of the county may represent many black slave owners whose holdings were limited to relatives: a spouse, some children, grandparents, an aunt or uncle, until their freedom was allowed by statutory law or mandated by constitutional law.

In America, chattel slavery was practiced. A chattel slave was property owned for life, whose children and grandchildren were automatically held in slavery. Persons held as slaves throughout all states in 1800 numbered 887,612. In 1793, Eli Whitney invented the cotton gin (engine), which made it easy to separate seeds from cotton fibers. Very quickly, the southern economy changed from tobacco farming to cotton, and the dependence on slave labor was highly reinforced. By 1860, slavery was limited to the South and numbered 3,950,546 persons. Large numbers of Indians were also enslaved and listed on the plantation manifests as blacks, as was anyone else held in slavery. Enslavement of Native people began in 1493 with the second expedition of Christopher Columbus to the Americas. Many Indians, 90-100 per cent depending on the area, died from diseases contracted from the Europeans. The Spanish census of 1516 estimated that there were only 12,000 natives left in Haiti, down from approximately 8 million before the Spanish conquest and 3 million in 1496. Colonials began looking for other sources of forced labor.

The first African slaves were brought to Jamestown in 1619 not in a Dutch ship as reported by John Rolfe, but in the English warship *White Lion*. The English captain carried letters of marquee issued by Dutch Prince Maurice, son of William of Orange. The *White Lion,* acting as a privateer, took the slaves off a Portuguese ship *San Juan Bautista*. Rolfe purchased several for use as laborers. They were treated as indentured servants, but according to the Law Library of Congress, throughout colonial days, there was no legal distinction between indenture and slavery. These types of servitude were not considered to be chattel or life-long. Such persons were baptized into the Anglican Church, marriages were legal, and an attempt was made to keep families together.

The first official slave owner in colonial America was an Angolan who adopted the name of Anthony Johnson. He was sold to slave traders in 1621 by an enemy tribe in Africa, and was registered as Antonio, a negro, in the official records of the Colony of Virginia. He went to work for a white farmer as an indentured servant. After the expiration of his contract, Johnson became moderately successful. By July 1651, he had five indentured servants of his own. In 1664, he brought a case before Virginia courts in which he contested a suit launched by one of his indentured servants, an African who adopted the name of John Casor. Johnson won the suit and retained Casor as his servant for life, legally making Casor the first official slave in America.

Throughout the 17th and 18th centuries, slaves contributed significantly to building the economic foundations of North America. Spanish and Portuguese engaged extensively in the slave trade. They worked closely with wealthy, brilliant, and powerful African kingdoms that produced the majority of slaves for export. There was a national identity rather than a sense of African identity. Ninety per cent of slaves were captured by Africans; ten per cent by Arabs or Europeans. A few nations in Africa were adept at the capture and sale of slaves. Ghana, in West Africa, was a major port of sale. Zanzibar was once east Africa's main slave-trading port, and under the Omani Arabs in the 19th century, as many as 50,000 slaves were passing through that city each year. It is estimated that between 11 and 18 million black African slaves crossed the Red Sea, Indian Ocean, and Sahara Desert, and 9.4 to 12.5 million Africans were sent to the Americas. The Trans-Atlantic Slave Trade Database says that between 1525 and 1866, 12.5 million Africans were shipped to South and North America and the Caribbean, with 10.7 million surviving the Middle Passage. Many slaves brought to America were from Arab North African countries. As with other slaves, names were changed, and the number is impossible to determine. It is believed that the destination of many of these Arab slaves was to Georgia, North and South Carolina.

There were also white slaves. When the Muslims failed to conquer Europe during the 8th century, they began raids along the coasts of Spain, Portugal, France, and Italy. In the eastern Mediterranean, Muslims captured and sold slaves from Slavic and Baltic states. The Byzantine-Ottoman wars brought large numbers of Christian slaves into the Islamic world. From the 16th to the 19th centuries, Muslim Corsairs (Barbary pirates) captured an estimated 800,000 to 1.25 million Europeans as slaves.

English sale of Irish as slaves began early in the 17th century during the reign of James the Sixth and First. The number of Irish sold exceeded a half million persons. Large numbers of Scots were also sold into slavery, with both Irish and Scots sold in North Africa and the Caribbean Islands. In America, some white slaves were indentured servants who earned their freedom, but only forty per cent completed their contracts and many continued as chattels. Orphaned white children were often sold into slavery. People with any color to their skin might be sold as mulattos. The Historical Society of Pennsylvania notes a Natchez newspaper article in which a man was using dyes to paint an orphan white girl of nine or ten years of age to make her a slave. The *Lebanon Courier* (Pennsylvania) in 1863 told of a man named Charles Grayson, with blue eyes, a sandy beard and straight, light hair, who had been a slave for seventeen of his twenty-three years. Rev. John H. Aughey told of preaching to slave congregations for eleven years, a third of whom were as white as he was. Rev. Calvin Fairbank described a woman as one of the most beautiful and exquisite young girls, sold at auction in Lexington, Kentucky, who was only 1/64th African. White slaves were generally branded by their masters to make escape more difficult. Some Asians were brought in as slaves after slave importation was illegal. They were listed as indentured servants, but the indentures never ended.

In the third paragraph of his Second Inaugural Address, March 4, 1865, President Lincoln said, "One-eighth of the whole population were colored slaves, not distributed generally over the Union, but localized in the southern part of it. These slaves constituted a peculiar and powerful interest. All knew that this interest was somehow the cause of the war…." There has long been contention that slavery was not the principal issue. However, Henry L. Benning, Georgia politician and future Confederate general, in 1849, wrote to his fellow Georgian Howell Cobb, "First then, it is apparent, horribly apparent, that the slavery question rides insolently over every other, everywhere—in fact, that is the only question which in the least affects the results of the elections." Lawrence Keitt, Congressman from South Carolina and delegate to the South Carolina secession convention, said during debates, "Our people have come to this on the question of slavery...I think it is the great central point from which we are now proceeding, and I am not willing to divert the public attention from it." John C. Calhoun said, "The defense of human liberty against the aggressions of despotic power have been always the most efficient in States where domestic slavery was to prevail." James H. Hammond, Congressman from South Carolina, in a speech before the U.S. House of Representatives, said, "the moment this House undertakes to legislate upon this subject (of slavery), it dissolves the Union. Should it be my fortune to have a seat upon this floor, I will abandon it...; I will go home to preach, and if I can, practice, disunion, and civil war...." The *Atlanta Confederacy* in 1860 stated: "We regard every man in our midst an enemy to the institutions of the South, who does not boldly declare that he believes African slavery to be a social, moral, and political blessing." This publication would have been astounded to think that there might be black Confederate soldiers, as would politicians such as Calhoun, Keitt, Hammond, Benning, and Cobb who were later evidently unaware of the real situation. That there were black Southerners in the Confederate military seems to defy logic.

As the war came to a close, the Confederate Government authorized the enlistment of blacks. General Orders, Number 14, issued March 23, 1865, stated: "The Congress of the Confederate States of America do enact, That, in order to provide additional forces to repel invasion, ...the President...is hereby authorized to ask for and accept from the owners of slaves, the services of such able-bodied negro men as he may deem expedient, ...to perform military service in whatever capacity he may direct. That the General-in-Chief be authorized to organize the said slaves into companies, battalions, regiments, and brigades, ...to be commanded by such officers as the President may appoint. That while employed in the service, the said troops shall receive the same rations, clothing, and compensation as are allowed to other troops...."

The act came too late. It was a desperate move that did not offer, as Gen. Cleburne had suggested, freedom in exchange for enlistment. In 1864, on January 2, Confederate Maj. Gen. Patrick Ronayne Cleburne wrote to the Commanding General of the Army of Tennessee the following:

> "We have now been fighting for nearly three years, have spilled much of our best blood, and lost, consumed, or thrown to the

flames an amount of property equal in value to the specie currency of the world. Through some lack in our system the fruits of our struggles and sacrifices have invariably slipped away from us and left us nothing but long lists of dead and mangled. Instead of standing defiantly on the borders of our territory or harassing those of the enemy, we are hemmed in to-day into less than two-thirds of it, and still the enemy menacingly confronts us at every point with superior forces. Our soldiers can see no end to this state of affairs except in our own exhaustion; hence, instead of rising to the occasion, they are sinking into a fatal apathy, growing wary of hardships and slaughters which promise no results. In this state of things it is easy to understand why there is a growing belief that some black catastrophe is not far ahead of us, and that unless some extraordinary change is soon made in our condition we must overtake it.

"We can see three great causes operating to destroy us: First, the inferiority of our armies to those of the enemy in point of numbers; second, the poverty of our single source of supply in comparison with his several sources; third, the fact that slavery, from being one of our chief sources of strength at the commencement of the war, has now become, in a military point of view, one of our chief sources of weakness.

"Our country has already some friends in England and France, and there are strong motives to induce these nations to recognize and assist us, but they cannot assist us without helping slavery, and to do this would be in conflict with their policy for the last quarter of a century.

"The immediate effect of the emancipation and enrollment of negroes on the military strength of the South would be: To enable us to have armies numerically superior to those of the North, and a reserve of any size we might think necessary; to enable us to take the offensive, move forward, and forage on the enemy. It would open to us in prospective another and almost untouched source of supply, and furnish us with the means of preventing temporary disaster, and carrying on the protracted struggle. It would instantly remove all the vulnerability, embarrassment, and inherent weakness which result from slavery.

"Therefore when we make soldiers of them we must make free men of them beyond all question, and thus enlist their sympathies also. We can do this more effectually than the North can now do, for we can give the negro not only his own freedom, but that of his wife and child, and secure it to him in his old home. To do this, we must immediately make his marriage and parental relations sacred in the eyes of the law and forbid their sale.

"It is said that slavery is all we are fighting for, and if we give it up we give up all. Even if this were true, which we deny, slavery is not all our enemies are fighting for. It is merely the pretense to establish sectional superiority and a more centralized form of government, and to deprive us of our rights and liberties. We have now briefly proposed a plan which we believe will save our country. It may be imperfect, but in all human probability it would give us our independence."

The situation was bleak for the Confederacy. Jefferson Davis had only two options. One was for Gen. Lee to unite with Gen. Joseph Johnston's army in the Carolinas and use the combined force to take on Sherman and Grant one at a time. The other option was to arm slaves, the last source of fresh manpower in the Confederacy. From many sources, the response was easy to predict. Virginia senator R.M.T. Hunter, president pro-tempore of the Confederate Senate, asked "What did we go to war for, if not to protect our property?" In a letter sent to Confederate Secretary of War James A. Seddon, January 1865, Howell Cobb wrote, "The day you make soldiers of them is the beginning of the end of the revolution. If slaves make good soldiers our whole theory of slavery is wrong…." Gen. Lee asked the Confederate government for help: "We must decide whether slavery shall be extinguished by our enemies and the slaves be used against us, or use them ourselves." Many responses like these were at odds with reality.

In the September 1, 2011, edition of *Harvard Gazette*, comments from Harvard historian John Stauffer were presented. Stauffer, Ph.D. from Yale, chair of the History of American Civilization Program and professor of both English and African-American Studies, Harvard University, opened the W.E.B. DuBois Institute's Fall Colloquium Series with a lecture on black Confederates.

He said that the number of slaves who fought and labored for the South was modest. Those who shouldered arms numbered more than 3,000 but fewer than 10,000, or no more than one per cent of the Confederate army. Black laborers for the Southern cause numbered from 20,000 to 50,000. Stauffer drew on one source, Frederick Douglass, whose life Stauffer studied for his 2008 book *Giants: The Parallel Lives of Frederick Douglass and Abraham Lincoln*. In August 1861, Douglass published an account of the First Battle of Bull Run and noted that there were blacks in the Confederate ranks. Later, he quoted a witness who said black Confederates had muskets on their shoulders and bullets in their pockets. Douglass also talked to a fugitive slave from Virginia who asserted that black units were forming in Georgia, South Carolina and Virginia.

Stauffer related the case of John Parker, a slave who joined the crew of a cannon firing grapeshot at Union troops at the First Battle of Bull Run. He was one of four slaves in the battery ordered by owners to fight for the Confederacy. All the while, recalled Parker, he worried about dying, prayed for a Union victory and dreamed of escaping to the other side. Many freedmen faced re-enslavement and made displays of loyalty which were really gestures of self-protection. There were, however, some Southern freedmen who identified with the slave-owning white plantation culture. After a question about this from the audience, Institute Director Henry Louis Gates, Jr., had one answer: "Black people are just as complex as anybody else."

Dr. Gates is Alphonse Fletcher University Professor and Director of the Hutchins Center for African and African American Research, Harvard University. A native of West Virginia, he received his bachelor's in history from Yale University and his Ph.D. from Claire College, University of Cambridge. In Concord, North Carolina, he watched as descendants of a black Confederate were honored with a special presentation and standing ovation. He had never heard the real story and thought it was a myth. His comment on leaving the ceremony, "Fellas, I was lied to." There is more to the story of black Confederates.

The First Louisiana Native Guard was the first official black regiment in the Confederate Army. The Guard was formed when Louisiana Gov. Thomas Overton Moore accepted into the state militia a regiment of 1,100 free black men, May 2, 1861. All the initial members were French speaking Creoles, including successful architects, brick masons, dentists, doctors, and carpenters. Three white officers were regimental commanders, but company commanders were Creoles chosen from the ranks of the unit. The unit never saw action and quickly switched sides when Louisiana was occupied by Federal troops.

Nelson Winbush, a recognized authority on black Americans in the Confederate military, estimates that there were 50,000 to 90,000 black combatants, including people in support roles. Mr. Winbush is a grandson of Louis N. Nelson, a black Confederate veteran who rode with Gen. Nathan B. Forrest. Forty-five slaves and free men of color served with Forrest. Gen. Forrest said in an interview in 1868 that there were no better Confederates than these men.

Black Confederates were not always regularly enlisted, nor were all white soldiers regular. Dr. Edward Smith, Dean of American Studies at American University, estimates that by February 1865, 1,150 black Americans had served in the Confederate navy. This number would equal approximately twenty per cent of this branch of service. Confederate Naval Regulations allowed a ship's captain a ratio of one black seaman to five white seamen. A higher percentage of black crewmen was allowed if the captain filed an exemption. Numerous exemptions were filed making it reasonable to conclude that the number of black sailors in the Confederate navy was higher than anticipated.

W.S. Lewis of Charleston County, South Carolina, served aboard the CSS *Atlanta* and the famous raider CSS *Alabama*. Years later, he was granted a soldier's pension. Skilled black pilots on Confederate gunboats were paid $80-$100, a good salary, and held officer's rank, although without the authority. Moses Dallas, who served with the Savannah Squadron from 1862-64, was considered the best inland pilot on the coast. His commander wrote the Confederate Secretary of Navy that the pay to Dallas had to be increased in order to retain him in service. Moses Dallas was on the expedition which captured the Federal gunboat USS *Water Witch*, June 1864, and was one of six men killed in action as they attempted to board the Union gunboat.

There are other examples of Black Confederates. In the *Journal of Negro History*, 1919, it was reported that "Seventy free blacks enlisted in the Confederate Army in Lynchburg, Virginia. Sixteen companies of free men of color marched through Augusta, Georgia, on their way to fight in Virginia. Kenneth W. Noe in his book *Perryville: This Grand Havoc of Battle*, published in 2001 by The University Press of Kentucky, referred to a May 1, 1863, letter reprinted in the Winchester (Indiana) Journal: "I can assure you of a certainty, that the rebels have negro soldiers in their army. One of their best sharpshooters, and the boldest of them all here is a negro."

In 1895 a former black Union soldier, Christian A. Fleetwood, a sergeant-major in the 4th U.S. Colored Troops, acknowledged that the south began using blacks as soldiers before the Union did. Two weeks after the fall of Fort Sumter, the *Charleston Mercury* records the passing through Augusta of several companies of the 3rd and 4th Georgia Regiment and of sixteen well-drilled companies and one Negro company from Nashville, Tennessee. A telegram from New Orleans dated November 23, 1861, notes the review by Gov. Moore of over 28,000 troops, and that one regiment comprised "1,400 colored men."

African Americans served in the Confederate States Marine Corps, in the Confederate Navy as members of the Savannah, the James River and the Wilmington squadrons, and as Confederate raiders. Men from the Savannah Squadron joined remnants of the Wilmington Squadron in a combat unit known as Tucker's Brigade assigned to Gen. Lee's army. During the Confederate withdrawal from the Richmond-Petersburg line, the Federal army cut off the rear of Lee's army in the Battle of Saylor's Creek. During the battle, Tucker's Brigade was the only Confederate unit which did not break under the initial Federal charge. After repulsing the charge, Tucker's Brigade, numbering 300-400 men, was surrounded by six Union divisions. Tucker's Brigade counterattacked, smashing the 37th Massachusetts Infantry into fragments and tearing into the 2nd Rhode Island in hand to hand combat. Withdrawing to a wooded area, the Brigade repulsed several more Federal attacks. Their performance was so intense and the damage they inflicted so devastating that the Union generals estimated the Marine Brigade (Tucker's Brigade) to number 2,000 men.

The Indianapolis *Daily Evening Gazette* reported on March 5, 1863: "During the fight the (artillery) battery in charge of the 85th Indiana was attacked by two rebel negro regiments." Federal Official Records, Series I, Vol XVI Part I, page 805: "There were also quite a number of negroes attached to the Texas and Georgia troops, who were armed and equipped, and took part in the several engagements with my forces during the day."

Federal Official Records, Series I, Vol XLIX, Part II, page 253; April 6, 1865: "The rebels (Forrest) are recruiting negro troops at Enterprise, Mississippi, and the negroes are all enrolled in the State." Federal Official Records, Series I, Vol. XIV, page 24, second paragraph: "It is also difficult to state the force of the enemy, but it could not have been less than from 600 to 800. There were six companies of mounted riflemen, besides infantry, among which were a considerable number of colored men." Colonel B. C. Christ, 50th Pennsylvania volunteer Infantry, official report of May 30, 1862, referring to Confederate forces opposing him at Pocotaligo, S.C.: "Sargt said war is close to being over. saw several negros fighting for those rebels."

The chief inspector of the U.S. Sanitary Commission, Dr. Lewis Steiner, reported that he saw about 3,000 well-armed black Confederate soldiers in Stonewall Jackson's army in Frederick, Maryland, and that those soldiers were "manifestly an integral portion of the Southern Confederate Army."

Levi Miller was a former slave who became a Confederate hero. He went to war with his master as a body servant and saved his life. Miller was voted by his regiment to be a full-fledged soldier. He exhibited bravery in battles in Virginia, Tennessee, Georgia, Maryland and Pennsylvania. During the fighting at Spotsylvania Courthouse, his former commander Capt. J.E. Anderson said of him, "Levi Miller stood by my side and no man fought harder and better than he did when the enemy tried to cross our little breastworks...." Levi Miller met several other negros that he knew either by friendship or as a relative. They attempted to get him to desert to the North, but he would not. At his death, his coffin was draped with the Confederate First National Flag at a hero's funeral service.

On the far side of Arlington National Cemetery, in a little known place, is the cemetery's largest monument. It is the Confederate Memorial that stands over the graves of Confederate soldiers. On this monument is a carving of a black soldier, not in chains, but in a Confederate uniform marching alongside fellow soldiers. The monument was designed by a former Jewish Confederate, Moses Ezekiel, who wanted to correctly portray the racial makeup in the Confederate Army.

The history web site of the 37th Texas Cavalry writes that The Confederate Burial Mound for Camp Morton at Indianapolis, Indiana, has bronze tablets which list the nearly 1,200 Confederates who died at that camp. Among those names are twenty-six black southerners, seven Hispanic southerners and six Indian southerners. At a time when those black southerners could have walked into the Camp Commander's office, taken a short oath and signed their name to walk out the gates as free men obliged to no one, they chose instead to stay even unto death. The history site concludes, "Your understanding of that choice is likely nonexistent."

A sense of understanding may be enhanced by an article written November 17, 1999, by economist, Libertarian and syndicated columnist Walter Williams. Concerning the Confederate battle flag and blacks in the Confederate military, he wrote that if the battle flag is a flag of slavery, the United States flag is even more so. Slavery thrived under the United States flag from 1776 to 1865. "The birth of both flags had little or nothing to do with slavery. Both flags saw their birth in a violent and proud struggle for independence and self-governance. If one sees the war for Southern Independence solely or chiefly as a struggle for slavery, then it's natural to resent the Confederate battle flag."

Williams challenged the assertion that Abraham Lincoln waged war against the South to abolish slavery as a fiction created by the victors. He said a more plausible source of North-South antagonism was presented in an 1831 speech by South Carolina Senator John C. Calhoun where the Senator said, "...the naked question is whether ours is a federal or consolidated government; a constitutional or absolute one; a government resting solidly on the basis of sovereignty of the States, or on the unrestrained will of the majority, as in all other unlimited ones, to which injustice, violence and force must ultimately prevail."

A significant source of Southern discontent was tariffs enacted to protect Northern manufacturing interests. Calhoun said, "the North has adopted a system of revenue and disbursement in which an undue proportion of the burden of taxation has been imposed on the South, and an undue proportion of the proceeds appropriated to the North."

Williams continued, "The blacks who served in the Confederacy no more fought to preserve slavery than their successors fought in World War I and World War II to preserve Jim Crow and segregation. They fought because their homeland was attacked and fought in the hope that the future would be better and they'd be rewarded for their patriotism." Dr. Williams is John M. Olin Distinguished Professor of Economics at George Mason University. His comments will elicit severe criticism for not following an established agenda, but the whole discussion of the Civil War and African Americans who served in both the Confederacy and the Union is a dialogue, long needed, that should enhance our understanding through realization of the facts.

Walter Williams was born in Philadelphia and lived in the housing projects. In the Army, he waged a one man battle against Jim Crow laws. In a court martial resulting from this, he argued his own case and was found not guilty. After military service, he earned a bachelor's in economics from California State University, a master's and a Ph.D. in economics from U.C.L.A.

Research in this area has been facilitated since 2010 by Black Confederate Soldiers website that focuses on connecting families with their ancestors' genealogical records and citations. Primary and secondary sources of information are made available to family historians. The website was reorganized in 2014 in order to provide consumable information for librarians and genealogists. Additional sources, other than those named in the article, are www.blackpast.org, Harry W. Tison, II, Michael T. Griffith, Andy Hall, and Winthrop University: Causes of the Civil War, New York Times.

Children and Youth as Soldiers

Many boys joined because they were orphans or runaways or they wanted to fight alongside their brothers and fathers. Some thought war was exciting, but soon learned about danger and horror. Forty-eight soldiers under the age of eighteen received the Medal of Honor and many remained in the Army after the war ended. Several had distinguished careers in the military. Drummer Boys had a crucial role in communicating battle commands. They also served as stretcher bearers bringing the wounded to medical care. Many drummers became soldiers. Thousands more enlisted and fought.

Most Civil War soldiers were between eighteen and thirty-nine years of age. It is estimated, however, that at least 100,000 Union soldiers were boys under the age of fifteen, and that about twenty per cent of all Civil War soldiers were under the age of eighteen. Since soldiers had to be at least eighteen to enlist, it seems obvious that many soldiers were not truthful about their ages. Boys often wrote the number eighteen on the bottom of their shoes and, when asked if they were over eighteen, would say they were. As casualties increased in the Civil War and more soldiers were needed, recruiters often did not ask for an enlistee's age.

Boy soldiers usually served as drummer boys, buglers, fifers, messengers, nurses, and scouts for the troops. They often assisted surgeons. These duties could be dangerous. Drummers, musicians, messengers and flag bearers were targets for rifle fire. During battles, many of these boys set aside those duties and joined the troops in combat. Many boys were killed in combat. Others were imprisoned in camps like Andersonville.

The youngest Confederate soldier to fight in the Civil War seems to have been Alex Gillenwater. He was from Tazewell, Virginia, and was one of the original Tazewell Boys. He joined on May 29, 1861, in Wytheville, Virginia, and became a member of the 45th Virginia Infantry, Company G. He served throughout the war.

Robert Henry Hendershot of Jackson, Michigan or New York, born sometime between 1847-1751, Hendershot was a fixture in camp in 1861 and moved south with the Jackson County Rifles either as a servant to Capt. Charles V. DeLand or as a stowaway. When he enlisted in the 9th Michigan in March 1862, Hendershot was a slight-framed boy four and a half feet tall. His unit moved south from Kentucky to Murfreesboro. When troops under Nathan Bedford Forrest attacked Murfreesboro before dawn, several 9th Michigan soldiers verified that Hendershot fearlessly exposed himself to enemy fire.

Hendershot received a severe wound at Shiloh. Soon after, at the end of July 1862, he was discharged from the army. Hendershot was retained by a Lt. Hogan, and later by Chaplain George Taylor, traveling with the 8th Michigan Infantry in the Army of the Potomac. He had been suffering from epileptic seizures and was ordered off duty and applied for his discharge. In December while Hendershot awaited his discharge, the Army of the Potomac was at Fredericksburg on the Rappahannock River. Engineers were attempting to build pontoon bridges over the river. There were delays in getting bridge materials. This gave time for General Lee's troops to get into position, and when the Union engineers were able to begin constructing pontoon bridges, Confederate sharpshooters kept them from working. The 7th Michigan Infantry volunteered to cross the river and drive the sharpshooters from their positions. Hendershot "joined" the unit by clinging to the gunwale of the first boat to cross and participated in the battle. His discharge came through about two weeks later.

Another soldier was John Cook, a fifteen-year-old bugle player who volunteered to operate a cannon during the Battle of Antietam. Cook later received the Medal of Honor for his actions during that battle.

The youngest Union soldier to fight in the Civil War was Edward Black, eight years old when he joined the Union army in 1861 as a drummer boy for the 21st Indiana Volunteers. He was captured at the Battle of Baton Rouge in 1862 but was freed when the Union army won the battle. He was discharged in September of that year, but reenlisted with the 1st Indiana Volunteer Heavy Artillery and was finally discharged in February 1866.

Elisha Stockwell from Wisconsin described his experience during the Battle of Shiloh in 1862: "I want to say, as we lay there and the shells were flying over us, my thoughts went back to my home, and I thought what a foolish boy I was to run away and get into such a mess as I was in. I would have been glad to have seen my father coming after me." And sixteen year old John Cockerhill described Shiloh: "I passed…the corpse of a beautiful boy in gray who lay with his blond curls scattered about his face and his hand folded peacefully across his breast. He was clad in a bright and neat uniform, well garnished with gold, which seemed to tell the story of a loving mother and sisters who had sent their household pet to the field of war. He neat little hat lying beside him bore the number of a Georgia regiment…. He was about my age…. At the sight of the poor boy's corpse, I burst into a regular boo hoo and started on."

Zouaves

There were over seventy Zouave units in the Union Army and at least twenty-five in the Confederate Army during the Civil War. These were not foreign troops, but were patterned on the French Zouaves that had been initiated in 1831 and were a development from Berber Zouaves, which the French had observed as being extremely fast moving and agile fighters. The French Zouaves included Berber, Arab, European, and Black volunteers.

The first Zouave unit in the United States was initiated by Elmer Edwin Ellsworth, a New York City law clerk. Having studied French Zouave manuals, he was appointed to lead the Rockford City Greys and turned them into the Zouave Greys. In 1859, they won the national military drilling competition in Chicago. Zouave fervency began, and more units were formed. After his friendship with President Lincoln began, Ellsworth's unit became the 11th New York Infantry Regiment, the Fire

Zouaves, which were sworn into Federal service May 7, 1861. Col. Ellsworth was the first Union officer to die in the Civil War. The 9th New York Infantry Regiment, the Hawkins' Zouaves, were the first Zouaves to officially enter the war. Also well known were the 5th New York Duryee's Zouaves. Famous Confederate units were Charleston's Zouave Cadets, the Louisiana Tigers, and Coppen's Zouaves. Zouave units were fearless, hard fighting infantry shock troops trained to lead attacks.

Zouave uniforms were not standardized. They generally consisted of baggy trousers, a short open front jacket, a sash, probably high top boots and possibly a fez or turban. Zouaves served as light infantry and fought in open order formations rather than the closed order formations, which were standard with other infantry units. Zouave units fought in every major battle of the Civil War. Photographs show a colorful variety of uniform styles.

Chapter Seven

Military Essentials

Civil War Ranks and Formations

When looking at the size of Civil War military units, it is important to remember that most Civil War units in the field were usually at twenty to forty per cent of their full strength. In looking at the sizes given below, it is important to decrease the number from twenty to even fifty per cent in the field. Also, due to casualties among the officers, units would often be commanded by an officer below the rank common for that position.

Infantry

The basic unit is the company, commanded by a captain.

A company had 100 men in two platoons, in four sections, in eight squads.

For a company in two platoons, the Captain commanded one and the First Lieutenant commanded the other. There was a sergeant for each section, and a corporal for each squad. The First Sergeant "ran" the whole company.

Battalions and regiments were formed by organizing companies together. In the volunteers, both Union and Confederate, ten companies would comprise a regiment, commanded by a colonel.

A regiment had the following staff: Colonel, Lt. Colonel, Major, Adjutant (First Lt.), Surgeon (Maj.), Assistant Surgeon, (Captain), Quartermaster (lieutenant) Commissary (lieutenant), Sergeant-Major and Quartermaster Sgt.

A brigade was formed from three to six regiments and commanded by a brigadier general. Sometimes, artillery would be attached to the brigade.

A division was composed of two to six brigades and was commanded by a major general. Cavalry was sometimes attached to a division.

A corps was commanded by a major general (Union) or a lieutenant general (Confederate) and was made up of two to four divisions. The number of corps in an army varied.

Examples:
Company, 100 men, Company A
Regiment, 1000 men, 38th NC Infantry
Brigade, 4000 men, 3rd Brigade (US)
Division, 12,000 men, Pender's Division
Corps, 36,000, IIIrd Corps (US)
Army, Confederate Army of Kentucky

Cavalry

The basic unit was the troop or company, organized much like an infantry unit, with a nominal strength of 100 men. If the troop dismounted for battle, one man in four would stay to guard the horses. In Union volunteers, twelve cavalry troops formed a regiment commanded by a colonel. Confederates used ten troops for a regiment. Union regulars used two troops to form a squadron, two squadrons to form a battalion and three battalions to form a regiment. Union cavalry was assigned to an infantry division. Confederates brigaded their cavalry.

Artillery

The basic unit of artillery was the battery, which had four to six guns. It was commanded by a captain and had four lieutenants, twelve or more sergeants and corporals and 120 or so privates. A Confederate battery usually had four guns and Union battery six guns. Batteries were divided into gun crews of about twenty men and into sections of two gun crews, with two or three sections per battery. A gun crew was commanded by a sergeant and a section by a lieutenant.

At the start of the war, both sides attached one battery to each infantry brigade, plus an artillery reserve under the army commander. By mid-1862, larger organizations were used. After 1862, it was normal for each infantry division to have an artillery battalion attached, with each corps or army to have two to five battalions in reserve. The Union used "heavy artillery" units of ten artillery batteries with about 1,800 men who had trained as both infantry and artillery.

Engineers

Both sides raised regiments of engineers, organized similar to infantry. They were expert in building forts, entrenchments, bridges, and other military construction. They were combatants but did not normally engage in fighting. They often continued to work on construction even during battle.

Sharpshooters

Union and Confederates both used sharpshooter units. Confederates used these as independent companies. The Union usually assigned them to skirmish duty, but allowed them to roam around the battlefield looking for advantageous positions.

Civil War Casualties

Guy Gugliotta, article in the *New York Times*, April 2, 2012:

> For 110 years, the numbers stood as gospel: 618,222 men died in the Civil War, 360,222 from the North and 258,000 from the South. But new research shows that these numbers were far too low. By combing through newly digitized census date from the 19th Century, J. David Hacker, a demographic historian from Binghamton University, has recalculated the death toll and increased it by more than twenty per cent to 750,000.
>
> The new figure is already winning acceptance from scholars. *Civil War History*, the journal that published Dr. Hacker's paper, called it "among the most consequential pieces ever to appear."
>
> The Union armies had from 2,500,000 to 2,750,000 men. The Confederate number is less accurate because of missing records, but the number may have been 1,250,000. Out of every 1,000 Federals in battle, 112 were wounded, and out of every 1,000 Confederates, 150 were wounded.
>
> Mortality was greater among Confederate wounded because of inferior medical service. People who died from wounds after the battle ended were considered to have died from illness and were not a battle casualty.

Civil War Paroles

Casualties at the Battle of Richmond included 519 Confederate soldiers wounded and 122 killed on the two days of the battle. There were 844 Union soldiers wounded, some of whom died in the days following the battle, and 206 killed. Battle casualties are listed as those killed during the battle. Those who die later as a result of the battle are listed as having died from illness. When the battle ended, 4,303 Union soldiers were prisoners. The iron fence at the Richmond Cemetery was around the courthouse on Main Street, Richmond. Union soldiers were held at the courthouse while their paroles were being printed.

Printing of these paroles may have been done at Mount Pleasant, the Solomon Smith House on Second and Water Streets in Richmond. The house overlooks downtown Richmond from a steeply sloping hillside. It was built for George Brown, the father-in-law of Solomon Smith, from 1835-40, with additions in 1852. Union soldiers were brought there to sign their paroles.

While the types of Civil War printing presses were of recent vintage, printing presses were not a new invention. Johannes Gutenberg was a German blacksmith and goldsmith. In 1439 he was the first European to use a printing press and movable type. Prior to this, copying of books and brochures had been done by hand or by engraved wooden blocks for printing. The Gutenberg Bible was the first substantial book printed in Europe with movable type. It was completed in 1454 or 1455. This Bible was a 42-line printing acclaimed for its high aesthetic and technical quality.

The first portable printing press of record was made in 1786 by Vittorio Alfini, a little press on which he could print a sonnet of fourteen lines. A "pocket printing office" was mentioned in Hamburg in 1772. The first press in America was set up at Massachusetts Colony's new college by Mrs. Jose Glover in 1638.

The type of press used to print the paroles in Richmond is not known today; however, it may have been portable. An alternative would have been a newspaper press, but the only Richmond newspaper, *The Messenger*, the latest of a series of short-lived publications, had closed earlier in 1862. The *Kentucky Rebel* had one edition in September 1862. The press used for both of these newspapers might have been available to print paroles. This press may have been a flatbed press, but it was too large to be moved easily. A cylinder press of 1812, a rotary press, 1840, or a Frank Press, 1850, were much too large to be moved quickly from one location to another. Location of the Richmond newspaper press has not been determined.

Types of portable printing presses used by the military were a new invention and they were generally used only through the era of the Civil War. Lowe and Adams presses were common, easy to use and very popular with both military and amateur printers during and after the Civil War. Besides paroles, they were used to print military orders, receipts and billheads, business receipts on letterhead paper. Both Lowe and Adams advertised "Every Man His Own Printer." The ability to communicate quickly in wartime had the possibility of profoundly affecting military actions and outcomes in the Civil War.

The Lowe Cone Press was invented and patented by Samuel W. Lowe of Philadelphia in 1856. This used a revolving cone-shaped roller. The Adams College Press, No. 4, a cylinder press, was patented in 1861 by Albert Adams of New York. Portable presses such as the Adams Cottage Press were inked by hand and did not use a frisket, an inner frame to hold the paper. They used a crank to press the paper against the type. There were also some self-inking systems, but these were not portable. Kits for the Adams Cottage Press were sold in five sizes to fit different needs and to enable the production of different sizes of documents. The kits included a press, type, rollers and ink. The Lowe press was lighter in weight than an Adams and was popular with pharmacists. It used a simpler frame and thin castings. Depending upon the style, an Adams press could weigh from 100 to 400 pounds. A Lowe press could weigh 12 to 120 pounds. Portable presses were very popular with Army and Navy both Federal and Confederate.

Paroles were common early in the Civil War. Lacking any means for handling large numbers of captured troops, both the Federal and Confederate governments relied on the traditional European system of parole and exchange of prisoners. The terms called for prisoners to give their word not to take up arms against their captors until they were formally exchanged for an enemy captive of equal rank. Parole was supposed to take place within ten days of capture. Sometimes parole camps were maintained where soldiers on parole could be kept by their own side in a non-combat role. Where there was no parole camp, parolees went home to await notice of their exchange.

The system grew increasingly complex, cumbersome and expensive as the war continued and the number of parolees increased rapidly. The paperwork was extensive. The prospect of being sent home caused some soldiers to allow themselves to be captured. Some parolees were permanently lost to the army when they failed to return to their units. The Federal authorities finally admitted that the parole system was prolonging the war. By 1863, the parole system was the Confederate army's principal means of maintaining troop strength. And by 1863, the Federal government had begun using black troops. The Confederate government refused to recognize these soldiers as prisoners of war. They reduced them to slavery and threatened to execute the officers who commanded them.

The first account of parole was February 18, 1861, when Federal troops in Texas surrendered to Confederate state forces. Federal troops paroled the first Confederate troops, 700 Missouri militia, May 10, 1861. The Confederates decreed that Union Maj. Gen. David Hunter and other officers would be held for execution as felons instead of prisoners of war because they had raised regiments of former slaves for Union service. December 28 and 30, 1862, exchange and parole of Confederate officers was halted by orders from Edwin Stanton, Secretary of War under Lincoln, and by Maj. Gen. Henry Halleck, general-in-chief of all Federal armies at that time. Gen. U. S. Grant issued an order on January 26, 1863, making invalid any paroles in the field offered by troops in his department. He wrote to Union Secretary of State William Seward August 19, 1864, "We ought not to make a single exchange nor release a prisoner on any pretext whatever until the war closes. We have got to fight until the military power of the South is exhausted, and if we release or exchange prisoners captured it simply becomes a war of extermination."

Confederate Gen. John Bell Hood proposed to Union Gen. William T. Sherman, August 27, 1864, an exchange of recently captured men, and Sherman agreed. On September 18, an exchange of invalid and sick prisoners began. Gen. Robert E. Lee on October 1, 1864, proposed to Gen. Grant an exchange of prisoners, but the discussion foundered on the question of paroling Union black troops. Gen. Grant did renew paroles February 2, 1865, beginning with men from Missouri and Kentucky. The alternatives to parole were the prison camps with their terrible conditions.

Prisons During the Civil War

Dix – Hill Cartel

The Dix-Hill Cartel failed not long after it was signed at Haxall's Landing on the James River, Virginia, because the Confederate Government refused to parole black prisoners and threatened to treat them as slaves and to execute their officers. The result was Civil War prisons. The articles of the cartel are listed after the section on prisons.

Although more than 150 places were used as prisons on both sides during the Civil War, only a few are notable. Generally, they fit into certain types: Fortifications, former jails, and penitentiaries, altered buildings, enclosures around barracks, enclosures around tents, and open stockades. Of the first type, a Confederate example is Castle Pinckney. The Union had Fort Warren in Boston Harbor, Fort Lafayette in New York, Fort McHenry in Baltimore, and the most dreaded for Southerners, Fort Delaware in the Delaware River.

The Union used the Alton, Illinois, and the Columbus, Ohio, penitentiaries for prisoners. The Confederacy's Libby Prison and the Union's Old Capitol and Gratiot Street Prisons were converted buildings. Others, all in the South, where tobacco factories were common and excellent for this purpose, were Ligon's in Richmond and Castle Thunder in Richmond and also a Castle Thunder in Petersburg. Buildings were also converted in Danville, Lynchburg, and Shreveport. Selma, Alabama, had Cahaba Prison, also called Castle Morgan. Union prisons that were enclosures around barracks included Johnson's Island, Camp Morton, Camp Douglas, Camp Chase, Elmira, and Rock Island. The Confederate Belle Isle and the Union Point Lookout prisons were enclosures built around tents. Prisons that were open stockades existed only in the South, and the most infamous was Andersonville. Others were Camp Lawton, Camp Ford, Camp Groce (a.k.a. Camp Liendo), and stockades in Salisbury, North Carolina, Macon, Georgia, and Charleston, Florence and Columbia, South Carolina. If both sides had agreed to the cartel, prisons might not have existed.

The Dix-Hill Cartel was negotiated between Major General John A. Dix, U.S. Army and Major General Daniel. H. Hill, C.S. Army, in July 22, 1862, to set down guidelines for how prisoners were to be exchanged between the Confederacy and the Union.

Article 1. In detailed form, this indicated that officers in the Army or the Navy would be exchanged for officers of equal rank.

Article 2. Local, state, civil and militia ranks held by persons not in actual military would not be recognized, the basis of exchange being the grade held in the naval and army.

Article 3. Captured settlers, teamsters and all civilians charged with disloyalty or any alleged civil offense would be exchanged for civilians in a similar position.

Article 4. All prisoners of war were to be discharged on parole in ten days after their capture, and the prisoners now held and those hereafter taken were to be transported to points mutually agreed upon. The surplus prisoners not exchanged were not permitted to take up arms again, nor to serve as military police or constabulary force in any fort, garrison, or field-work held by either of the respective parties, nor as guards of prisons, depots or stores, nor to discharge any duty usually performed by soldiers, until exchanged under the provisions of this cartel. The exchange was not considered to be complete until the officer or soldier exchanged for had been actually restored to the lines to which he belonged.

Article 5. Each party upon the discharge of prisoners of the other party was authorized to discharge an equal number of their own officers or men from parole, furnishing at the same time to the other party a list of the prisoners discharged and of their own officers and men relieved from parole, thus enabling each party to relieve from parole such of their own officers and men as the party may choose. The lists thus mutually furnished would keep both parties advised of the true condition of the exchange of prisoners.

Article 6. The stipulations and provisions above mentioned were to be a binding obligation during the continuance of the war. It did not matter which party may have the surplus of prisoners, the great principles involved being, first, an equitable exchange of prisoners, man for man, officer for officer, or officers of higher grade exchanged for officers of lower grade or for privates, according to the scale of equivalents; second, that privateers and officers and men of different services may be exchanged according to the same scale of equivalents; third, that that all prisoners, of whatever arm of service, were to be exchanged or paroled in ten days from the time of their capture, if it be practicable to transfer them to their own lines at that time; if not, as soon thereafter as practicable; fourth, that no officer, soldier, or employee, in the service of either party, would be considered as exchanged and absolved from his parole until his equivalent has actually reached the lines of his friends; fifth, that the parole prohibited the performance of field, garrison, police, guard or constabulary duty.

Soldiers' Leisure Time

A good reference is *The Soldiers of the Civil War* by William C. Davis. The book focuses on the daily routine of soldiers: Drill, camp chores, meals, songs, games, rules they broke and punishments, and the ways they occupied their free time. Soldiers participated in all kinds of activities such as boxing, broad jumping, leap frog, wrestling matches, foot and horse races, and louse races. There was even one instance of a bowling game played with cannon balls. The number one activity was playing cards. Common card games were poker, twenty-one, keno, and euchre. At the time, playing cards did not have numbers on them, just the symbols and suits. Music was almost always popular, from informal singing around the campfire to formal balls with dancing. In the winter, games were ice skating, sledding, building snowmen, and snowball battles. Extensive information is available online. See also Judith Giesberg, Ph.D. *Sex and the Civil War*, Thomas P. Lowry, M.D. *The Story the Soldiers Wouldn't Tell*, and James McIver *God Rest Ye Merry Soldiers: A True Civil War Christmas Story*, Christmas during the Civil War.

Soldiers spent a lot of time writing letters. For many of them, being in camp was the first time they had been outside their small, rural communities. It was not uncommon in a unit of 1,000 men for them to be writing 600 letters a day. Many were well written, but some were spelled in phonetics that were hard to understand. A Union soldier wrote to his wife, "I am well at the present with the exception I have got the dyerear (diarrhea) and I hope these lines will find you the same." A New York farmer wrote, "My country, glorious country, if we have only made it truly the land of the free... I count not my life dear unto me if only I can help that glorious cause along. A farmer from the 47th Alabama wrote, "I confess that I gave you up with reluctance. Yet I love my country dearly. The war in which we are unfortunately involved has been forced upon us. We have asked for nothing but to be let alone. I intend to discharge my duty to my country and to my God."

Soldiers sometimes had pets or they looked after the unit's mascot. Their pay was small, but they often spent it at sutlers near camp where they bought fruit, pocket knives, paper for letters or playing cards at high prices. Chess and checkers were very popular.

Many soldiers had Bibles to read. In the Union Army, if a soldier did not have a Bible, he could receive one from the U.S. Christian Commission. The American Bible Society gave Bibles to both sides. It shipped

Bibles to Maryland Bible Society and Washington City Bible Society, who smuggled them into the South. There was also The Bible Society in Nashville and the Confederate States Bible Society.

Some soldiers wrote hospital and camp newsletters. There were literary and debate societies in camp. Many kept journals. And there were church meetings. When any unit was in camp for a long period of time on either side, there would likely be a tent meeting and revival. Soldiers on both sides relied on these activities to help them relieve the boredom.

Playing cards also relieved the boredom. In America, there began to be restrictions against cards since they were viewed as a distraction to religious observance and were not in line with strict religious practices. Included in the restrictions against cards were also dice, games of chance, drinking, keeping of horses and horse racing, cock fighting and billiards. George Washington had restrictions on the use of cards for his soldiers. Massachusetts passed a tax on cards in 1785. Ben Franklin and his brother were early importers of playing cards. Ben Franklin was postmaster in Philadelphia. He placed ads in the local paper and playing cards could be purchased at the local post office. The Franklins were printers and made their own cards for sale. Key centers of card manufacturing in America were Boston, Philadelphia and New York.

Solitaire was played during the Civil War. Dick and Fitzgerald published a book of Fireside Games in 1859 on how to play solitaire and other games one could play alone. Blackjack was also popular.

Whist was a trick-taking card game from England, which was widely played during the 18th and 19th centuries. Whist was a game of tactics and strategy with four players and a deck of fifty-two cards similar to today's related games of duplicate bridge and contract bridge.

On July 1, 1862, Congress passed the Revenue Act of 1862, which included a five cent playing card stamp, a broad program of additional taxes to offset the rising war expenditures and establishment of the Office of Commissioner of Internal Revenue. The most significant aspects of the law were: 1. authorization of the first federal income tax; 2. creation of the Bureau of Internal Revenue under the Treasury Department; 2. use of adhesive tax stamps.

Marbles

Games played with marbles are ancient in origin. Little white marbles and round pebbles have been found in paleolithic caves. Stone balls and pillars have been found in Egypt dating to 4000 B.C. Early Greeks played marbles games with nuts. There are many references to marbles games played with nuts in Roman literature. Cherokees still play the very old game of Cherokee Marbles with marbles the size of billiard balls.

Marbles made from various forms of clay were introduced about 1800. Commercially made marbles date from Akron, Ohio, toward the end of the 19th Century for clay and early 20th Century for glass. There is evidence from archeological excavations at many Civil War battle sites that soldiers played marbles. Usually clay could be rolled between the palms of the hands into a reasonably round shape and baked in front of a fire.

Baseball

The earliest known mention of baseball in the United States was in Pittsfield, Massachusetts, where a 1791 city law banned the playing of the game within eighty yards of the town meeting house. The first team to play baseball under modern rules was the New York Knickerbockers, a social club founded in 1845. The club members, including Alexander Cartwright, formulated the "Knickerbocker Rules" which included both rules for playing the game and organization guidelines.

The first known competitive game between clubs under the new rules was played at Elysian Fields in Hoboken, New Jersey, on June 19, 1846. In 1857, sixteen New York area clubs formed the National Association of Base Ball Players. Aided by the Civil War, membership grew to almost 100 clubs by 1865 and to over 400 by 1867. During the Civil War, soldiers from different parts of the United Sates played baseball together spreading its popularity and leading to a more unified national version of the sport. They used the New York "Knickerbocker" rules, and these form the basis of our baseball rules today.

President Lincoln had learned to play baseball before his election and loved the game. There was even a baseball field constructed on the White House lawn. Early baseballs were handmade with a rubber core from melted shoes or some other hard core, wound with yard, and covered with hand-stitched brown leather. The size of balls varied. Bats also varied greatly. The first ones were made from wagon tongues, then players realized that round bats worked better. Bats were handmade according to what the batter wanted.

On July 4, 1862, Confederate soldiers at the Salisbury Prison yard cheered on Union troops as they battled on the grassy field—playing baseball. During the day, there was music, reading of the Declaration of Independence, sack and foot races, and baseball. The players were Union prisoners of war. Salisbury Prison in North Carolina became a prime venue for spreading the popularity of baseball. Confederate soldiers sometimes joined in the games. Their commanders encouraged this as a way to keep men alert. Baseball provided amusement, exercise, diversion and camaraderie. Confederate and Union stood surrounded the field shoulder to shoulder. On July 4, 1862, the contest ended when nine innings had been played. The score was 11-11.

Soldiers' Personal Care

In the Civil War, soldiers relied upon a laundry woman in camp to wash their clothes and do most of the mending. This woman, called a laundress, was one of the most respected and highest paid persons in camp because of her important work. She was also in charge of the men who assisted her in providing clean clothes for officers and troops. The Union Army's 1861 Military Handbook specified that only a woman of good character could serve as laundress. Each woman had to obtain a "Certificate of Good Character" from Army headquarters. The woman was probably married to one of the soldiers or she was the mother of one of them. Her fees were deducted from soldiers' pay at fifty cents, from unmarried officers at one to two dollars and from married officers at four dollars a month.

Soldiers also carried their own mending kits. One of the last gifts given to a departing soldier by his mother, sister or a female relative was a "housewife," a pocket sewing kit. It was made of cloth that would roll and fit easily into his pocket or knapsack. It would contain a reel of thread, several sizes of needles for sewing and for darning, straight pins and a few buttons. After battles, soldiers often needed to repair torn uniforms, split seams or buttons, which were lost. Soldiers were also expected to sew on military insignia.

Horses

If the Civil War was costly for humans, it was a catastrophe for horses and mules. There were approximately 3.4 million horses in the North, 1.7 million horses in the South and an additional 800,000 in Kentucky and Missouri. Whereas two per cent of all the people in the

United States died in the war, about twenty per cent of the 7.4 million horses and mules were destroyed. Horses were "used up" by hard work and malnourishment, and needed to be replaced every seven months. About half were returned to civilian use, while the other half died, requiring constant replacements for both sides. Confederate battlefield needs competed with farming and transportation of food and materiel. Ultimately, the depletion of Southern horses determined the strategies of immobilized Confederate armies accelerated by the collapse of the Southern economy.

Horses came into military service two ways. Officers and cavalry provided their own mounts. Quartermasters were responsible for procuring horses for artillery and transportation of wagons. Confederate cavalrymen were reimbursed forty cents per day for the use of their horses. Horses killed in action resulted in the owner being reimbursed at the appraised value on the date of muster. By 1864, a prized cavalry horse was valued at $3,000.00. Artillery employed twelve per cent of the horses. Battery horses had to pull cannons into battle and wait patiently while they fired and were being fired upon. On paper, each battery required about a hundred horses to haul its six guns, six caissons, three or four wagons and a battery forge. Mules could be used, but they often bucked and rolled during combat.

For the South, transportation of food, forage, ammunition, camp gear, and other supplies fell to the four-horse wagons. They each carried about a ton of supplies. The North preferred six-horse teams, which could pull 3,500 pounds. Southern transportation was deficient at the start of the war and deteriorated throughout the war, requiring continual reallocations and reductions of what was moved. As the Civil War continued, finding horses became increasingly difficult. Farmers might expect their horses to be taken as an army moved through the area.

Horses were fed fourteen pounds of hay and twelve pounds of oats, corn, or barley a day. It was possible to graze horses, but they required two and a half to four acres of grassland and about seven acres of grain crops each to equal the nutrition. Any army with 25,000 animals required 150 square miles of good pasturage. Horse shoes were also a scarcity. In addition to suffering from poor nutrition, exhaustion and the lack of shoes, horses also contracted a contagious respiratory disease. There was no cure and destroying infected animals was the only remedy. Excerpted from "Southern Horse," by Keith Miller, *Civil War Times*, February 2006.

Horse shoes date to the early domestication of the horse. Working animals were exposed to many conditions that would cause breakage or excessive hoof wear. Around 1000 A.D. case bronze horseshoes with nail holes became common in Europe. By the time of the Crusades, 1096-1270, horseshoes were made of iron and were so valuable that they were often accepted instead of coins to pay taxes. From the need for horseshoes, the craft of blacksmithing became of the staple crafts of medieval and modern times.

In 1835, the first U.S. patent for a horseshoe manufacturing machine capable of making up to sixty shoes per hour was issued to Henry Burden. With the coming of the Industrial Revolution, horseshoe production reached new heights. A machine to cast shoes on a large scale was introduced. During the Civil War, Northern armies had a machine to forge horseshoes that gave them a distinct advantage over Southern armies.

The great need in the Civil War for horses changed horse racing forever, starting with the re-capture of *Asteroid.* Woodburn Stud was a farm in Woodford County owned by Robert A. Alexander. Its top thoroughbred was *Asteroid.* Confederate raiders invaded Alexander's farm just across the county line from Lexington and Fayette County, and they took a prized animal. *Asteroid*_was a half-brother of the great runner *Kentucky,* sired by the horse Lexington. When Alexander realized the Confederates had *Asteroid,* he quickly organized a posse to go after the raiders. His men found the horse with the famous Confederate guerrilla Sue Mundy near the Kentucky River. Sue Mundy was a young man named Marcellus Jerome Clark, who adopted the name of a fictional female Confederate raider whose exploits embarrassed Union authorities in Kentucky. Alexander's men offered a ransom of $250 for *Asteroid* because, they maintained, the children were crying after their pet horse had been taken. Not knowing the horse's identity, Mundy returned the horse reluctantly, saying it was the finest horse he had ridden.

As some of the darkest days of the Civil War brought widespread death and destruction, an equine hero was rising to prominence at the new Saratoga Race Course in New York. Most things from the South at that time were held in contempt, but this racehorse was an exception. He was *Kentucky*, a half-brother to *Asteroid*. Bred in Lexington at Ashland Stud, *Kentucky* was an 1861 foal sired by *Lexington* out of the Glencoe mare *Magnolia*. *Kentucky* was sold to John R. Hunter, chairman of The Jockey Club and influential in Saratoga racing's formative years. *Kentucky* made his three-year-old debut in the Jersey Derby in 1864. During the Civil War, Lexington, Kentucky, was one of the cities in American with organized thoroughbred racing. The old Kentucky Association track in downtown Lexington operated continuously during the war. Churchill Downs did not open until ten years after the war ended.

In the early days of the sport of horse racing, after the Civil War, many African Americans were influential. In the first Kentucky Derby, *Aristides* was trained by African American Ansel Williamson and guided to victory by Oliver Lewis, one of fifteen black jockeys in that race. Fifteen of the first twenty-eight Kentucky Derbys were won by black jockeys, and five were trained by black trainers. Most famous of the black jockeys was Isaac Murphy, considered one of the greatest riders in American history. He was the first jockey to win three Kentucky Derbys, and won an astonishing forty-four per cent of all races in which he rode. He is buried in Kentucky Horse Park next to Man O' War.

The Thoroughbred is the horse breed best known for horse racing. While the term could be applied to any purebred horse, it technically refers only to the Thoroughbred breed. These horses are considered "hot-blooded" and are known for their agility, speed and spirit. The Thoroughbred was developed in the 17th and 18th centuries when English mares were crossed with three stallions *Arabian*, *Barb* and *Turkoman*. All modern Thoroughbreds trace their pedigrees to these three stallions. The first Thoroughbred horse in the American colonies was *Bulle Rock*, imported in 1730 by Samuel Gist. Two important Thoroughbreds imported during the Revolutionary War were *Diomed* and *Messenger*. A son of *Diomed* was *Sir Archy*, the first outstanding stallion that was born in America.

The Morgan horse is one of the oldest American breeds. It is compact and very versatile. The Morgan saw extensive use in Civil War cavalry. It was later used as a coach horse and in harness racing. The quarter horse excels in sprinting very fast at distances up to about a quarter of a mile. It was extremely useful in working on ranches. The

Tennessee Walker was developed in the South for use on farms and plantations. It was a very popular riding horse because of its calm disposition, surefootedness, and smooth gait. It was developed from Narragansett Pacers, Canadian Pacers, and the Spanish mustang. There was no preferred horse for cavalry. Civil War cavalry horses needed to be at least fifteen hands tall, weigh at least 950 pounds, 4-10 years of age, and well broken to bridle and saddle. Cavalry also had artillery.

The Standardbred is a breed best known for the ability to race in harness at a trot or pace instead of under saddle at a gallop. Developed in North America, the breed is now recognized worldwide. In the 17th century, the first trotting races were held in the Americas, and by the 18th century, there were official courses for horses in harness. Several breeds have contributed to the Standardbred, including *Narragansett Pacer*, *Canadian Pacer*, Thoroughbred, *Norfolk Trotter*, Hackney and Morgan. The most notable sire was the Thoroughbred_*Messenger,* which came to the United States in 1788. His offspring were found to be good trotting horses. Standardbreds tend to be more muscled with longer bodies. They have more placid dispositions. They are considered people-oriented and easy to train.

Mules

Over a million mules were used in the Civil War. Their specialty was pulling wagons. Mules are sturdy and durable. They can perform work in harsh situations and require less food than horses. They are sure footed and can carry heavy loads for longer distances. Mules were not used for cavalry, artillery, or for ambulances. They could take ammunition toward the front, but not too close. Mules have a strong sense of self-preservation. They can be nervous and skittish. The sound of cannon would frighten them. In battle, they were very difficult to control. They would panic and bolt. The terms "stubborn as a mule" and "kick like a mule" were very appropriate.

Chapter Eight

Weapons

The long rifle was a type of weapon used in early America by both military and civilians. It is characterized by an unusually long barrel, sometimes more than four feet in length. This length was often matched to the height of the user. The Pennsylvania rifle, the Kentucky rifle and the Tennessee hog rifle are all variants of the long rifle. Pennsylvania and Kentucky rifles are basically identical. Initially the weapon of choice on the frontier was a smooth bore musket. Often called a "Brown Bessie," it was easy to load but was quite heavy. The long rifle was developed from the German Jager rifle, well known for hunting. The changes were a smaller caliber to conserve lead and powder and a longer barrel, which made for easier gripping

The long rifle originated on the American frontier in the early 1700s and continued its development technically and artistically until it passed out of fashion in the mid to late 19th century. However, extensive use and manufacture of long rifles continued in the Appalachian Mountain counties of Virginia, Tennessee, Kentucky, and North Carolina well into the 20th Century. A long rifle was made entirely by hand. Increasingly frontiersmen began using rifled guns with helical grooves in the barrel. The smooth bore had an effective range of less than 100 yards. A rifle in the hands of a skilled shooter could hit a man-size target at 300 yards or more. The helical groove allows the bullet to rotate rapidly, balancing the turbulence of the bullet and keeping it straight on line. The longer barrel gave slow-burning black powder more time to burn, increasing the muzzle velocity and accuracy. Small calibers were preferred to conserve lead, with a .36 to .45 caliber being common. Black powder caused extensive wear on the barrel, resulting in an enlarged barrel. A long rifle might later be re-bored and re-rifled to .50 caliber.

In addition to accuracy and distance, another reason for the popularity of these guns was because of how light and graceful they were.

A long rifle was owned by almost every family on the frontier. For them, rifle shooting was a way of life. It was used for safety, for securing food, and for recreation in shooting matches on weekends and holidays.

The Kentucky rifle style was also used in flintlock pistols, called Kentucky Pistols. These were matched in caliber to a rifle owned by the same user to simplify bullet molding. A Kentucky Pistol was slimmer than other pistols and had the same barrel style and graceful lines of a long rifle. This pistol was quite accurate and had superb balance. One is shown in the section on pistols.

The Tennessee hog rifle differs from the Pennsylvania and Kentucky style usually in its simplicity. These rifles were produced in areas of the Southern Appalachians less populated and often far removed from sources of supply. Many of the extras such as a brass patch box were eliminated.

Among the earliest documented long rifle makers were Martin Meylin and other Mennonites in Pennsylvania, Adam Haymaker in the northern part of the Shenandoah Valley of Virginia, Moravian gunsmiths in the Christian Springs area of Pennsylvania, and Moravians in the Salem area of North Carolina. There is evidence that the first high quality Kentucky rifles were made by Jacob Deckard. Rifle shops were located all along The Great Wagon Road from Pennsylvania, down the Shenandoah, into the Cumberland Gap and the Yadkin River Valley.

During the American Civil War, the rifle was the common weapon found on the battlefield. Many of the rifles during this time were loaded with a small lead musket ball or with a minie ball and black powder. Most rifles were muzzle loaded and were common in both Union and Confederate military.

In the decades leading up to the Civil War, numerous advances had been made in weapon design. The flintlock, which had been used for around 200 years, was being replaced with the caplock. Rifles had been in use for many years, but prior to the Civil War rifles had rarely seen military use. The black powder at the time quickly fouled the barrel, making reloading slower and more difficult. Black powder also quickly obscured the battlefield, which led military leaders to conclude that greater range offered by the rifles did not outweigh the drawbacks. The invention of the minie ball solved the slow loading problem, which allowed for rifles to replace the muskets.

A rifle is a weapon designed to be fired from the shoulder, with a barrel that has a helical groove or pattern grooves (rifling) cut into the barrel walls. The raised areas of the rifling are called "lands," which make contact with the projectile, imparting spin around an axis corresponding to the orientation of the weapon. When the projectile leaves the barrel, this spin lends gyroscopic stability to the projectile and prevents tumbling, in the same way that a properly thrown American football or rugby ball behaves. This allows the use of aerodynamically-efficient pointed bullets (as opposed to the spherical balls used in muskets) and thus improves range and accuracy. The world "rifle" originally referred to the grooving and a rifle was called a "rifled gun".

Muzzle loading rifles are loaded from the open end of the barrel. A measured quantity of black gunpowder is put into the barrel, either with a measuring powder flask or by dropping premeasured solid pellets of black powder into the barrel. A bullet or ball is placed in the end of the barrel and pushed down firmly and evenly to rest on top of the powder load by using ramrod, which is normally stored underneath the barrel when not in use. Breech loading rifles were developed in the 19th century. A breech loading weapon is a firearm in which the cartridge or shell is inserted or loaded into a chamber integral to the rear portion of a barrel above the trigger. The main advantage of breech loading was the faster reload time.

Muskets were smoothbore, large caliber weapons using ball shaped ammunition fired at relatively low velocity. Due to high cost and great difficult of precision manufacturing and the need to load readily from the muzzle, the musket ball was a loose fit in the barrel. Consequently, the ball bounced off the sides of the barrel when fired and the final direction on leaving the muzzle was unpredictable, resulting in inaccuracy.

The performance of early muskets was effective for the styles of warfare at the time, whereby soldiers tended to stand in long, stationary lines and fire at the opposing force. Precise aiming and accuracy were not necessary to hit an opponent. Muskets were used for comparatively rapid, imprecisely aimed volley fire, and the average solider could easily be trained to use one. The (muzzle-loaded) rifle was originally a sharpshooter's weapon. Since rifles were used by sharpshooters who did not routinely fire over other men's shoulders, long length was not required to avoid the forward line. A shorter length made a handier weapon in which tight-fitting balls did not have to be rammed so far down the barrel.

Sharps rifles were a series of large bore single shot rifles that began with a design by Christian Sharps in 1848. They have historically been known for long range and high accuracy. The initial rifle was patented September 17, 1848, and manufactured by A.S. Nippes at Mill Creek, Pennsylvania (Philadelphia). The 1851 model was brought to the Robbins and Lawrence Company of Windsor, Vermont. Rollin White of the R&L Company invented the knife-edge breech block and self-cocking devise. This is referred to as the First Contract for 5,000 carbines. The Second Contract in 1851 was for 15,000 rifles and the Sharps Rifle Manufacturing Co., was built in Hartford, Connecticut, on R&L property. The Model 1851 was replaced in production by the Model 1853.

The military Sharps was a falling block rifle, using a percussion cap with a pellet primer feed. This devise held a stack of pelleted primers and flipped one over the nipple each time the trigger was pulled and the hammer fell, making it easier to fire a Sharps from horseback. The Sharps was used by marksmen, notably the Berdan's Sharpshooters,. The Sharps was breech-loading, and many officers were concerned that breech-loaders would encourage soldiers to waste ammunition. The Sharps was expensive to manufacture and only 11,000 Model 1859s were produced. The carbine version was very popular with the cavalry of both Union and Confederate armies and was issued in much larger numbers than the full length rifle. The falling block action made it easier to convert to the new metallic cartridges developed in the late 1860s.

The Mississippi Rifle was developed by Eli Whitney Blake, nephew of Eli Whitney, producing a Model 1851 at the Harpers Ferry Armory. It was nicknamed the Mississippi Rifle during the Mexican War after its use by the First Mississippi Rifles under then Col. Jefferson Davis. The Model 1851 weighed nine pounds, four ounces. It delivered a very accurate ball at 1,200 feet per second up to 1,100 yards.

Other rifles used to a lesser extent were the Henry had a copper or brass cartridge. The power was comparable to military pistols. It used a .44 caliber bullet. The Spencer was the first successful repeater used in the United States. The seven-shot model was produced in both rifle and carbine versions. The Model 1855 Colt Revolving Rifle and companion carbine were repeaters with the defect that several chambers often discharged at the same time. The Whitworth was designed by Sir Joseph Whitworth and manufactured in Manchester, England, United Kingdom. It featured a unique hexagonal shaped bullet with a matching hexagonal barrel that gave it superior accuracy. It was capable of hitting a target beyond 1,000 yards.

The Springfield Model 1861 was a minie-type rifled muzzle loading musket, single-shot shoulder arm used by the Federal army and marines during the Civil War. It was the most widely used US Army weapon, and was favored for its range, accuracy, and reliability. The barrel was thirty-eight inches long, firing a .58 caliber minie ball, had a total weight of nine pounds, with a normal effective range of 200-300 yards. It used percussion caps. Trained troops were able to fire three rounds a minute, while maintaining accuracy up to 500 yards. It was a three bands rifle (meaning of bands is written below). The Springfield was aimed using flip-up leaf sights. There were two leafs (using the singular leaf with an s for clarity), one for 300 yards and one for 500 yards. With both leaves down, the sight was set for 100 yards. By the end of the war, 1.5 million Springfields had been produced at the Springfield Armory in Massachusetts. With high demand, the armory opened its weapons patterns to twenty private contractors, most notable of which was Colt. Officers of both armies preferred the Springfield because the machine-made parts were easy to change.

The Enfield Pattern 1853 rifle–musket was a .577 caliber minie-type muzzle loading weapon used by the British Empire from 1853-1867. Americans liked it because the caliber allowed the use of .58 ammunition. The term rifle-musket meant that the rifle was the same length as the musket it replaced, because a long rifle was thought necessary to enable the muzzles of the second rank of soldiers to project beyond the faces of the first rank of soldiers. The thirty-nine inch barrel had three grooves, with a 1:78 rifling twist, and was fastened to the stock with three bands. The Enfield had an adjustable ladder rear sight with steps for 100 yards, which was the default or battle-range, 200 yards, 300 yards and 400 yards. For distances beyond that, an adjustable slip-up sight was graduated from 900 to 1,250 yards. The Enfield was originally produced by the Royal Small Arms Factory at Enfield, England, U.K. The Confederates imported more Enfields than any other small arm, eventually buying over 900,000 of these.

The Austrian-made Lorenz was imported by both armies. The Lorenz was designed by Lieutenant Joseph Lorenz and introduced into the Austrian Army in 1854. American purchases were from several sources, including Hapsburg armories in Vienna and private arms makers in Vienna and Ferlach. The Lorenz was a rifle-musket with a thirty-seven and a half inch barrel secured with three bands. It was made with two styles of rear sights, a non-adjustable block calibrated to hit a target up to 300 paces, and a leaf sight adjustable up to 900 paces. Some were furnished with elevating screws for a range up to 800 yards. In 1862, a version was developed with a steel barrel rather than iron. Quality of Lorenz rifles varied.

The invention of the minie bullet in the 1840's solved the slow loading problem, and in the 1850's and 1860's rifles quickly replaced muskets on the battlefield. Many rifles, often referred to as the rifled muskets, were very similar to the muskets they replaced, but the military also experimented with other designs. Breech loading weapons proved to have much faster rate of fire then muzzle loaders, causing military forces to abandon muzzle loaders in favor of breech loading designs in the late 1860's. In the late 19th century, rifles were generally single-shot and breech-loading.

When the American Civil War broke out in April 1861, neither the North (360,000 small arms) nor the south (240,000 small arms) had enough weapons to fight a major war. Stockpiles of rifles and handguns carried by individual soldiers were limited. Soldiers were often forced to use older smooth bore and flintlock muskets, simply because the newer rifles were not available in sufficient quantities. Many soldiers were forced to use their own personal hunting rifles, which were typically Kentucky or Pennsylvania type rifles. The rifles, while more accurate than smoothbore muskets, had been designed for hunting, and fired smaller caliber ammunition.

To combat the arms shortage, the Union and Confederacy both imported large quantities of rifles from Europe, with each side buying whatever they could. The South, with low cash reserves, only brought 50,000 by August 1862, while the North had bought 726,000. Accordingly, during the first two years of the war soldiers from both sides used a wide variety of rifles, including many that were over fifty years old and were considered to be obsolete. At the same time, Northern rifle and gun manufacturers such as Sharps, Colt, Remington and the

United States Armory at Springfield, Massachusetts, quickly increased their production of rifles; Springfield alone increased its annual output from 20,000 to 200,000. The North was thus able to supply its own small arms needs, while the South had to continue to rely on foreign sources, eventually purchasing 580,000 rifles.

Shotguns

Shotguns were used by both Union and Confederate cavalry. These shotguns may been muzzle-loading, but breech-loading models were available. James Fennimore Cooper wrote that frontiersmen in Kentucky were the first to use the term shotgun. Previously, these types of weapons were called scatterguns, fowling pieces, or simply fowlers. Shotguns are smooth bore.

Joseph Manton, 1766 1835, London, England, a gunsmith and hunter, is considered to be the father of modern shotguns. By 1770, reliable Damascus shotgun barrels were readily available. By 1790, double-barrel flintlocks were available. Hammerless and percussion shotguns were made in the early 19th century. Breech-loading shotguns were available by the middle of the 19th century. Breech-loading shotguns used thick paper shells in the 1850s and brass shells in the 1860s. The earliest American made shotguns were manufactured by E. Remington and Sons. The New York company was formed by Eliphalet Remington in 1816.

Double-barrel shotguns were the most efficient weapon used by cavalry. They were versatile, using a single slug, buck shot or a combination. Barrels were often sawed shorter to produce a wider pattern and terrible damage at short range. Percussion or caplock shotguns would not misfire in wet or damp weather.

Pistols

Many different pistols, or revolvers or handguns as they were called at the time, were used throughout the Civil War by both the North and the South. Sometimes the exact same model and version of a handgun would be used by both sides, or the hand gun would be built to specifications set forth by the respective faction. Generally speaking, the Confederate troops were always outnumbered by the North in both manpower and available weapons to use. This caused the Confederate troops to use many captured weapons throughout the war. If there was any handgun used the most by Union troops it would have to be the Colt models 1851 and 1860 army versions, as well as the Starr revolver. For the Confederate troops it would be either of the Colt models or the Remington model 1858 revolver. The large majority of Civil War soldiers did not have a pistol or revolver. These were not issued to the infantry soldiers. Revolvers or handguns were issued to cavalryman, and officers. Some Artillery units may have had pistols issued for the gunner. Officers were issued handguns, or they would buy their own.

Colt Percussion Revolvers

Similar in size and appearance to the Colt Army, the main difference of the Colt Navy was the change in caliber from .44 to .36 and the fact that it was primarily issued to the Navy.

Starr Model 1848

Starr Arms Company in 1858 began manufacturing very innovative and genial .36 and .44 caliber revolvers. This revolver was designed by Eban Townsend Starr, son and grandson of Nathan Starr, junior and senior, famous Connecticut sword makers and rifle makers. The U.S. Ordnance Department began purchasing these for the Western Theater, but in 1863 forced the company to change from double-action to single-action, after which Starr sold 23,000 of these to the federal government.

Remington 1858 Patent

Remington Repeating Arms Company also made revolvers during the Civil War. The most common was the Remington Model 1858. This pistol was highly favored by troops. The Remington had a quick cylinder release catch, which made reloading much faster. It was used in large quantities during the war.Remington New Model, 1863-1875. All three models of Remington revolvers were nearly identical in size and appearance. Noticeable changes were in the cylinders, hammers and loading levers. All three models were very accurate. This revolver came in army .44 caliber, navy .36 caliber and pocket .31 versions. The navy had a 7 1/2 inch barrel, and the army had an 8 inch barrel. Front sight was a German silver cone.

Confederate and Union cavalry were known to carry as many loaded pistols as possible, often carrying eight, with extras purchased or found on the battlefield. They carried more loaded cylinders in bandoleer bags and coat pockets. The largest caliber possible was preferred, and a barrel of 7-9 inches was the choice, adding velocity – effective distance and impact, plus accuracy from the longer sighting length of the barrel.

Bullets

Almost as soon as the war ended, historians began studying the factors that led to so much bloodshed and concluded that the introduction of the rifled musket was the primary cause of the staggering casualty rates. The rifle musket combined the best features of the smoothbore musket and the Kentucky flintlock rifle. It could be loaded quickly and easily, while its long, grooved barrel gave it an effective range up to four times that of a smoothbore, with similar improvement in accuracy. An experienced soldier could load and fire up to four rounds a minute. Of all the wounds treated by Union Army doctors throughout the war, ninety-five per cent were caused by small arms fire. Less than one percent were attributed to bayonets and swords and about four percent to artillery shells and shrapnel. It was not just the accuracy or frequency of fire that killed or maimed so many soldiers, but the characteristics of the ammunition.

The minie ball (properly pronounced "min-YAY" after its developer, French Army officer Claude-Etienne Minie, but pronounced by Americans as minnie ball), was not a ball but rather a conical-shaped bullet. James Burton, an armorer at the Harpers Ferry Arsenal, simplified the design and developed a hollow-based .58 caliber lead projectile that could be cheaply mass produced. Minie balls were slightly smaller in circumference than the inside of the barrel, so they could be dropped in quickly. When fired, the base of the bullet expanded and gripped the rifle grooves, which imparted a spin to the bullet and gave it greater range and accuracy, at a speed of 950 feet per second.

Unlike a solid ball, which could pass through the human body intact, leaving an exit wound not much larger than the entrance wound, the soft, hollow-based minie ball flattened and deformed upon impact, while creating shock wave through the body. It didn't just break bones, it shattered them. It didn't just pierce tissue and internal organs, it shredded them. And if the ragged, tumbling bullet had enough force to completely go through the body, which it often did, it tore out an exit wound several times the size of the entrance wound.

During the Civil War, many bullets were made primarily in factories. A factory worker, using a machine, could make as many as 3,000 bullets an hour. Prior to 1860, a soldier sometimes needed to make bullets by hand in the field. This not only took a long time, but also meant a soldier could only make a few bullets an hour. (Often, bullets in museums are white in appearance. When a lead bullet is buried in dirt for a long time, it will often rust to a whitish color. This is created by the chemical process of oxidation.)

Ammunition for Civil War small arms was more varied than the weapons themselves. The period of the early 1860s was one of great ammunition development. Patentees constantly bombarded ordnance officers with new bullet and cartridge ideas for standard arms. Weapons inventors and manufacturers, most notably carbines and pistols, were inclined to make weapons that required special, patented cartridges.

There was also a great variety of ammunition because neither the North nor the South had a central laboratory or arsenal for fabricating small arms ammunition. Although the Confederacy made an effort at Macon, Georgia, the war did not last long enough for that facility to be fully established. In the North, it does not seem that a central facility was even considered. Civil War arms ammunition ran the gamut, from simple to complex. It was possible to load most weapons with loose powder and ball, but this was seldom necessary. Both Federal and Confederate ordnance departments were more than able to supply the needs of their troops in the field.

Civil War bullets were manufactured in several ways. Casting was the least satisfactory method. It required that the lead and mold both be extremely hot to prevent layering and air bubble entrapment, which impaired the accurate flight of the bullet. Round balls were made by machines using pressure or compressions, making balls more uniform in size and weight, smoother and more solid, increasing accuracy.

With the adoption by the U.S. Army of the minie ball, a machine for their production was ordered to be constructed at the Allegheny Arsenal, Pittsburgh, Pennsylvania. By 1863, these machines were also in operation in Benicia, California, Frankford (Philadelphia), St. Louis, Watervliet, New York, and Allegheny arsenals.

The most common ammunition used with muzzleloaders was the paper wrapped cartridge. The bullet and powder were encased in paper, and it required the soldier to open the cartridge and pour the powder down the barrel, then the bullet free from paper was rammed down the barrel. Combustible cartridges were best suited for breech-loading carbines and rifles. The cartridge case was made of thin nitrated paper, linen, membrane, collodion, or another substance that would be completely consumed by the powder charge explosion. It did not need to be opened to expose the powder.

The most advanced types of ammunition were those that were internally primed, such as the rim-fire, pin-fire, cup-fire and teat-fire. Several steps were used to produce these bullets with metal casing.

In the great variety manufactured, there were some really interesting bullets. The Williams Cleaner was a federal bullet. A thin zinc disk was attached to the base of the bullet that, upon being fired, would flatten and take the rifling, scraping away the fouling built up in the bore. The patent was applied for in May 1861, and granted in December,

The buck and ball cartridge was designed for the Revolutionary War. During the War of 1812, it was standard military issue. It contained a .69 caliber round shot and three additional buckshot of .31 caliber. The larger shot was intended to strike the primary target, with the buckshot scattering and causing additional injury. During the Civil War, these cartridges were manufactured in the millions. Buck and ball specimens have been found at every Civil War battlefield. Recently a walnut tree fell in the Richmond Cemetery. As it was being cut apart for removal, a buckshot from a buck and ball was found lodged in the wood. The wood split from around the buckshot.

The Shaler three-piece conical bullet was a .58 caliber bullet invented by Ruben and Ira Shaler of New York. After discharge, the three sections were intended to spread apart with greater accuracy than the buck and ball. There are five known variations of the Shaler that are generally associated with the Army of the Potomac.

In November 1861, a letter written to the Federal War Department offered the sale of Gardiner's explosive shell. With Samuel Gardiner's bullet, the cavity within the shell was packed with an explosive compound of phosphorus and fulminate. It was fused to explode in one and a fourth seconds after ignition. In 1862, Gardiner had a successful test of the bullet at West Point. While there was some support for purchasing Gardiner's, General James Ripley, who headed the Ordnance Department, was shocked by the barbarism of the round. A comment from the Ordnance Department was "We think it is enough to shoot a man, without afterward blowing him up." As word of the exploding bullet spread, public sentiment mounted to disallow its use.

Swords

The American Civil War saw a dramatic shift in tactics from wars in the past, including the first real combat use of such the rifled musket. These weapons, more accurate than the smoothbore weapons to have come before them, caused the demise of the edged weapons that had before dominated warfare. Fighting moved from close range, melee battle, and hand-to-hand to medium range shootouts and long range artillery duels.

Nevertheless, both Southern and Northern forces were issued with a variety of swords depending on their fighting style; cavalrymen, infantry, artillerymen, marines, and officers had distinct weapons issued to them with the intention, once the initial exchange of artillery and musket fire had abated, of defeating the enemy. Cavalrymen, in particular, accustomed to covering ground quickly and attacking enemy infantry from a mounted position, were issued with a variety of single-edged sabers designed for slashing and hacking. However, the American Civil War included advancements in projectile weaponry including the deployment of the first Gatling guns, machine guns that essentially rendered cavalry charges both obsolete and suicidal. Nevertheless, such tactics and the associated weaponry remained the mainstay of western armies until the First World War.

The use of edged weapons did not die out so easily. Around about the time of the American Civil War, the sword bayonet was being developed. This twenty-three inch blade mounted on the end of a rifle or musket turned the slow-to-reload medium range weapon into an effective spear for close range work. Though the sword gradually lost favor, the bayonet has been successfully deployed by modern armies.

The Model 1840 Noncommissioned Officers' Sword was based on a German infantry sword used by British troops during the Napoleonic

Wars. The sword had a thirty-one inch blade, a cast brass hilt resembling the more expensive wire-wrapped leather grips, and a leather scabbard rather than the steel used by cavalry troopers and officers.

Swords and sabers were an important part of every officer's dress uniform on both sides of the Civil War. Among the enlisted men in the Union army, however, only sergeants, cavalrymen, select artillerymen, and musicians were issued swords, and rather plain ones at that, since they were designed more for fighting than dress. The swords issued to officers tended to be much more ornate and served as a symbol of rank rather than a fighting weapon. Only the sabers carried by cavalry and light artillery officers were actual weapons, though they weren't used as often as rifles and sidearms.

The vast majority of regulation swords issued to Union soldiers were patterned on weapons of the French army, and most were made by private firms or purchased from foreign manufacturers. European sword makers provided nearly all officers' blades, which were based on an 1850 pattern. It was also common for citizens and military subordinates to give specially made presentation swords to officers as tokens of appreciation for exceptional service or bravery. Most of these ornate swords, which were quite expensive, were for formal occasions rather than actual fighting.

Swords held much greater appeal among Confederate soldiers because they harkened back to an era of chivalry and romance, an era that was still in effect in the midcentury South. As in the North, swords were both a symbol of rank and a fighting weapon, though they were rarely used. Instead, cavalry and artillery forces relied on sidearms for self-defense because they were reliable and effective. Confederate infantry officers commonly wore swords but used them in combat only when absolutely necessary.

The **Model 1840 Cavalry Saber** was based on the 1822 French hussar's saber. Unlike its replacement the Model 1860 Light Cavalry Saber, the M1840 has a ridge around its quillon, a leather grip wrapped in wire (rather than grooves cut into the wooden handle), and a flat, slotted throat. It is forty-four inches long with a thirty-five inch blade and weighs roughly two and a half pounds.

The M1840 was designed for slashing and because of its heavy flat-backed blade was given the nickname "Old Wristbreaker." It was adopted due to the army's dissatisfaction with its predecessor—the model

1833 dragoon saber, the first cavalry sword adopted by the US Army. The iron-hilted M1833 was based on a Napoleonic-era British sword used by heavy cavalry and reputed to be only good for cutting butter.

The 1840 saber was used during the U.S.-Mexican War by US Cavalry. The main contractors were Ames of Cabotville, Horstmann, and Tiffany, but due to the large number of swords required, at least 1,000 were made in Germany by S&K and imported. Some troopers used Prussian sabers as an alternative, which in contrast to the M1840 had straight blades. When production ceased in 1858, over 23,700 had been made. During the Civil War, it continued to be issued to Union Cavalry and was more readily available than the M1860.

The **Model 1860 Light Cavalry Saber** (also known as the M1862 as this was when the first 800 were issued) was used by US cavalry from the American Civil War until the end of the Indian wars. Some were still in use during the Spanish-American War. It was forty-one inches long with a thirty-five inch by one inch blade and weighed two pounds, four ounces alone or three pounds, ten ounces with an iron scabbard. The M1860 saber received its name to distinguish it from the larger and heavier Model 1840 Heavy Cavalry Saber that it replaced. Like its predecessor, it had a brass guard, leather-wrapped grip and steel scabbard, but unlike the M1840 it was smaller and easier to handle.

By the end of the Civil War over 300,000 1860 sabers had been produced: 200,000 by Ames, 32,000 by Roby, and many more by firms such as Tiffany and Co, Glaze, Justice, and Emerson and Silver. M1860s were carried not only by cavalry, but also by many infantry and staff officers as the regulation Model 1850 Army Staff & Field Officers' Sword.

Knives

Knives may be made with fixed blades for which a sheath is used to carry the knife, or they made be folding blades. Pocket knives are folders. They may have been termed clasp knives. A common fixed blade knife in the Civil War was the bowie knife. This is usually pronounced BOO-ee. This was a fighting knife used by Colonel James Bowie in the early nineteenth century. It became popular after his use of that style of knife in the Sandbar Fight, a 1827 duel on a Mississippi River sandbar across from Natchez. The first bowie was designed by Rezin Bowie, brother of James. The most famous version of the bowie was designed by Jim Bowie and made by James Black, Arkansas, in 1830. According to an 1847 article, the bowie knife was originally designed to fill the need for a wearable, convenient close combat weapon—a short sword much shorter than the saber or other swords of the day, yet still possessing a heavy blade. It was used in a slashing attack.

Frank G. Carpenter, a distinguished 19th Century journalist and author, wrote a lengthy profile of Cassius Marcellus Clay, from Whitehall in Madison County, Kentucky. He referred to Clay as the foremost bowie-knife fighter of the 19th Century. In his autobiography, Clay does not mention writing a manual on bowie knife fighting. No one recalled ever seeing a copy.

The earliest known pocket knives were found at Hallstatt and dated back to 600 B.C., made with a bone handle and crude, yet simple, folding blade design. First century Romans created the first folding pocket knife. These were for easy carrying for soldiers. The Roman pocket knife was about three inches long when shut, made without a spring or nail nick, the groove used to open the blade. The handles were often elaborately carved. One pocket knife surviving from the first century features an ivory handle skillfully carved into the shape of an armored gladiator.

Until the 18th century, the only kind of pocket knife generally available was a jack knife, a heavy tool with one blade that closed into a groove in the handle. This knife was designed in the 16th Century by Jacques de Liege of France.

In the early 17th century, knives were made with a puzzle locking mechanism, some very intricate. The puzzle knife was quickly superseded by a back spring mechanism, still popular today. Obadiah Barlow began making barlows in the late 17th century. Later, cutlers began using springs to secure the blade in both the open and closed positions. This provided a safer, firmer tool. As the craft improved, multi-bladed tools began to appear. Improved steel resulted from the use of coke, bar iron, and crucible melting resulted in better knife blades. Modern steelmaking began in 1858 with Henry Bessemer's pig iron process, letting him produce large quantities cheaply. Pig iron has a very high carbon content.

The penknife was the very popular. A penknife was a specialized pocketknife with one blade opening at each end of the handle. The smaller of the two blades was used to trim and sharpen quill pens. Throughout the 18th and 19th centuries, anyone who wrote had to own a penknife. Foreign makers common during the Civil War were from Solingen, Germany; Sheffield, England in the United Kingdom; or perhaps an individual carried a Sabatier brand from Thiers, France. The single blade folding fruit knife, first made in the 18th century was also popular. Used for cutting fruit, the blade was usually of gold, silver or silver plate, which would better resist the corrosion of acid in fruit.

The Sheffield cutlers in the 19th Century began fitting pocket knives with other tools. Buttonhooks, files, leather borers, tweezers, gimlets, saws, and specialized blades were common. The Norfolk Sportman's Knife, manufactured in 1851, was fitted with seventy-five blades. Joseph Rogers and Sons, Ltd, introduced in 1822 a knife with 1,822 blades, and a new blade was added each year until the year 2000. An extremely popular fixed blade was made by Wade and Butcher from Sheffield from 1819-1918. The butcher knife, made by many companies, continues to be popular today.

American knives from the Civil War period were often made by cutlers operating small businesses. Until the 20th century, all knives were made by hand. In addition to James Black, other notable cutlers were Daniel Searles, New Orleans, and John Russell, Massachusetts, whose Green River Knives began to be popular in 1840.

> There were many large knives in use, fixed blade and folders. The first bowie knife designed by Rezin Bowie for his brother James Bowie as a hunting knife was possibly smithed in 1827 by a blacksmith Jess Clift from an old file. It was 9 ½ inches long, 1 ½ inches wide and had a crossguard (finger guard). Knives of a variety of styles were referred to as bowie knives, including many knives made before 1827.

Cannons

There were two general types of artillery weapons used during the Civil War: smoothbores and rifles. Smoothbore artillery refers to cannons that are not rifled. Smoothbores included howitzers and guns. Further classifications were based on the type of metal used, typically bronze or iron, either cast or wrought, with some examples of steel produced. Additionally, the artillery was often identified by the year of the design in the Ordnance Department records.

Six pound guns were made of bronze. Twelve pound Napoleons were bronze, as were twelve pound and twenty-four pound field howitzers, twelve pound mountain howitzers and the fourteen pound James Rifle. The ten pound and twenty pound Parrott rifles were iron, as was the twelve pound, breech loading Whitworth rifle. The three inch ordnance rifle was wrought iron. A weapon was referred to as a particular "pounder" based on the weight of the projectile it was capable of firing.

Wrought iron has a low carbon content. It also has fibrous inclusions called "slag," giving it a grain like wood. Wrought iron is tough, malleable, ductile, and easily welded. Cast iron is made from pig iron and has a high carbon content. It is brittle, but has excellent machinability and is resistant to deformity and wear.

It was standard practice to mix guns and howitzers into batteries. Six pound field guns were typically matched with twelve pound howitzers, nine and twelve pound field guns with twenty-four pound howitzers. Smoothbore guns were designed to fire solid shot projectiles at high velocity over low trajectories in the open. The barrels were longer and called for higher charges of powder. By far the most popular smooth gun was the Napoleon, generally the 1857 model. It was lighter weight than previous models and could be pulled by a six-horse draft. It used a heavier projectile than earlier models because of the larger bore.

The Napoleon was named after Napoleon III of France. It was widely admired for its safety, reliability, and killing power, especially at close range. The napoleon was first used in America in 1857. The federal version can be recognized by the flared front end of the barrel. Confederate napoleons were produced in at least six variations, most of which had straight muzzles. There are, however, eight Confederate catalogued survivors with muzzle swells. There are four iron Confederate napoleons from the Tredegar Iron Works.

Howitzers were short barreled weapons designed to fire explosive shells at a higher trajectory of possibly five or six degrees elevation. They had a shorter range. Howitzers were the weapon of choice if opposing forces were concealed behind fortifications or hidden by the terrain. Howitzers used lower powder charges.

While rifling in cannon, as in rifled muskets, caused the projectile to spin and increased the accuracy, adding rifling to the barrel made it more difficult and expensive to manufacture and increased the length of the tube. Most rifled guns in the Civil War were muzzle loaded, but a small number of breech loaded guns were used. Muzzle means it was loaded from the front end of the barrel. Breech means the projectile was loaded in the back end of the barrel.

The three-inch ordnance rifle (76 mm) was the most widely used rifled gun during the Civil War. It was invented by John Griffen and was extremely durable with a barrel made of wrought iron. These were primarily made at the Phoenix Iron Company of Phoenixville, Pennsylvania. The three-inch ordnance rifle was deadly at any distance under a mile.

The Parrott rifle, invented by Robert Parker Parrott, was manufactured in different sizes, from ten pounders to the rare three hundred pounder. Parrotts were made with a combination of cast iron and wrought iron. The cast iron improved the accuracy but was brittle enough to fracture when fired often. A large wrought iron reinforcing band was overlaid on the breech to reinforce it. James rifles were an early solution to the need for rifled artillery at the start of the war. With a process invented by Charles T. James, small smoothbores were reworked with rifling. Although quite accurate, bronze rifling would wear quickly, and these weapons were not favored for very long. The Whitworth was designed by Joseph Whitworth and made in England. It was a rare gun during the Civil War, but it was an interesting forerunner of modern artillery in that it was breech loaded. An engineering magazine wrote in 1864 that the Whitworth fired ten shots with a lateral deviation of only five inches. This was a very high degree of accuracy. While there were several reasons for variance, a velocity of 1,440 feet per second was common for a cannon projectile.

Mountain Howitzer

U.S. Model 1841 Mountain Howitzer was a twelve pound, smoothbore with a 3.3" powder chamber and a bronze tube, with a weight of approximately 220 pounds, The first model was produced in 1835 and standardized in 1841. It had a range of 1,000 yards at 5 degrees of elevation. Shell fragments might reach an additional 300 yards.

Ammunition was a shell, a hollowed cannonball filled with black powder, Spherical Case Shot, same was similar with shell containing .69 caliber lead balls; Canister was tin cylinder filled with 148 .69 caliber lead balls packed in sawdust. All ammunition was fixed, meaning the powder charge of one half pound of cannon grade black powder was attached directly to the round with a wooden sabot. A sabot is a "shoe" that is sealed to the ammunition in order to trap propellant gases. This raises the muzzle velocity of the projectile. When the sabot encountered air, it tore apart.

The mountain howitzer was a small, lightweight cannon used where larger field pieces were unable to pass due to narrow, roads, lack of roads or rough terrain. It was originally designed for mountain use with a "pack carriage." It disassembled and fit onto three mules or horses. The pack carriage did not use a limber, but would have the gun on one animal, the carriage on a second and the ammunition on a third. The carriage weighed 157 pounds, and each wheel weighed sixty-five pounds. Mountain howitzers were used by artillery and infantry units, but their portability made them especially suited for use by cavalry. A small, portable forge was carried to shoe horses or repair small metal items. It weighed only 31.5 pounds with a bellows weighing 18.25 pounds.

A prairie carriage was adapted which had a limber and caisson. A limber is a two-wheeled cart that supports an artillery piece by carrying ammunition in a chest that is called a caisson. Prairie carriages had two caissons which could be detached from the limber.

The pack carriage was small, narrow and lightweight with a 38" wheel designed to be taken apart. The prairie carriage had a 42" wheel and a wider wheel base which prevented it from flipping over as easily.

A mountain howitzer was really light weight in comparison to other twelve pounders. The field howitzer was heavier than a mountain howitzer with a field carriage. The field howitzer weighed 788 pounds with a carriage weighing 900 pounds. A twelve pound napoleon smoothbore field gun weighed over 1,200 pounds with a 1,100 pound carriage.

A field howitzer could fire a projectile about two hundred yards further than a mountain howitzer. A napoleon could fire a projectile 1,600 yards. Time fuses were used in howitzer shells. They were fuse paste packed into paper or wood. Each fuse had a different color for a different time. Another common time fuse was the Bormann, which had a fuse trail laid onto a round flat metal like a coin and pressed onto another round metal. Numbers to show seconds or part of seconds were on the outside. A mountain howitzer used a six-man gun crew, two or three persons less than a crew for a larger field piece. The first model was scaled down to a six pound version, less reliable than the twelve pound model.

Chapter Nine

Remembering the Civil War

Causes

A cause is a person or thing which gives rise to an action, condition, situation or phenomenon, such as "the cause of the argument or accident is not clear." Or a cause is a principle, aim, or movement, which through deep commitment, a person is prepared to defend or advocate, as in "she devoted her life to the cause of children's health."

One notable type of cause is a cause célèbre, an issue or incident that arouses widespread controversy, outside campaigning, and heated public debate. The term is most commonly used in relation to celebrated legal cases. This designation originated in 1763 in a 37-volume collection of well-known French court decisions of the 17th and 18th centuries. Cause célèbre was used after that in the English language, but became much more common in the United Kingdom after the 1894 conviction in France of French artillery officer Alfred Dreyfus for espionage, a case that attracted worldwide attention. This followed other scandals hinting that the French Republic was in danger of collapse.

Sometimes public attention can obscure the facts rather than clarify them. John Humffreys Parry, in his book *Whistler v. Ruskin: An Attorney's Story of a Famous Trial*, wrote, "The true story of many a cause célèbre is never made manifest in the evidence given or in the advocates' orations, but might be recovered from old papers when the dust of ages has rendered them immune from scandal."

For many people, the cause célèbre of the U.S. Civil War is slavery, and for a few, it is the only cause. All other suggestions of cause are argued against vehemently. A person's opinion on cause strongly influences that individual's perspective on whether any commemoration, either ceremony or battle reenactment, or any reenactor participating in an event, or any symbol of the former Confederate States of America is to be tolerated without protest.

There is ample evidence to support the advocating of slavery as the singular cause of the Civil War. The Confederate Constitution explicitly protected slavery. The articles of secession of the Southern states repeatedly point to slavery along with other, often related, reasons for leaving the Union. The articles from South Carolina lean heavily on the Declaration of Independence as a legal justification for secession, and on events leading up to and through the composition of the Constitution establishing our government. Slavery was mentioned a half dozen times and is shown to be of primary concern even though other arguments are more substantial in their wording. Of significance is the statement, "A geographical line has been drawn across the Union, and all the States north of that line have united in the election of a man to the high office of President of the United States, whose opinions and purposes are hostile to slavery." It states that Lincoln has declared that no government can endure half slave and half free, and the public believes that slavery must face ultimate extinction.

The articles from Georgia, along with a recitation of other grievances, mention slavery over a dozen times. Abolitionists, Republicans, and their allies were condemned for attempting to subvert institutions, excite insurrection and servile war in Georgia. The articles from Mississippi, as though in a power point presentation, state, "Our position is thoroughly identified with the institution of slavery—the greatest material interest of the world. Its labor supplies the product which constitutes by far the largest and most important portions of commerce of the earth…a blow at slavery is a blow at commerce and civilization."

Texas noted in her articles that the United States proposed to the free, sovereign, independent Republic of Texas that on March 1, 1845, Texas should become a member of the United States, knowing at the time that Texas was a slave-hold commonwealth. Texas complained that the United States excluded Southern States with their institutions from the territories bordering the Pacific Ocean. The articles also complained that the United States had not protected the people of Texas from the murderous frays of banditti from Mexico or from Indian savages. Texas asserted "that the servitude of the African race, as existing in these States, is mutually beneficial to bond and free…."

In a brief ordinance, Virginia stated that the commonwealth had ratified the Constitution of the United States "having declared that the powers granted under the said Constitution were derived from the peo-

ple of the United States, and might be resumed whensoever the same should be perverted to their injury and oppression; the Federal Government, having perverted said powers, not only to injury of the people of Virginia, but to the oppression of the Southern Slaveholding States."

In a short time, eleven states left the Union: South Carolina, Mississippi, Florida, Alabama, Georgia, Texas, Virginia, Arkansas, North Carolina, and Tennessee. For all of them, slavery was a concern; however, the background of the delegates to conventions and legislatures must be considered. Property qualifications for office had ended in 1860, but at the end of that year and early 1861, the incentive was still strong to elect those with property. Not all property owners had plantations, but propertied officials either owned slaves or had the means to afford them. Members of the secession conventions were voting their personal interests. Four slave states did not secede: Kentucky, Missouri, Maryland, and Delaware. Secession was approved in parts of Kentucky and Missouri. In New Jersey, slavery had been abolished in 1846, but four counties retained "apprentices for life," which the Federal census listed as slaves. Having legally abolished slavery, New Jersey did not secede.

Kentucky was an anomaly. It had the third highest number of slave owners, 38,000. Virginia and Georgia ranked first and second, but Kentucky had almost as many slave owners as Georgia. Like most slave states, there were not many large farms or plantations; 22,000 of Kentucky's slave holders owned four or fewer slaves. Slaves made up 19.5 per cent of the commonwealth's population.

The Commonwealth of Kentucky was bordered by three slave states and three free states. It was connected by railroad to Tennessee and to Ohio. Its rivers accessed the lower South and the East Coast. Kentucky's most ardent proponents of slavery came from the state's south and west regions. In these sections, lifestyle most resembled that of the lower South. A leading export was slaves being sold into the other slave states. In Kentucky, instead of cotton, rice and sugar being major crops, tobacco and hemp were the cash crops. This tobacco was not burley, however, which did not appear commercially until after 1866. In the north and east of the state, Kentuckians were ideologically and economically moving away from slavery. The economy was diversifying. More people were growing grains and cereals, breeding horses, cattle, and swine or turning to manufacturing. At first, Kentucky tried to remain neutral. Unionists backed neutrality because they disap-

proved of both southern secession and northern coercion of southern states. Others leaning toward the Confederate cause backed neutrality because they feared that if Kentucky chose a side, she would choose the Union.

As states began seceding in December 1860 and May 1861, Kentucky Governor Beriah Magoffin issued a formal proclamation of neutrality and advised people in the state to remain at home and away from the fight. Magoffin did not think slavery was a moral, stoical, or political evil, but he opposed secession for two reasons. He believed sectional differences could be worked out through mediation. And, he feared an invasion of the state if Kentucky left the Union.

Slavery as a cause encompassed several aspects. For some, the emphasis might be lifestyle, for others there was social control or economics. The profitability of slavery is an enduring economic question. Since workers were paid nothing, a business that used slaves ought to have been profitable. This should have been true even if slaves were loaned to a business such as the large slaughter house and meat packing plant in Madison County employing at maximum eighty-three slaves. In such a case, slave owners were paid for services rendered by slaves.

Robert Fogel and Stanley Engerman in their book *Time on the Cross*, suggested that slavery in the South was lucrative for plantation owners. Alfred Conrad and John Meyer calculated the rate of return on investing in slaves. In their study, slave capital earned at least equal returns to those other forms of capital investment. Rate of return on slaves could be as high as thirteen percent. Contrary to this, economist John Elliott Cairnes reckoned that slavery stifled economic growth in the South. Slaves were generally prohibited from education, and as workers they were reluctant to learn and use new farming techniques. Soils were depleted more quickly. Southern farms lost competitiveness to Northern farms.

Ralph Anderson and Robert Gallman wrote that slavery inhibited trade within the South, and as a result, stifled the growth of towns and villages. Slave owners found it easier to produce something themselves rather than spend scarce money to buy it. Eugene Genovese said that antebellum South was not focused on seeking a profit. Slave owners were more interested on flaunting their vast plantations and huge reserves of slaves than they were on profits. Rational economic decisions were sacrificed to lavish lifestyle.

Economies that relied on slaves may have, over the long term, been at a disadvantage. The economic contradictions of slavery may have led to its inevitable demise. However, slavery had effects on other economies. Douglass North, a Noble Prize recipient, argued that the expansion of Southern plantation slavery encouraged development of the Midwest through the South's demand for certain foodstuffs. And, the need for credit on plantations may have promoted the growth of banking.

A study of plantation profitability by Jan Richard Heier, Auburn University, shows that Southern states generated an unprecedented amount of wealth through production of vast amounts of cotton, sugar and tobacco. From 1820 to 1860, products grown in the South made up eighty per cent of the value of all exports from the United States. In 1860, cotton exports alone reached $192 million. This cotton ran the textile mills of the United Kingdom and New England.

Southern agricultural reformer Thomas Affleck, in his study, *The Cotton Plantation Record and Account Book*, first published in 1847 or 1848, outlined accounting methods. Because of the size and scope of Southern businesses, sophisticated accounting systems should have been used, and some owners did use these. Others wrote down business activities infrequently, often only once a year. This fed the perception that plantations were crude business ventures. This fostered a belief that plantations were not profitable, which was far from the truth. In that context, an attack on slavery was an attack on Southern businesses and wealth.

While the productivity of slave labor was undeniable, by the late 1700s, production was deteriorating and prices declining. It was the patent of the cotton engine in 1794 by American inventor Eli Whitney that ultimately transformed Southern economy and prosperity. Prior to this, separating cotton seeds from fiber was highly labor intensive, but the cotton gin changed this. The need for cheap labor, specifically labor from slaves, grew rapidly. Threats to slave labor were threats to the economy and each threat had to be addressed and repulsed.

From the Northern perspective, this came to be viewed at the Great Slave Power Conspiracy. In his 1949 book *Fettered Freedom*, Russel B. Nye said that it was not until after 1845 that the various abolitionists developed an effective way to bring together all their arguments under one common heading. Abolitionists came to the conclusion that there existed a secret agreement among slaveholders to foist slavery upon the nation, destroy civil liberty, extend slavery into the territories, including more enslavement of white persons, reopen the slave trade which had in itself been quite lucrative, control Federal policies and form a controlling national slave aristocracy. This greatly shaped Northern and Western thought on slavery. The aggressive attitude of the Southerners in Congress fueled this suspicion. After the Compromise of 1850, Slave Power became a primary object of attack by abolitionists.

Frank L. Owsley in a 1941 article entitled "The Fundamental Cause of the Civil War: Egocentric Sectionalism" blamed both sections to some extent. He said there were three basic manifestations of that egocentric sectionalism in 1861. First was the habit of the dominant section, which had the larger share in the control of the Federal government of considering itself the nation and its people the American people. It considered the minority group as a faction, with its interests, institutions, and way of life as un-American, unworthy of friendly consideration and the object of attack.

The second manifestation was the perennial attempt of both sections to gain or maintain political ascendancy over the federal government by destroying the sectional balance of power. The third and most dangerous was the failure to observe comity of sections. That is, the people in one section failed to respect the people in the other section. By the spring of 1861, this created a state of mind in the Southern people in which they felt it both abhorrent and dangerous to continue to live under the same government with the people of the North. So profound was this feeling among the bulk of the Southern population that they were prepared to fight a long and devastating war to gain separation.

Arthur Schlesinger in a 1922 essay entitled "The State Rights Fetish" said that writers and teachers were accustomed to use the phrase as if it furnished a fundamental explanation of the leading up to the Civil War. Readers are likely to get the impression that the state rights theory was a peculiar product of the South. Prior to the Civil War, however, almost every state at some point had declared its own sovereignty and denounced as almost treasonable any similar declarations by other states. Economic interest or some other local advantage usually determined the attitude of states and parties toward constitutional construction.

The first declaration of state rights appeared in the Virginia and Kentucky resolutions of 1798 and 1799 drafted by Madison and Jefferson as a protest against the Federalists in Congress passing the Alien and Sedition Acts and other laws that seemed to violate a clear reading of the Constitution. Senator Robert Toombs of Georgia in a speech before his state legislature in 1860 blamed economic policy. He said that from the beginning of the Union, Northern states had a desire and purpose to use the Union for their own benefit. They demanded a monopoly of ship-building and got a prohibition against the sale of foreign ships to U. S. citizens. They demanded a monopoly of the coastal trade in order to get higher freights than they could get in open competition. Fishermen in Massachusetts and New England received public funding on their catching codfish, Northern production of iron, wood, spinning and weaving of cloth all received Federal protection.

James M. McPherson in *Ordeal by Fire: The Civil War and Reconstruction*, 1982, said the United States, particularly the North, was undergoing modernization, heavy investment in overhead capital; rapid increases in output per capita resulting from technological innovation and the shift from labor intensive to capital intensive production; urbanization; expansion of education, literacy and mass communications; a value system that emphasized change rather than tradition, and a shift from rural toward cosmopolitan and pluralistic.

The South was the great exception to much of the modernization. Southern economy grew, but it did not develop a substantial commercial and industrial base. Southern economy was labor intensive and upward mobility was impossible for the half of the Southern labor force that was held in slavery. Southern commitment to education was weak and nearly half of its people were illiterate. Antebellum Southern agriculture underwent little technological change after the cotton gin.

James G. Randall in a 1947 revisionist interpretation entitled "A Blundering Generation," said the movement toward war tends to be explained in terms of great forces, something elemental which is understandable and is an explanation for war. He maintained that these broad national urges dignified war-making. Writers talk about such a grand cause in which a whole section was drawn into war as though everyone in the section believed in that cause. He said that this was a great fallacy.

He said it was hard for Southerners to accept the victory of a sectional party in 1860, even though it was no part of the Republican program to end slavery in the South. Southerners cared little for taking slaves into the territories, and Republicans cared so little that they did not prohibit slavery in territorial laws of February and March 1861. If one word were selected to account for the war, it would not be slavery or economic grievance or state rights or diverse populations, it would be fanaticism, on both sides, accompanied by misunderstanding, misrepresentation and politics.

He said that other revisionist historians have correctly pointed out that little was actually at stake. Slavery did not go into New Mexico or Arizona. Kansas, after having been opened to slavery for six years, had only two slaves. The Dred Scott decision declared an already repealed law unconstitutional. John Brown's raid had no significant support in the North and roused no visible enthusiasm among Southern slaves. American society was still new and was ill equipped to meet any shocks, however weak. As Henry James has noted, it was a land which had "No sovereign, no court, no personal loyalty, no aristocracy, no castles…no great universities nor public schools, no political society—in short, no resistance to strain."

Michael F. Holt in his 1978 *The Political Crisis of the 1850s*, rejected slavery and cultural differences as causes of the Civil War. He said that for at least thirty years, political leaders had recognized that the way to build political parties, create voter loyalty, gain support and win elections was to find issues or positions on issues, which distinguished them from their opponents. The most successful tactic was to pose as a champion of republican values and to portray opponents as anti-republican, unlawful, tyrannical or aristocratic. Politicians agitated and exploited sectional grievances in order to build a winning party.

While there are many viewpoints on what caused the Civil War, there seems to be no disagreement with the opinion expressed on occasion that if people from Africa had not been brought to America, there would have been no war. Even though many in the North were opposed to slavery, there was some hesitancy from many in fighting the war. Some people did not believe the federal government had the right to enter a war over slavery. For others, while abolition of slavery began in Europe in the last quarter of the 18th century, this was still a relatively new concept. The earliest abolitions were in Portugal in

1777 and in Scotland in 1778. France ended the slave trade in 1818, Upper Canada in 1819, Hawaii initially in 1819, Brazil in 1831 and the Ottoman Empire in 1847. After years of promotion by William Wilberforce, the United Kingdom stopped slave trade in 1807 and ended slavery throughout the empire in 1834. Russia ended slavery in 1861.

In both the North and the South, many people had a loyalty to their own states that was much stronger than to the Union. Some Northerners doubted that it was right for one state to invade another. Many Southerners joined the war to protect their state or their own home. Cherokees in North Carolina and the tribes in Indian Country found themselves surrounded by Confederate troops or on occasion, Union troops, and knew they should either join or risk loss of land. None of the Indian tribes had a strong affinity for either the Union or for the new Confederate government.

Others understood President Lincoln's position. The war was fought to restore the Union. Abraham Lincoln was very much opposed to slavery. He told a correspondent in 1864, "If slavery is not wrong, nothing is wrong. I cannot remember when I did not so think, and feel." In his 1860 Cooper Union address, his research indicated to him that the Framers of the Constitution wanted to place slavery on a course to ultimate extinction. He believed that most of the Framers thought slavery was an evil that contradicted the ideal of equality. At Gettysburg, he envisioned a nation dedicated to equality in a nation that had a "government of the people by the people and for the people.

Abraham Lincoln was devoted to the Declaration of Independence and the Constitution, which though written eleven years apart, he saw as one continuous process. He said, "I have never had a feeling politically that did not spring from the sentiments embodied in the Declaration of Independence." His strongest complaint against slavery was that it showed how far the nation had fallen from its founding ideals. "Near eighty years ago we began by declaring that all men are created equal, but how from that beginning we have run down to the other declaration, that for some men to enslave others is a sacred right of self-government."

Though opposed to slavery, he took his oath of office as President seriously, to preserve, protect and defend the Constitution of the United States. He looked at the opening paragraph which expressed the six reasons for establishing this government, the first of which was to form a more perfect union. He reasoned that if some states were allowed to secede, then it would be a less perfect union. He looked at the Declaration as setting the ideals, and at the Constitution as doing precisely what such a document should do, to show how the government addressing those ideals is to be constituted, designate its component parts, how they are assembled and the basic law under which the government shall operate. Since the Constitution was an embodiment of the ideals of the Declaration, the specific ideal that all men are created equal had to be what the Framers intended for everyone in the Republic.

When President Lincoln eventually moved against slavery in the Emancipation Proclamation, while it mirrored his beliefs about slavery, it was done with the first intent to further the cause of preservation of the Union. The United Kingdom and France had questioned the federal embargo of Confederate ports. Their cotton supplies were low, but Egyptian cotton began to meet this need. The French and British concern was that the Civil War was keeping both countries from selling many of their civilian goods in the states. If the Civil War were not about the abolition of slavery, they might consider recognition of the Confederate States of America as a legitimate government.

President Lincoln's concern was that if he issued as Commander in Chief a proclamation declaring freedom for the slaves, how would Kentucky react? He had previously said that if the Union lost Kentucky, he did not think the Federal government could hold Missouri or Maryland, and he thought that the war was lost if he lost all three of these states. He recalled his minister to Russia, Cassius M. Clay, to return to Kentucky where the General Assembly would be in session to ascertain if Kentucky would secede. Clay assured him that it would not. The Civil War, which had not begun as a war against slavery from the Union standpoint, moved in that direction after January 1, 1863.

President Lincoln understood that the proclamation was an executive order and could be reversed by the next president. It was essential that an article of amendment to the Constitution should be introduced and adopted which ended slavery. The 13th article of amendment, which was ratified December 6, 1865, abolished slavery. The 14th amendment, ratified July 9, 1868, granted citizenship and over-turned the Dred Scott ruling. It states that "all persons born or naturalized in the United States, and subject to the jurisdiction thereof, are citizens of the United States...." It specifically did not apply to American Indians. While they were born in the United States, it was reasoned that they were subject to the laws of their own tribal governments. The 15th amendment, ratified February 3, 1870, granted the right to vote by prohibiting persons from being denied the franchise (right to vote) because of race, color or previous condition of servitude.

In a 1988 guest editorial in *The Daily Tar Heel*, H.S. Robinson wrote, "I do not intend to denigrate the honor of the Confederate armies. I admire their courage and loyalty as much as I despise the destruction and hatred that the war engendered.... Let's honor the dead for their sacrifice and, yes, let them lie under the flag for which they fought. The majority of them honestly did not believe they were fighting for slavery. But for God's sake, let's acknowledge that the only nobility to be found in the noble lost cause were the small commonplace nobilities of heroic men and women." This has application in both South and North. In the final analysis, for the approximately 96 per cent of the southern population which did not own slaves, there was no cause célèbre, but la raison de la guerre. The war came and they fought to defend themselves, protect their families and preserve their homes.

Flags

The Confederate battle flag is a controversial, often inflammatory icon (person or thing that is revered or idolized) of American culture. It is important to understand that symbols like what people have learned. The battle flag was not the national flag of the Confederacy, though it was incorporated into the second and third national flags. The Confederate battle flag was not an official flag at the Battle of Richmond, Kentucky, in 1862. Gen. Kirby Smith carried a flag of the Army of East Tennessee, renamed the Army of Kentucky as he entered the commonwealth. His flag was the flag of Scotland. Gen. Cleburne used a blue flag with a white border and white circle in the center. It appears to be the pattern upon which the twentieth century flag of the Commonwealth of Kentucky was designed. There was not been any special flag for Gen. Churchill.

The first Confederate national flag was also known as the Stars and Bars serving from March 4, 1861 to May 1, 1863. It was designed by the Prussian artist Nicola Marschall in Alabama and resembles the flag of the Austrian Empire. The Stars and Bars caused confusion at the First Battle of Bull Run because of its similarity to the U.S. flag. It was the Confederate national flag used at Second Bull Run and the Battle of Richmond, both fought the same weekend. The second national flag, used from May 1, 1863 to March 4, 1965, was called the "Stainless Banner." It was designed by William T. Thompson and William Ross Postell. The third national flag, called the "Blood-stained Banner," was adopted March 4, 1865. It had a red vertical end bar suggested by Major Arthur L. Rogers who maintained that the pure white field could be mistaken for a flag of truce. The First National continued to be used throughout the war.

The flag which has become the center of attention in very recent years was the battle flag of the Army of Northern Virginia, 52 inches square for infantry, 38 inches square for artillery and 32 inches square for cavalry and the rectangle version used by the Army of Tennessee. While navy blue was used for the Northern Virginia flag, a lighter blue was used for the Confederate naval jack. The Army of Northern Virginia was commanded by Gen. Robert E. Lee. After the war, he distanced himself from divisive symbols of the Civil War writing in a letter to the Gettysburg Battlefield Memorial Association, "I think it wiser moreover not to keep open the sores of war." At his request, there were no flags, Confederate or otherwise, displayed at his funeral.

The Reversal Flag, a trans-Mississippi flag with colors reversed, was used by Gen. Richard Taylor after the capture of western Louisiana in 1864. The flag had been made in Cuba and the colors were reversed evidently because of misunderstanding of the description and instructions. Gen. Taylor was the son of President Zachary Taylor.

After the Civil War, the Battle Flag of Northern Virginia, the flag that is usually thought to be the Confederate national flag and is associated with the Confederacy today, turned up occasionally at events to commemorate soldiers, though not often. It was not until 1948 that use of the battle flag re-emerged, probably when Strom Thurmond ran for president under the newly founded States Rights Democratic Party, also called the Dixiecrats. The party platform was clear: "We stand for the segregation of the races." At campaign stops, Thurmond used the American flag, state flags and the Confederate battle flag. Use of the flag again surfaced after *Brown vs Board of Education of Topeka, Kansas* in 1954. This was a Supreme Court ruling ordering desegregation of public schools. In 1961, to honor the 100th anniversary of the beginning of the Civil War, South Carolina lawmakers raised the Confederate battle flag over the State House. In 2000, it was moved next to a soldiers' monument under the *2000 Heritage Act*.

The October 2015 edition of *Civil War Times* has two excellent opinion columns on the battle flag. Emmanuel Dabney, National Park Service curator, battlefield guide and devoted Southerner said in a presentation about the flag that "this symbol has an accretion of meanings across time and across different people. It is true that many Confederate troops did not own black people, but the Confederate leaders did not stutter when it came to their support of slavery and white supremacy. The flag represents a gamble to create a separate slaveholding republic." He mentions the 1948 Dixiecrats who opposed Harry Truman's civil rights plank in the Democratic Party platform.

Dabney continues that for African Americans, the flag represents those who denied service at a lunch counter, equal education or access to the ballot box. Removing the flag does not change the fact that disproportionate numbers of minorities are in jails. Nor does it mitigate the unfairness of the justice system. He states that "we also need to make sure we do not further contribute to divisiveness."

Lars Prillaman writes in the same edition that the Confederate battle flag does not belong anywhere near a public statehouse. It should be displayed within its historical context at museums, reenactments or other living history events. But he added that after a lengthy discussion in his home, his small battle flag was furled. He says, "I now feel as though I've hidden away my lineage in a dresser drawer. It's a battle I can't win. I'm sorry, all you Prillaman boys in the 57th Virginia Infantry, who laid it all on the line so many times, captured at the Angle at Gettysburg…I believe you wrong in your cause, but you fought for that cause with your every fiber because at heart you were Americans."

What ought to be clear at this point is that once symbols are set aside, real issues, lingering and deeply held, need to be addressed by people of all races and opinions. For all of them, the truth needs to be confronted even if it doesn't match their agendas or prejudices. Change will continue to be painful as we inch toward that goal of the Declaration of Independence, "We hold these truths to be self-evident, that all men are created equal, that they are endowed by their Creator with certain unalienable Rights, that among these are Life, Liberty and the pursuit of Happiness. That to secure these rights, Governments are instituted among Men, deriving their just powers from the consent of the governed, That whenever any Form of Government becomes destructive of these ends, it is the Right of the People to alter or to abolish it, and to institute new Government, laying its foundations on such principles and organizing its powers in such form, as to them shall seem most likely to effect their Safety and Happiness."

Statues

In 1850, Henry Clay of Kentucky began working on what would become his last great compromise. He had been a National Republican. His political party at this time was called the Whig Party. For two years he negotiated, traveled and spoke, forging a series of agreements that would become known as the *Compromise of 1850*. He died in 1852 before the legislation was enacted by Congress. Stephen A. Douglas, leader of the Democratic Party, worked tirelessly until each provision of the extensive compromise was enacted into law. He understood what politicians have known before and since, that in representative governments such as our republic, leadership requires the ability to speak, to persuade, to negotiate and to compromise.

There have been several modern working relationships that are legendary. Each week, Democratic Senate Majority Leader Lyndon Johnson had lunch with Republican Senate Minority Leader Everett Dirksen. As President, Lyndon Johnson did not have enough votes from the Democratic Party to pass civil rights legislation. He contacted Senator Dirksen, who was able to deliver Republican votes to pass the civil rights laws. When Ronald Reagan, a Republican, was President, Thomas "Tip" O'Neill, a Democrat, was Speaker. They described themselves as two Irishmen who knew when to argue and when to have lunch. After President Reagan was shot, he was in his hospital room much worse than the public realized. Tip O'Neill came to his hospital room, took Reagan's hands and knelt beside his hospital bed. They recited the 23rd Psalm together. It was a friendship which made government work. A few years later, the working relationship between Democratic President Bill Clinton and Republican Speaker Newt Gingrich also allowed people with different points of view to work together. That sense of cooperation is lacking today. Any politician who dares negotiate on controversial legislation risks defeat at the ballot box.

Compromise is needed on the issue of Confederate statues. No one seems to be providing the common sense required. In his book *Lee, The Last Years*, Richmond, Kentucky, resident, Charles Bracelen Flood, now deceased, wrote that after the Civil War, Robert E. Lee promoted conciliation. When a man in Richmond, Virginia, solicited donations for a monument to Stonewall Jackson, Lee declined to contribute. He believed that Confederate monuments would keep alive the passions and memories of the war which he was working to eradicate. He said, "All controversy, I think, will only serve to prolong angry and bitter feelings, and postpone the period when reason and charity may resume their sway." He publicly and repeatedly advised people to move past the war, embrace peace and became model citizens of the United States.

A solution might be rather simple. Instead of being reactive when statues are threatened, supporters need to be pro-active. Agree to removal, but insist that cities place all statues, Confederate and Union, in Civil War parks. Have interpretive signs such as the one in front of the restored slave house at Battlefield Park. Tell the whole story. Tell all the causes of the war. Include a memorial to the freedom of slaves, but get it correct. The first slaves were Natives who were kidnapped by ships patrolling the American coast, and they continued to be enslaved in large numbers. Africans shipped to America on the terrible ships made up the bulk of the slaves. Few things in history compare to the despicable conditions of the Middle Passage. Irish women and Scottish women were imported in sizable numbers as slaves. Asians, particularly Chinese, were brought in as slaves. The category "indentured servant" was used to cover enslavement after importation of slaves was illegal. Remember also all those orphaned children who were captured, enslaved and branded. History parks might in time address treatment of American Indians and boarding schools for Indian children. Honor Native people. Honor those men and boys who fought in the Civil War.

History parks would turn highly negative situations into positive learning opportunities. They could serve to attract visitors to cities, benefit the economy and might finally enable Americans to address those issues which were left unresolved after the Civil War. There are economic and educational benefits, as well as enhancing civic awareness, to have a park also highlight local history. A park could be a small area in town or along a walking trail. The same benefits would be derived from a museum whether located in an entire building or a section of a building, in conjunction with the park, dedicated to local history. A museum regardless of size would help to inform the community and attract tourists.

Reenactors

The centennial of the Civil War held in 1961-65 was essentially a "whites only" event. There was an on-going conflict over Civil Rights. There was also a Cold War that led many people to want to present to the world a united American front devoid of controversy. Federal law establishing a centennial commission encouraged each state to create its own commission. The National Park Service used the centennial to successfully lobby Congress for funds to landscape and reinterpret the battlefields. The Postal Service issued a series of stamps. The first national commission chair, U.S. Grant III, wanted to emphasize large-scale events such as battle reenactments that he thought would appeal to the public. This creation of reenactments was the major legacy of the centennial. The Civil War sesquicentennial commemorated between 2011 and 2015 successfully promoted inclusion of the many different groups of people who participated in the U.S. Civil War, including African Americans, American Indians, Asians and Pacific islanders, Latinos, Canadians and many Europeans. The battle reenactment continues to be popular.

There is no pretense that reenactments actually restage the original battle. At the Battle of Richmond, that would require us to hold a cavalry event on August 29 and a series of three battles on August 30 beginning about 7 a.m. and continuing for twelve hours. The event here is a thirty-minute engagement, which in 2015 had twenty-four horses, fifteen cannon and 300 reenactors. There is a battle scenario that was carefully written to exclude any action contrary to the original event August 29-30, 1862.

Some people insist that reenactments are merely Southerners hoping each event will somehow restore the old Confederacy. The evidence does not support this. In 2015, there were 111 Union reenacting units and eighty-three Confederate reenacting units. For the Union, eighteen of these units are from Pennsylvania, fifteen are from Illinois and twelve are from Texas. Of the Confederate units, Virginia has by far the most with seventeen, Tennessee with eleven, Kentucky with nine and Georgia with eight. For some people, this is camping with a theme, but others are very much interested in history, accuracy and educating the public. There are several excellent groups at the Battle of Richmond who are interested in engagement with visitors and attempt to be authentic. The 12th U.S. Colored Heavy Artillery attends each year. This unit is professional in appearance and is featured in the nine-minute Civil War in Kentucky. There are a few American Indian reenacting units for Civil War events. They schedule participation in those areas where Native units fought.

There are several types of reenacting from Colonial wars, the Revolutionary War to World War Two. Renaissance festivals are a type of reenacting, in effect staging a living history. Mountain Man gatherings are reenacting, celebrating the Rocky Mountain Rendezvous of 1825 through 1840 and experiencing how our ancestors survived on the American frontier. For all of these, reenacting can be an expensive hobby. A Civil War reenactor can easily expect to spend $3000; cavalry and artillery exceed this. Specialized units like medical or topographical engineers have their own unique costs. Some Civil War units acquire a second set of uniforms and will "galvanize" either Union or Confederate as needed to assure there are enough participants in both armies. An Ohio unit that attends the Battle of Richmond weekend is able to galvanize as Confederate, Union or Home Guard. While original weapons might be usable, authentic reproductions are purchased, and these can be a major expense. In addition to uniforms, there are also camping equipment needs, food supplies, travel and usually insurance.

The sesquicentennial has given African American reenactors the opportunity to reclaim history. The Grand Review of the Armies that marched along the streets of Washington, D.C., following the war contained only white troops. Black troops held their own parade in Harrisburg, Pennsylvania, in November 1865, celebrating not only the end of the war, but also the end of slavery. That reinterpretation of the Civil War in the sesquicentennial continues with the ongoing debate over whether the war was mainly fought over slavery or other issues. Ken Burns' 1990 documentary film "The Civil War", successfully acknowledged the roles of both free and enslaved blacks in the conflict. This followed the 1989 movie "Glory", which highlighted the

54th Regiment Massachusetts Volunteer Infantry, one of the most celebrated African American units that fought in the Civil War. The first military unit of freed slaves was the First South Carolina Volunteers. When Richmond, Virginia, fell, colored troops were the first Union soldiers to enter the city, and they escorted Abraham Lincoln into the Confederate capital. Today the mission of black reenactors is to publicize the fact that African Americans were an essential part of the Civil War and the Union's victory.

Mel Reid, a reenactor and retired National Park Service manager, has a home filled with souvenirs and memorabilia illustrating black Civil War fighters. He said, "When I was growing up, the only thing we heard was Lincoln freed the slaves. But if you look, you'll see that most historians now say that if it wasn't for these black soldiers, the North might not have won the war. These guys were freedom fighters. That's what our people should know and that's why we do this."

There are about 50,000 Civil War reenactors. Of this number, about a thousand are black participants, according to Hari Jones, curator of the African American Civil War Museum in Washington, D.C. *Time Magazine* states that the number of reenactors reached its peak in about 1986 but has been on the decline since that year. The number is still high. Civil War movies rely on reenactors to fill the ranks. Well known Civil War movies are "Glory," "Gettysburg." "Gods and Generals" and "Field of Lost Shoes." Other important movies are "Red Badge of Courage," "Friendly Persuasion," "Horse Soldiers," "Shenandoah" and "The Good, the Bad and the Ugly." .

Warren Lambert

The First Berea Provisional Volunteer Inactive Unorganized Reserve Confederate States Light Irregular Dismounted Horse Cavalry Brigade never won any battles or lost any battles, because it never fought any battles. This fictitious brigade was dreamed up on an afternoon in December 1954, by Warren Lambert, a school teacher, Bill Barbour, a laundry supervisor, and Murray Shearard, an insurance agent, as they loafed in a local store and the talk drifted to the possible pleasure of belonging to just one organization that required no dues or responsibilities. The brigade was born, the three commissioned themselves brigadiers and the fun began.

As soon as the word spread that Berea had an army brigade that required no duties, volunteers for service were numerous. In addition to the three original brigadier generals, within a week other commissioned officers included Brig. Gen. Oscar Gunkler, Brig. Gen. Herbert Hays, Lt. Col. Jack Blanton and Lt. Col. Eugene Kilgore. Their uniforms are near the authentic Confederate uniform of 1862 as ordered by the adjutant general, and an officer is ready to don his uniform at a moment's notice, as the brigade is prominent in all local parades, public celebrations and functions. The story of the brigade might end if the mirth and frivolity of the nonsensical organization had not spread as far as Washington, D.C., where it caught the interest of a man who appreciated the spirit of fun-loving people, to the extent that he wanted to be a part of it.

John A. Waters of Washington, D.C., wrote a letter to Lambert asking for a captaincy in the fictitious military organization. Lambert consulted with other officers and sent him one. A few weeks later Lambert received a review of commission from authority that purported to be from the Adjutant and Inspector General's Office for the Confederate Secretary of War. The Secretary of War in Richmond, Virginia, forwarded an order promoting Lambert to lieutenant general, and ordered him to form the Thirteenth Confederate Army Corps, taking in all portions of the Department of the West. This appealed to Lambert who decided to comply with the order and set about to acquaint himself with the Confederate Army organizational procedure.

For about a year work has progressed on the project with the idea that this army might have a single serious purpose of furnishing drill teams and uniform parade units for the coming commemorations of the battles of the Civil War as planned for the hundredth anniversary of each battle. Lambert stated that the army will have absolutely no political or social purpose. And it will not be involved in any way or in any kind of contemporary question. The new corps is being organized according to and as accurately as details can be found in official records of the "War of the Rebellion."

After many years of research, Dr. Lambert completed *When the Ripe Pears Fell, the Battle of Richmond, Kentucky,* which was fought on August 29-30, 1862. This was published by the Madison County Historical Society in 1995. The book was dedicated to his grandfather Oscar B. Lambert, Sergeant, Company I, Thirty-Third Regiment, Wisconsin

Volunteer Infantry, and his great-grandfather Philip Hayes, Confederate States Cavalry, unit unknown. It was the first attempt to bring all the aspects of this battle into one book. Warren's research notes are archived in the Hutchins Library of Berea College.

Dr. Warren Lambert was Professor of History and Political Science and former chair of the History Department at Berea College where he had been a faculty member since 1953. There was often a waiting list to get into his classes. On the last day of his Civil War class, he came to the classroom in a Confederate lieutenant general's uniform with saber. He would lay the saber on the desk and announce that he would now take questions but must be addressed properly as General Lambert. He was a specialist on Russian History and the U.S. Civil War. Warren was a native of Fairfax, South Dakota. He received his bachelor's degree from Berea College in 1948, his master's degree in 1957 and doctorate in 1974 from the University of Kentucky. Dr. Lambert was the 1992 recipient of the college's prestigious Seabury Award for Excellence in Teaching. He also received the Berea College Alumni Association Award of Special Merit in 1994.

Warren Lambert was a U.S. Army veteran. He served as a secretary to U.S. Representative Francis H. Case of South Dakota, and was later associate editor of *The Berea Citizen*. He was active in the Kentucky Historical Society and was a founding member of the Madison County Civil War Round Table. He was Police Judge Pro-Tem for the City of Berea and dean of instruction for the American Legion Bluegrass Boys' State, an annual event directed by Dean of Men Paul Seyfrit at Eastern Kentucky University. Warren Lambert died in 2002 at the age of 75.

A Hero in Homespun

Most of the time, it is not a good idea to use a novel or short story fiction to acquire historical data. Sometimes, however, the novelist may be aware of some unique information and the interpretation of facts may be excellent. If the work of fiction has a "fact" that no other sources have, be cautious. If all the other information in the writing is accurate, the probability increases that the remaining "fact" is also true. The closer in date the writing is to the original incident recorded, the greater possibility that the author may have information that was locally known or not included in official reports and letters. For example, there is no written report that the Rogers House was hit by cannon on August 30, 1862. An examination of the south side of the house, confirmed recently by two colonels and a major general, strongly suggests from the random pattern of bricks replaced, that the house was hit by fragments from an exploding howitzer shell.

An example of historical fiction was found in Hutchins Library archive, Berea College, early in 2015. It tells about the Battle of Richmond. The novel begins, "How much of this book is history and how much is fiction will be apparent to readers familiar with the history. To extend popular knowledge of the Civil War as it affected a large but almost unrecognized body of our people, this volume has been written. The form of fiction has been employed to permit a larger use of incident and personal experience, and to allow greater freedom of treatment, but the historical background is believed to be true to fact."

William E. Barton, *A Hero in Homespun. A Tale of the Loyal South.* Boston, New York and London: Lamson, Wolffe and Company. 1897.

A clue to accuracy of this book may be this biographical information. The Rev. William Eleazar Barton (1861-1930) was one of the early twentieth century's most prominent writers and lecturers on the life of Abraham Lincoln. He traveled in Kentucky, Indiana and Illinois visiting Lincoln sites and interviewing surviving Lincoln relatives and acquaintances, and he went as far as California and England to collect information and conduct genealogical research on the Lincoln family. Barton was born in Sublette, Illinois, did his undergraduate studies at Berea College, and then obtained his divinity degree from Oberlin Theological Seminary in 1890. He served churches in Tennessee, Ohio and Massachusetts before becoming pastor of the First Congregational church in Oak Park, Illinois, a position he held until his retirement in 1924. In 1928, he accepted an appointment as lecturer at Vanderbilt University.

In 1932, Barton's collection of 3,500 books and manuscripts on Abraham Lincoln and the Civil War era was acquired by the University of Chicago. The collection included most of the significant works on

Lincoln published since his presidency, many of them signed copies, first editions of the printings of a number of Lincoln's pre-presidential speeches, seventy-five volumes from Lincoln's law library and other important works. Manuscripts included briefs, pardons and commissions in Lincoln's handwriting, letters from Mary Todd Lincoln and letters written by members of his cabinet and other notable political and military figures of the time. There were also portraits, photographs and paintings.

Excerpt from *A Hero in Homespun*

(Page 234) "On the western slope of Big Hill there is clear and beautiful spring, whose waters ripple in a cool rill all the way down the mountain side. When the retreating soldiers came to this, they halted for water, and here a handful of the old troops made a stand, supported by the braver ones that were new. Here again the enemy came upon them, but, met in the narrow mountain pass by a determined body, they were repulsed, and their superior numbers driven back, and under cover of this advantage, the Union soldiers retreated to the foot of the hill.

"A week later occurred the forgotten battle of Richmond. The terrible struggles about the Confederate capital later in the war drowned out all memory of another Richmond. But here, in the edge of the blue grass, a few miles from the Big Hill fight, occurred what was up to that time the greatest battle in Kentucky, and one whose results struck terror to the heart of the entire North.

"General Nelson was not dismayed by the defeat of his troops at Big Hill. He left General Manson in charge of the army, with instructions to oppose the Confederate advance, and to fall slowly back to the Kentucky River, while he prepared to make (Page 235) a stand at his own well-chosen position. He was driving about in a buggy, selecting points to be occupied by his troops, when he heard the sound of the cannonade. Lashing his horse into a run, he hastened to Lancaster, ten miles on the way, where he secured a fresh horse and pushed on. Over six feet high, and bearing his three hundred pounds lightly, he was one of the most commanding figures of the war, and those who saw him that day lashing his horse furiously along the Richmond pike fell back before him.

"As Nelson approached Richmond, the firing, instead of receding, came nearer, and he knew that it boded ill for his army. The Union forces, under General Manson, had gone out to meet the Confederates, and taken position beyond Richmond, a few miles toward the Big Hill. Behind their slender defenses of fence rails stood the new men, and against them, hardened to service and flushed with victory, came the hosts of Kirby Smith. To have won their way inch by inch up the steep side of the Big Hill had been to them a thing of little difficulty; and now to meet their foe upon the level and face to face, they counted hardly worth the name of fighting. With a yell and a volley, they came to the attack, while the Union soldiers with set teeth awaited the onset.

There was a short struggle and a sharp one, and the dead and wounded were on every side. The Confederate artillery came up, and belched out its fire and sent its round shot bowling over the rolling fields and tearing through the ranks. The raw recruits fought bravely against great odds until there (Page 236) fight became a hand-to-hand contest, and then the Union soldiers broke and retreated toward the town.

"As Nelson came into Richmond, he was met by the retreating soldiers. He was in a frenzy. The defeat of his army meant the surrender of Lexington and Frankfort, perhaps also of Louisville and Cincinnati. He drew his sword and ordered the fugitives to halt. He cursed the women who ran to him for protection, and threatened the life of every man who did not turn back. The soldiers feared him more than the enemy, and gathered to his support. Only one man withstood his authority. A soldier from Indiana, making toward the rear stopped when ordered by Nelson to return, and held up a wound arm, "But, General, I'm wounded." he said.

"The infuriated Nelson struck him over the head with his sword and pushed on. The poor fellow fell against a fence, and holding himself up, leaned his wounded head upon the fence, which showed his blood stains for nearly a year. When, a month later, Nelson was shot dead by an Indiana officer, the people of Richmond looked at the stains upon the fence, and thought his death a retribution for his striking a wounded Indiana soldier.

"Furious as Nelson was, he was yet able to display great military genius. He selected a new position, and gathered the fugitives to maintain it. Just outside the little city, in the cemetery, he rallied his men. Hiding behind tombstones, and protecting themselves behind the fence, they made a desperate stand. But again the rebels pressed upon them in front and flank, while their cavalry threatened the (Page 237) rear. Their guns seemed never empty. Their yell was terrible to hear. The gaps in their ranks seemed to heal as fast as made. Nelson's utmost efforts were unavailing. His men broke and ran, leaving on the field five hundred dead and twelve hundred wounded. That in its day was an awful roll of dead and wounded, and showed how hot had been the struggle ere the new troops gave way. Nelson left no stone unturned to redeem the fortunes of the day. When his soldiers had been driven from the cemetery and through the town, and he himself was wounded, he rallied them for a last desperate stand upon the Lancaster pike; but all in vain. His men were hopelessly routed. They fled beyond Camp Nelson to Lexington and then on north, hardly stopping till they reached the Ohio River; and Kirby Smith pushed on into the rich bluegrass region, where he captured hundreds of fine horses and gathered stores of provisions, and his men lived on the fat of the land."

This book was originally published in 1897 and copies may be found at used book sources. Reprints are available and were reproduced from the original artifact. A Hero in Homespun *is considered to be culturally important and part of the knowledge base of civilization as we know it.*

Sources

Chapter One

Kentucky Weather, 1862

How Tornadoes and Severe Weather Affected the South During the Civil War by Timothy W. Troutman and Mark A. Rose of the National Weather Service.

Kentucky Climate Center, Western Kentucky University, a partner of National Climate Services.

Environmental History Resources, Dr. Jan Oosthoek, Brisbane, Research Assistant, Asia Pacific Centre for Sustainable Enterprise, Griffith University, South East Queensland, Australia.

Red Ice Creations, an independent site headquartered on the west coast of Sweden, online at redicecreations.com.

D. Warren Lambert, *When the Ripe Pears Fell*, 1995.

Christopher L. Kolakowski, *The Civil War at Perryville*, 2009.

B. Kevin Bennett, J.D., LTC (Ret.), *Blue and Gray* "Battle of Richmond, Ky.", 2009.

Stuart W. Sanders, *Perryville Under Fire*, 2012. American Meteorological Society.

The Battle of Richmond

Bobrick, Benson. The Master of War: The Life of General George H. Thomas. 2009.

Brown, Kent Masterson, editor. The Civil War in Kentucky: Battle for the Bluegrass State. 2000.

Cleburne, P.R. Report on the Battle of Richmond to E. Kirby Smith. September 1, 1862. Official Records of the War of the Rebellion, Volume 16, Chapter 28, Pages 944-946.

Eaton, Dr. Clement. Jefferson Davis. 1977.

Ellis, Dr. William E., Dr. H.E. Everman, Jr., and Dr. Richard D. Sears. Madison County: 200 Years in Retrospect. 1985.

Foote, Shelby. The Civil War. 1958.

Garcia, Pedro. "The 1862 Battle of Richmond: The Confederacy in the Balance," Warfare History Network. November 14, 2015.

Halstead, Murat. Dispatch to the Cincinnati Commercial on the Battle of Richmond. August 30, 1862.

Harrison, Lowell H. The Civil War in Kentucky. 1975.

Hattaway, Herman and Archer Jones. How the North Won: A Military History of the Civil War. 1983, Illini Books Edition, 1991.

Henry, Robert Selph. The Story of the Confederacy, with a forward by Douglas Southall Freeman. 1931, revised in 1936.

Hess, Earl J. The Civil War in the West: Victory and Defeat from the Appalachians to the Mississippi. 2012.

Horn, Stanley F. Article on the Battle of Richmond. Civil War Times Illustrated. February 1966.

Keegan, John. The American Civil War. 2009.

Lambert, Dr. D. Warren. Quoted by Dorris and Dorris in Glimpses of Historic Madison County, Kentucky. Pages 149-151. 1955.

Lambert, Dr. D. Warren. When the Ripe Pears Fell. 1995.

Leigh, Phil. Editorial, New York Times. September 3, 2012.

Morgan, John Hunt. Telegram to Edmund Kirby Smith. July 16, 1862.

Parks, Joseph H. General Edmund Kirby Smith C.S.A. 1954, 1982.

Seyfrit, Phillip. Battlefield Park Superintendent: Interpretive Brochures. 2009.

Shaler, Nathaniel Southgate. "The Battle of Richmond as told in 1884. Kentucky: A Pioneer Commonwealth. 1884.

Stewart, Bruce H., Jr. Invisible Hero: Patrick R. Cleburne. 2009.

Suhr, Robert Collins. "Confederate High Tide in the Bluegrass State." America's Civil War, January 1999.

See also the following DVDs:

Long Road Back to Kentucky: The 1862 Confederate Invasion. Written and hosted by Kent Masterson Brown, attorney, Lexington, Kentucky, 2007.

The American Civil War, with Course Guidebook. Professor Gary W. Gallagher, University of Virginia, 2000. The Great Courses. Lecture 14.

Chapter Two

History of Masonry in Madison County, Kentucky, 1812 – 1913, Robert R. Burnam.

Chapter Three

Margaret Elizabeth Clewell left a narrative of her services as a nurse to the 21st North Carolina Regiment. This rare, unpublished document was found in Perkins Library, Duke University. Parts of A Volunteer Nurse are available online. Also of interest: A Union Woman in Civil War Kentucky, The Diary of Frances Peter, edited by John David Smithand William Cooper, Jr. 2000. 1862-1864. Gratz Park, Lexington, Kentucky.

There are many books on Walt Whitman. Relating to the Civil War, look at WWII History Magazine, "Walt Whitman's Civil War: Stories of the Wounded," "Walt Whitman's Civil War Poetry," National Humanities Center, live online professional development seminars for history and literature teachers. Walt Whitman's America: A Cultural Biography, David S. Reynolds, 1996. Walt Whitman and the Civil War, Ted Genoways, 2009.

Chapter Four

Glimpses of Historic Madison County, Kentucky, Jonathan and Maude Dorris, pages 123-126.

Chapter Five

Inventory of Burials: Berea (Kentucky) Cemetery, Inc., Jerry Parrish Dimitrov and Charles Cortlandt Hay III, Madison County History Society, 1993, the web site Find A Grave, www.findagrave.com, and the research of Bill Williams.

Chapter Six

American Indians in the Civil War

The American Indian in the Civil War, 1862-1865. Annie Heloise Abel, 1992.

American Indians and the Civil War. Official National Park Service Handbook. Robert K. Sutton and John A. Latschar, editors.

Between Two Fires: American Indians in the Civil War. Laurence M. Hauptman, 1995.

Blood Moon: An American Epic of War and Splendor in the Cherokee Nation. John Sedgwick, 2018.

The Blue, The Gray & The Red: Indian Campaigns of the Civil War. Thom Hatch, 2003.

The Civil War in the Smokies. Noel Fisher, 2005.

Medicine Bags and Dog Tags: American Indian Veterans from Colonial Times to the Second Iraq War. Al Carroll, 2008.

Storm in the Mountains: Thomas' Confederate Legion of Cherokee Indians and Mountaineers. Vernon H. Crow, 1982.

The Union Indian Brigade in the Civil War. Wiley Britton, 1922.

Warrior in Two Camps: Ely S. Parker, Union General and Seneca Chief. William H. Armstrong, 1978.

Foreign Soldiers in the Civil War

Sources include *The Autobiography of Nicholas Said*; Amir N. Muhammad: *Muslim Veterans of American Wars*, 2007; Edward E. Curtis IV: *Muslim Americans in the Military: Centuries of Service*, 2016; *The Gettysburg Compiler* from the Civil War Institute at Gettysburg College.

The Black Brigade of Cincinnati

Library of Congress, John M. Trowbridge, Center of Excellence for the Study of Kentucky African Americans, PBS, Federal Government Archives, University of Michigan Library, Berea College Hutchins Library, teachingamericanhistory.org, biography.com, City of Cincinnati Smale Riverfront Park and the City of Fort Wright (photographs), Ian Delahanty,

"So Nearly White: The Fight to Commission a Black Officer," werehistory.org

Suggested reading: Zora Neale Hurston, Barracoon: The Story of the Last "Black Cargo," published in 2018, fifty-eight years after the author's death.

Zouaves

Books on Zouaves (zu ahv or zwahv) are available online. In print are *American Zouaves 1859 -1959* by Daniel J. Miller, *American Civil War Zouaves* by Robin Smith, *Zouaves: The First and the Bravest* by Michael J. McAfee, *We Came to Fight* by Patrick A. Schroeder, other unit histories, CivilWarAcademy.com, *America's Zouaves*, Robert W. Lebling at Academia.com; warhistoryonline.com, American Battlefield Trust, and a Zouave training manual written by Elmer E. Ellsworth is available online and in print. Chasseur units with uniforms similar to zouaves were used for scouting and skirmishing.

Chapter Seven

Civil War Paroles

Sources include: Smithsonian National Museum of American History, Kenneth E. Behring Center; The University of Texas at Austin, Harry Ransom Center; The University of Houston College of Engineering, by John H. Lienhard; High Beam Research, by Joan Boudreau, and Letter Press Commons: Briar Press, core contributor; and a brief biography of Johannes Gensfleisch zur Laden zum Gutenberg.

Horses

See Horses and Mules in the Civil War by Gene C. Armistead and a chapter from the 1888 book Hardtack and Coffee by John D. Billings.

The Madison County Historical Society says on its web site that the first racetrack in Richmond was probably located on land that is now the Richmond Cemetery. Cassius Marcellus Clay owned the land in the southern part of Madison County, an area known as The Glade. In the 1840s, he began to develop a community of people who, like himself, were opposed to slavery. By the 1850s, The Glade was known for its population of emancipationists and for its racetrack.

Chapter Eight

The Bullet That Changed History, by Pat Leonard, New York Times, August 31, 2012; William Williams, utilizing his private collection of Civil War bullets.

Chapter Nine

D. Warren Lambert, *When the Ripe Pears Fell*, 1996

Kenneth A. Hafendorfer, *The Battle of Richmond, Kentucky*, 2008

Lambert and Hafendorfer are available at Battlefield Park Visitors Center.

The Civil War at Perryville: Battle for the Bluegrass, Christopher L. Kolakowski, 2009

Perryville under Fire, Stuart W. Sanders, 2012

The Civil War in Appalachia, collected essays edited by Shannon H. Wilson and Kenneth W. Noe, 1997.

Arguing About Slavery: John Quincy Adams and the Great Battle in the United States Congress. William Lee Miller, 1995.

Lincoln and His Wife's Home Town. William H. Townsend, 1929.

Reflections on the Civil War. Bruce Catton. John Leekley, ed., 1981.

With My Face to the Enemy: Perspectives on the Civil War. Edited by Robert Cowley, 2001.

The Civil War as a Theological Crisis. Mark A. Noll, 2006.

Upon the Altar of the Nation: A Moral History of the Civil War. Harry S. Stout, 2006.

Documentary DVD *You Don't Know Dixie*, The History Channel, 2011.

The War of the Rebellion: a compilation of the official records of the Union and Confederate armies. U.S. Government Printing Office, 1880-1901. These 128 volumes may be viewed in *The War of the Rebellion: The Civil War CD-ROM*, 1996.

Master Edition: The War of the Rebellion searchable page perfect DVD-ROM, 2011

Concerning Civil War railroads, consult *The Railroads of Kentucky, 1861-1865*, Jessie Munday, Master's Thesis, 1925, University of Louisville, available online.

Battlefield Park Visitors Center may have copies of the magazine *Blue and Gray* "Battle of Richmond, Ky." B. Kevin Bennett, J.D., LTC (ret.), 2009.

Some scholars may wish to consult two books by Thomas P. Lowry, M.D.:

The Story The Soldiers Wouldn't Tell, 1994, and *Sexual Misbehavior in the Civil War*, 2006. Also, Judith Giesberg, Ph.D.: *Sex and the Civil War*, 2017.

Of further interest:

Joshua H. Leet and Karen M. Leet, *Civil War Lexington, Kentucky*, 2011, and a brief book by J. Winston Coleman, Jr., *Lexington During the Civil War*, 1968. This is a rare book.

Religion in Antebellum Kentucky, John B. Boles, 1976.

There are many excellent books on slavery, including the autobiographies, which have been mentioned. Also look at the following which are selected from my library: Dan Jordan and Michael J. Walsh, *White Cargo: The Forgotten History of Britain's White Slavery in America*, 2007; Larry Koger, *Black Slaveowners*, 1985, and Andres Resendez, *The Other Slavery: The Uncovered Story of Indian Enslavement in America*, 2016.

Also from my library:

Africans and Their History. Joseph E. Harris, 1972.

The African Experience. Roland Oliver, 1991.

Before the Mayflower. Lerone Bennett, Jr., 1962, Fifth Edition, 1982.

Been in the Storm So Long: The Aftermath of Slavery. Leon F. Litwack, 1979.

The Negro in the Making of America. Benjamin Quarles, 1964.

Rebels Against Slavery: American Slave Revolts. Patricia E. McKissack and Fredrick L. McKissack, 1996.

To Be A Slave. Tom Feelings, 1968, numerous editions

Juneteenth, also known as Freedom Day, Jubilee Day, Emancipation Day, began as a Texas celebration and has now become national. On June 19, 1865, in Galveston, Texas, Union Gen. Gordon Granger announced that persons formerly held in slavery in Texas were now free. Freedom of slaves had been proclaimed in areas in rebellion against the United States effective January 1, 1863. Texas remote and enforcement of *Emancipation Proclamation*_had been slow.

About the Author

Paul Rominger

Paul Rominger, Ph.D., from Berea, Kentucky, now lives in South Carolina. He has a bachelor's degree in History and master's degrees in Secondary Education and in School Administration. His doctoral work includes a dissertation on the Establishment Clause of the United States Constitution concerning a lawsuit by Planned Parenthood against the Duval County, Florida, Board of Education involving a seventh grade health education text. He has attended Reading and Research Seminars in History at Oxford University, the Colonial Williamsburg Teacher Institute, and the Civil War Trust Teacher Institute.

Paul has a Kentucky Rank 1 Teaching Certificate with lifetime endorsements for School Superintendent and for Grades 7-12: History and English. He was inducted into Kappa Delta Pi honorary education society and Phi Delta Kappa professional education fraternity. He was certified by the Kentucky Personnel Cabinet as Education Academic Program Consultant and as Historic Preservation Coordinator.

Paul was in education for thirty years as a high school and middle school history teacher and in administration. He served as Executive Director of The Battle of Richmond Association, a 501c3 nonprofit, and as Associate Director of Battlefield Park Visitors Center and Museum. He was appointed to the Madison County Visitors and History Board. Paul was President of the Madison County Historical Society, Board Chair of the Richmond Pow Wow Association, a 501c3 nonprofit, and Treasurer of the Madison County Civil War Round Table and the Central Kentucky World War Two Round Table. In the Kentucky Conference of the United Methodist Church, he served on the Bishop's Committee on Program and Arrangements, as Native Advocate, and on the Committee on Race Relations. He has served as Secretary of the Berea College Alumni Chapter of South Carolina.

Paul is enrolled in the Cherokee of Georgia Tribal Council, a state tribe, has served several terms on its council, and represented the tribe for two terms on the Georgia Council on American Indian Concerns. He received the Outstanding Volunteer of the Year recognition from the Girl Scout Council of Savannah and the Silver Beaver Award from Okefenokee Boy Scout Council. He earned Wood Badge, received Vigil Honor from the Order of the Arrow, and God and Service Recognition from The United Methodist Church. Paul has letters of commendation from the Lt. General, U.S. Army, Director of the Army National Guard, and the 7th Command Sergeant Major, Army National Guard, for volunteer support and service to families of the Georgia National Guard.

Index